Trade friction and economic policy

T0312238

Trade friction and economic policy

Problems and prospects for Japan and the United States

Edited by
RYUZO SATO and PAUL WACHTEL

The right of the
University of Cambridge
to print and sell
all manner of books
was granted by
Henry VIII in 1534.
The University has printed
and published continuously
since 1584.

CAMBRIDGE UNIVERSITY PRESS

Cambridge
New York   New Rochelle   Melbourne   Sydney

CAMBRIDGE UNIVERSITY PRESS
Cambridge, New York, Melbourne, Madrid, Cape Town, Singapore, São Paulo

Cambridge University Press
The Edinburgh Building, Cambridge CB2 8RU, UK

Published in the United States of America by Cambridge University Press, New York

www.cambridge.org
Information on this title: www.cambridge.org/9780521344463

First published 1987
This digitally printed version 2008

A catalogue record for this publication is available from the British Library

Library of Congress Cataloguing in Publication data
Trade friction and economic policy.

1. Japan – Commerce – United States. 2. United
States – Commerce – Japan. 3. Japan – Economic policy –
1945–   . 4. United States – Economic policy –
1981–   . I. Sato, Ryuzo, 1931–   . II. Wachtel,
Paul.
HF3828.U5T73   1987   382'.0952'073   87–11694

ISBN 978-0-521-34446-3 hardback
ISBN 978-0-521-06705-8 paperback

Contents

Foreword

Over the past year or so, I have reflected frequently about two words used in the appellation for this volume: *trade* and *friction*. I have heard them often, particularly during my visits to Japan, where they seem to have become the accepted shorthand way of summarizing the current, somewhat strained state of bilateral trade relations between Japan and the United States.

They are, I think, good words, particularly *friction*. After all, besides being a synonym for a conflict or a clashing, it conveys the impression of a rubbing together of two bodies that produces heat. And, certainly, we know that the current "rubbing" between the United States and Japan is having the effect of producing some heat, especially in the halls of Congress, where pressures for protectionism appear so strong.

But before we lament too much the heat that trading tensions are producing, it is important to remember that with friction often light emerges. Indeed, our primordial ancestors took it for granted that it was virtually impossible to get one without the other.

Today, of course, the wonders of modern science and technology are such that in the physical world we can now produce "cold light." In the world of social sciences and politics (dare I say political economics?), however, we are really still in the Dark Ages. Hence, we have to recognize that when facing the kinds of subjects dealt with in this volume, the cost of getting some light on the issues may be the generation of some heat. The trick is to dissipate the latter while preserving the insights and images that the former permits. The distinguished group of scholars, government officials, and business leaders who have contributed to this volume have turned this trick well. The result is a volume that is, I believe, informative, balanced, and to the point.

Richard R. West

vii

Preface

In addressing a problem as complex and multidimensional as trade friction and economic policy between Japan and the United States, one must know where to begin and what one can realistically expect to accomplish. With respect to the first point, an appropriate beginning seemed to be in assembling a multitalented group of experts from both Japan and the United States to discuss the problems involved and to suggest solutions. The list of contributors to this volume is distinguished; it includes leading academics, businessmen, and government officials from both Japan and the United States. The result, we feel, is a volume that is balanced, first, in the sense that Japanese–U.S. trade friction is examined from the perspective of both sides and, second, in the sense that both theory and policy are put to effective use.

What can one realistically expect to accomplish in a conference volume of this type? At its best, such a volume can serve as a useful input into policy decision making. As the Japan–U.S. Center's first conference volume, we hope that our efforts have had this effect.

The purpose of this volume is to examine the problem of trade friction and economic policy. As is evident from its title, the volume addresses the major issues affecting Japanese–U.S. trade friction and discusses policy options for dealing with trade friction.

Trade friction comes in a variety of forms. First, there is friction that results from the closing of one's markets to outside competition. Second, there is friction created by market instability from supply restriction and rationing of demand. Third, market invasion by unwanted foreign goods competition is yet another source of friction. Fourth, friction may result from direct movement of factor inputs such as American lawyers and doctors seeking employment opportunities in Japan. Fifth, the absolute level of trade imbalance can itself be a cause of friction. Sixth, inequitable sharing in the cost of international public goods such as defense and direct foreign aid to developing countries can lead to friction. And seventh, friction inevitably results from differing social and cultural factors.

As we examine U.S.–Japanese trade friction, it becomes obvious that trade relations suffer significantly from each of these factors. Japanese–U.S. trade friction is a complex, multidimensional issue. Furthermore, the wide variety of factors responsible for this trade friction may act in concert so as to multiply the problem. Where mere disagreement as to market accessibility exists, friction may not be so great. But when this basic disagreement is compounded by widely different social and cultural attitudes, huge trade imbalances, and so on, the problem can easily assume major proportions.

Today, the Japanese and American people observe each other very closely but do not understand each other adequately. We hope that this volume will contribute to the understanding of not only the political economics and business practices of Japan and the United States but also of the structural and institutional factors that have shaped our economies.

We have benefited from a great deal of help and support from a large number of people, but we would particularly like to thank Dr. John Rizzo, Sandra Weren, and Ann Barrow, all of the Japan–U.S. Center, for their efforts in helping to organize this volume. Thanks are due also to the review committee of Cambridge University Press for their advice, involvement, and interest. And last but not least, we would like to thank our volume contributors, without whom this first step in resolving bilateral trade problems between Japan and the United States could not have been taken.

Ryuzo Sato

Contributors

HARRY P. BOWEN Assistant Professor of Economics and International Business, Graduate School of Business Administration, New York University, New York, NY 10006

ROBERT CUMBY Associate Professor of Economics and International Business, Graduate School of Business Administration, New York University, New York, NY 10006

M. THERESE FLAHERTY Associate Professor of Production and Operations Management, Graduate School of Business Administration, Harvard University, Boston, MA 02163

BARBARA GOODY KATZ Associate Professor of Economics, Graduate School of Business Administration, New York University, New York NY 10006

PAUL KRUGMAN Professor of Economics, Massachusetts Institute of Technology, Cambridge, MA 02139

RICHARD C. MARSTON Professor of Finance, The Wharton School, University of Pennsylvania, Philadelphia, PA 19104

MASAYA MIYOSHI Senior Managing Director, Keidanren (Japan's Federation of Economic Organizations), 9-4 Otemachi 1-chome, Chiyoda-ku, Tokyo 100, Japan

YOSHIO OKAWARA Advisor to the Japanese Ministry of Foreign Affairs and Executive Advisor to the Keidanren (Japan's Federation of Economic Organizations), 2-1 Kasumigaseki 2-chome, Chiyoda-ku, Tokyo 100, Japan

MASAHIRO OKUNO-FUJIWARA Associate Professor of Economics, University of Tokyo, 5-3-1 Hongo Bunkyo-ku, Tokyo 113, Japan

THOMAS A. PUGEL Associate Professor of Economics and International Business, Graduate School of Business Administration, New York University, New York, NY 10006

RAMA V. RAMACHANDRAN Associate Professor of Economics, Southern Methodist University, Dallas, TX 75275

RUTH S. RAUBITSCHEK Assistant Professor of Management, Graduate School of Business Administration, New York University, New York, NY 10006

PAUL A. SAMUELSON Institute Professor, Massachusetts Institute of Technology, Cambridge, MA 02139; Long-Term Credit Bank of Japan Visting Professor of Political Economy, Graduate School of Business Adminstration, New York University, New York, NY 10006

MITSUAKI SATO Executive Director, Jetro Tokyo, Tokyo 105, Japan

RYUZO SATO Director, The Center for Japan–U.S. Business and Economics Studies; C. V. Starr Professor of Economics, Graduate School of Business Administration, New York University, New York, NY 10006

ROY C. SMITH General Partner, Goldman, Sachs & Co., New York, NY 10004

HERBERT STEIN Senior Fellow, American Enterprise Institute, Washington, DC 20036

KOTARO SUZUMURA Professor, The Institute of Economic Research, Hitotsubashi University, Kunitachi, Tokyo 186, Japan

DAVID G. TARR Visiting Senior Economist, The World Bank, Washington, DC 20433; Senior Economist, Federal Trade Commission, Washington, DC 20580

SHUNICHI TSUTSUI Assistant Professor of Economics, University of Georgia, Athens, GA 30602

KAZUO UEDA Senior Economist, Institute of Fiscal and Monetary Policy, Ministry of Finance, 3-1-1 Kasumigaseki, Chiyoda-ku, Tokyo, Japan

PAUL WACHTEL Chairman, Economics Department, Graduate School of Business Administration, New York University, New York, NY 10006

RICHARD R. WEST Dean of Graduate School of Business Administration, New York University, New York, NY 10006

LAWRENCE J. WHITE Professor of Economics, Graduate School of Business Administration, New York University, New York, NY 10006

CHAPTER 1

Introduction

PAUL WACHTEL

The issue of trade friction and general tensions concerning economic policy between the United States and Japan is not a new one. For almost 20 years the issue has appeared in popular economic discussions. Sometimes events make the frictions more heated than at other times, but there is usually some manifestation of the issue. This volume presents the proceedings of a conference held in 1986, a year in which the policy frictions between the two allies were particularly heated. However, the issues discussed are of broader interest than the crises reported in the daily press. Indeed, the conference program and discussions attempt to put these crises in perspective and thereby contribute to our understanding of economic policy in a constructive manner.

The chapters presented here address three broad questions that are the source of the three topical groupings in the table of contents. The questions are:

What are the sources of trade friction?
What are the appropriate macroeconomic policy responses?
What are the appropriate trade policy responses?

That these questions are posed does not presume that there are definitive answers. In fact, the very issue of whether friction exists or whether there is any substantive basis for the apparent frictions expressed in both countries needs to be explored. In addition, it is possible that no response is the appropriate policy action. Indeed, some of the views expressed in this volume favor little or no policy response.

The essays in this volume are a combination of research papers, policy speeches, and discussions presented at a conference sponsored by the Center for Japan–U.S. Business and Economics Studies at the Graduate School of Business Administration at New York University. The conference was held on April 10 and 11, 1986, in New York and was organized by the editors. Although the essays have very different formats, ranging from academic studies to luncheon speeches, they have been prepared for publication in a form that we hope will be readable to everyone. This introduction will provide a guide for the interested reader to the issues, ideas, and conclusions of the essays.[1]

The sources of trade friction

The first chapter in Part I is perhaps the most timely. It is by Yoshio Okawara, the former Japanese Ambassador to the United States and a member of the Advisory Group on Economic Structural Adjustment for International Harmony – the Maekawa Committee. The committee was a high-level government group formed to make recommendations on how to alleviate Japanese–U.S. trade frictions. The commission's report was made public shortly before the conference, and Ambassador Okawara summarizes and evaluates the policy initiatives recommended by the Maekawa Committee.

Okawara acknowledges that eliminating the trade surplus is desirable but that it is important to do so without adversely affecting Japan's economy. To accomplish this requires nothing less than a combination of industrial restructuring of the Japanese economy and strong stimulus to domestic demand in Japan. Although a realignment of exchange rates and international cooperation on trade issues would be helpful, Okawara emphasized the need for long-term solutions. The Japanese economy must be restructured away from its export orientation and toward production geared to meeting domestic demand. These changes take time, so that substantial progress in reducing the trade imbalance and improving trade relations may be some time off. Nevertheless, Okawara is confident of the willingness of the Nakasone government to bring about such changes even in the face of political opposition in Japan.

A more formal analysis of the sources of trade friction is presented in the chapter by Paul Krugman of the Massachusetts Institute of Technology. He bluntly states that the economic tension between Japan and the United States owes little to Japanese trade and business practices. Instead he attributes the friction to the speed with which the large surplus occurred in response to changing terms of trade in the world economy. This is a rather optimistic interpretation because it

[1] One of the essays was not actually presented at the conference. The chapter by Paul Samuelson is based on a public lecture sponsored by the Japan–U.S. Center at the NYU Graduate Business School in December 1985. In addition, one of the papers presented at the conference was not available for publication. It is "Japanese Worker's Skills and Shopfloor Techniques in Comparison with the U.S." by Kazuo Koike of Kyoto University. It was discussed at the conference by John Rizzo and Paul Wachtel, both of NYU.

implies that changes in exchange rates will lead to a gradual correction of the imbalance. Krugman is confident that the problem will be solved in the long run by the revaluation of the yen to about its current level. Thus, no new initiatives are called for. Patience and exchange rate stability around existing levels will bring about a correction to the imbalance of trade flows.

Trade frictions heated in the 1980s because an unusual set of circumstances combined to result in the very rapid emergence of an enormous bilateral trade imbalance. These were the increase in energy prices, which led to a deterioration of Japan's terms of trade, and an overvalued dollar in world financial markets. Since 1985, both the dollar and the price of oil have fallen precipitously, which will cause the imbalance to shrink and frictions to disappear. Thus, Krugman does not put much credence in the idea that there are structural aspects of the two economies that need to be changed. The contrast between Krugman's view and the Maekawa recommendations endorsed by Ambassador Okawara is startling.

A mediating point of view is expressed by Masaya Miyoshi of the Keidanren (Japan's Federation of Economic Organizations). Like Krugman, Miyoshi regards the allegations that Japan engages in unfair trade practices as groundless. He attributes the recent trade frictions to the unanticipated size of the imbalance of trade and resulting panic in the United States over America's apparent decline in international competitiveness. However, Miyoshi is not willing to rely on exchange rate realignment and coordinated macroeconomic policies to change the situation. He instead advocates a role for structural change in both economies as a necessary part of the process.

The structural changes that Miyoshi emphasized are different from those suggested by Okawara. He called for increased export efforts by American industry. In his view the issue is not barriers to the Japanese markets but the need for American industry to develop marketing efforts abroad. Miyoshi places the burden on the United States to change the structure of business activity while Okawara places a greater burden on Japan to change the structure of domestic demand. Miyoshi and Okawara are in agreement that the devaluation of the dollar is not sufficient to reduce the trade frictions that have emerged.

The final chapter in this part of the volume is a historical overview of one of the possible sources of trade friction. It is very common in the United States to blame Japanese industrial policy for creating an economic structure that inhibits fair trade or creates barriers to Japanese markets as it promotes economic growth. Kotaro Suzumura of Hitotsubashi University and Masahiro Okuno-Fujiwara of the University of

Tokyo and the University of Pennsylvania provide a thorough review and critique of Japanese industrial policy in the post–World War II period. Their analysis calls into question the popular notion that industrial policies in Japan have played a critical role in promoting its extraordinary economic development. They conclude that these policies have been at best neutral and possibly even counterproductive.

Suzumura and Okuno do not only contend that Japanese industrial policy is not the cause of trade friction. They go on to imply that industrial policy in Japan has been generally ill-conceived. The chapter presents two basic reasons for this conclusion. First, Japan's industrial policy has, for the most part, been advisory in nature. Thus, it is only followed when private incentives to do so are present. Second, the welfare criteria adopted for determining which industries to assist lack any compelling theoretical motivation. The criteria used have been basically ad hoc. Nevertheless, the authors do not acknowledge a completely laissez-faire approach. They suggest that there is a role for industrial policy in such areas as information dissemination and the promotion of cooperative research and development efforts.

Trade friction and macroeconomic policy

The second part of this volume deals with issues of macroeconomic policy in Japan and the United States. The part begins with discussions of macroeconomic policy and the relationships between the two countries by two prominent American economists. The first is by Nobel laureate Paul Samuelson, Institute Professor at MIT and the first Long-Term Credit Bank of Japan Visiting Professor of Economics at NYU's Japan–U.S. Center. The second is by Herbert Stein, formerly chairman of the President's Council of Economic Advisors and currently at the American Enterprise Institute. Stein is confident that the frictions of the early 1980s will give way shortly to an era of trade harmony. Samuelson warns that although the frictions associated with the large trade deficit are likely to diminish, they will not disappear quickly, and a protectionist reaction is a real possibility.

Samuelson attributes the current situation to the natural post-war development of the Japanese economy. He argues that protectionist trade policies would not be a beneficial way of responding to the growth in the international economy. He blames the macroeconomic policy of the Reagan administration for the overvaluation of the dollar in the early 1980s and views the decline since February 1985 as fortuitous. However, Samuelson is not at all sure that the coordination of fiscal and monetary policies among major countries will maintain stability.

A more optimistic interpretation of events is presented by Herbert Stein. He notes that trade frictions have emerged before and have disappeared as well, and he forecasts that by 1988 the appropriate title for a conference will be trade harmony. Like Samuelson, he blames the U.S. macroeconomic policies of the 1980s for the trade deficit. Those policies led inevitably to large capital inflows, and a trade deficit is a necessary corollary to capital inflows. Although this situation is detrimental to some industries, avoiding it would have hurt other industries. In addition, the overall performance of the U.S. economy has been rather good. Finally, Stein views a number of developments already underway as sufficient to make the frictions disappear. These include an emerging willingness by Japan to save less and export less, the revival of the European economies, and a willingness by the United States to reduce the government deficit.

The next chapter is a review of trade relations and macroeconomic developments in Japan and the United States by Roy Smith, a general partner of Goldman-Sachs who has been active in their business relations with Japan for many years. Smith shows how the current situation is the logical consequence of macroeconomic policies over a long period. He views the trade deficit as a persistent and troublesome problem. In his view, it could be managed better, and steps could be taken to ameliorate the problem. Smith does not think that the Japanese propensity to save will change nor will the Japanese attempt to reduce their growth rate as a means of reducing the American trade deficit. He does suggest several steps that will enable the two economies to better cope with the situation. These include further steps to deregulate Japanese financial markets, efforts by Japan to cycle financial surpluses to other countries besides the United States, and continued growth of Japanese direct investments in the United States.

The final chapter in this part is on the effects of exchange rate intervention and the yen appreciation that began in 1985. It is by Kazuo Ueda of the Ministry of Finance and Osaka University. Ueda is particularly interested in the effects on exchange rates and the trade balance of the famous G5 (the group of five major central banks) meeting in September 1985. At that time the United States and Japan agreed to appreciate the yen through monetary intervention. Ueda emphasizes that political realities are likely to constrain any strong fiscal actions by either country. His concern is whether monetary intervention will be successful. His conclusion is that intervention will be helpful only if macroeconomic policy can also provide stable underlying economic conditions.

If U.S. real economic growth averages only 2% per year over the next decade, then Ueda estimates that the American budget deficit will soar and the long-run equilibrium yen exchange rate will plummet. On the other hand, 4% real growth in the United States would make it possible to maintain the deficit-to-GNP ratio at the current level. Ueda supports the use of foreign exchange interventions such as that implemented after the G5 meeting; he recognizes that political realities restrain the more structural changes that would be brought about with fiscal policy.

The use of trade policy

The chapters in this part are on two recent applications of trade policy that resulted from concern about U.S.–Japanese trade relations. The first is a detailed analysis of the costs and benefits of an important American trade barrier. David Tarr of the Federal Trade Commission and the World Bank analyzes the 1985 steel import quota program. The second is an analysis of trade practices and government policies in the semiconductor industry. Thomas Pugel of New York University analyzes the efforts of the American industry to seek protection and the attempts of both governments to evolve a cooperative policy. Although the two industries under study here are very different, neither author finds much support for market intervention, which interferes with free trade.

Tarr describes the history of trade policy in the United States for the steel industry. Since 1969, the industry has enjoyed a significant amount of protection from imports. Most recently the United States and its trading partners have agreed to restrict steel imports to less than 20% of domestic consumption. Tarr shows that consumers are paying significantly higher prices as a result of the quotas. These higher prices represent transfers from consumers to the steel producers and workers and also to overseas producers. His estimates indicate that each job in the steel industry saved by the quota costs consumers $114,000 and costs the American economy $81,000.

In contrast to the steel industry, the semiconductor industry is one where both technology and industrial structure are changing very rapidly. Consumption and trade in the industry grew rapidly for over a decade until 1984. At that time the worldwide industry entered a recession that spawned severe trade friction between the United States and Japan. Pugel presents a detailed summary of the various actions taken by producers and by governments since late 1984. At that time the trade frictions turned into formal trade actions against the Japanese firms and government.

Pugel describes trade actions of three different types. First, in 1985 several American firms brought dumping suits against Japanese exporters. Pugel describes and evaluates the procedures for examining these allegations by the International Trade Commission and the Department of Commerce. The second form of trade action was the efforts of American firms to protect their intangible assets, basically chip design and process technology. Finally, the U.S. industry and government have made formal allegations of unfair trade practices to the Japanese government. Pugel finds little basis for the allegations of unfair trade practices, although he is sympathetic with efforts to protect proprietary designs and processes from infringement.

Conclusion

A reading of the entire conference volume provides an interesting perspective on the agreements and disagreements concerning issues of trade friction and economic policy. Some authors fear that the trade deficit could have a devastating impact on the American economy, while others view it as relatively benign. Some are confident that the appreciation of the yen will have a strong impact on the deficit, while others doubt this. However, there seems to be widespread agreement that restrictive trade policies are not a worthwhile means of reducing the trade deficit.

The conference participants also agreed that the dollar had been overvalued. A few even ventured to suggest what the equilibrium exchange rate should be. Both Paul Krugman and Richard Marston offered the figure of 140 yen to the dollar. Japanese participants suggested that such a high value for the yen would be too disruptive to the Japanese economy to be acceptable.

A final point of discussion at the conference was simply whether allegations of trade friction are justified. Although many feel that Japanese markets are to some extent closed to foreign competition, these barriers have been diminishing. Trade friction should emerge only if such barriers are increasing, which is not the case. Similar thoughts were expressed concerning allegations of unfair trade practices by Japanese exporters. Although they may exist, there is no indication that they are becoming more of a problem. What then is the source of the apparent friction?

The consensus view is that trade friction arises because of the rapid growth of Japanese exports of highly visible manufactured consumer goods. Trade friction seems to be the consequence of Japanese product innovation and productivity improvements that result in the trade imbalance. Although governments should be careful to ensure that instances of unfair trade practices do not emerge, it does not follow that direct policy initiatives to interfere with free trade are advisable. The macroeconomic equilibrating process will lead to the gradual disappearance of the trade imbalance and with it the perceptions concerning trade friction. Thus, the consensus view is basically an optimistic one.

Many of the chapters are followed by comments that were prepared for the conference. These discussions provide some valuable additional insights the reader should not overlook. Finally, this volume is only one of several such volumes sponsored by the Center for Japan–U.S. Business and Economic Studies at NYU on related topics. Readers of this volume are more than likely to find the others of interest as well.

PART I

Sources of trade friction

CHAPTER 2

Restructuring the Japanese economy from a global perspective

YOSHIO OKAWARA

Trade friction between Japan and the United States is an obvious fact. What is far less obvious is how each nation will address this problem. In this chapter, I would like to discuss how Japan proposes to alleviate the trade friction that has resulted from an enormous Japanese surplus on its current account and a correspondingly enormous U.S. current account deficit.

In addressing this problem, one is at first confronted by its sheer enormity. How are we to deal with the huge external imbalances facing the global economy today? How can we literally restructure the Japanese economy in a manner that will alleviate international friction while preserving domestic tranquility? Japan's approach to this admittedly large and complex issue has been three-fold. First, efforts, must be made to improve market access and increase domestic demand. Second, exchange rate realignment should be implemented. And finally, efforts must be made to restructure Japanese industry along more productive lines by gradually shrinking economically depressed industries.

In the course of the past year, important and encouraging developments have already occurred on the world economic scene. Cooperative efforts to realign exchange rates have been more or less successfully implemented, interest rates have declined, and new initiatives to address the debt situation have emerged. A series of measures have been adopted by Japan to improve market access and expand domestic demand, and European efforts to redress structural rigidities are at least being discussed. Finally, recent oil price declines are also considered to have beneficial effects in general, although the full impact on oil-producing and debtor countries is yet to be assessed.

It is also true, however, that a number of serious problems remain that, if not properly addressed, could threaten the sustainability of world economic growth. The predominant cause of our current difficulties is the international trade imbalance, particularly with respect to

11

Japan and the United States. This huge trade imbalance, $148.5 billion deficit for the United States and $56.0 billion surplus for Japan in 1985 (all time historic highs for both countries), is a danger not only for the management of our economies but also for the prosperous development of the world economy.

Over the past year Japan, under the leadership of Prime Minister Nakasone, has exerted itself vigorously in unprecedented and systematic efforts to redress this imbalance and assume a role befitting its place in the international economic community.

In order to reduce the huge current account surplus, we have redoubled our efforts in tackling the question of market access in order to dispel doubts about the openness of our markets or the fairness of our trade practices. The MOSS (market-oriented, sector-selective) process and the Action Program have been the two major vehicles for our recent efforts in this regard.

The Joint Report by Foreign Minister Abe and Secretary of State Shulz of January 10, 1986, on MOSS concluded that "important progress has been achieved as a result of the MOSS discussions for the four sectors . . . telecommunications, medical equipment and pharmaceuticals, electronics, and forest products." In a press briefing wrapping up the meeting with Foreign Minister Abe, Secretary of State Shulz remarked that "a great deal has been accomplished" and cited "very substantial purchases" by Japan as evidence of that success. The MOSS process will be continued. Furthermore, while MOSS is a bilateral discussion between the United States and Japan, it certainly will benefit the entire world.

The Action Program was introduced in July 1985 to further open Japanese markets. It was hoped that this program would alleviate criticisms sometimes voiced by foreigners that Japan's market access initiatives are really nothing more than nice-sounding words. The program has led to radical improvements in market access, including large-scale tariff reduction and drastic changes in the standards and certification systems and in import procedures. More specifically, tariffs for 1,849 items have been reduced or eliminated, 56 out of 88 standards and certificate cases listed for improvement have already been implemented (with others to follow), and a variety of measures dealing with capital markets, services, and import promotion have been executed in order to enhance access of foreign products. While it is difficult to describe quantitatively the degree of implementation, roughly speaking, I would say that more than 70% of the 3-year program has already been implemented.

Paralleling these market access efforts, Japan has been grappling with more general macroeconomic conditions in an attempt to do its part in redressing the basic trade imbalances of the world economy. Movements toward better alignment of exchange rates and measures to expand domestic demand are the two major areas of importance in this regard. Japan is firmly committed to making efforts to sustain the trend of the strong yen, though many of its industries are complaining about the hardships caused by the sudden and exceptionally rapid rise of the yen.

As for domestic demand, government forecasts indicate that Japanese economic growth in fiscal year 1986 will be achieved solely through domestic demand expansion.

Structural readjustment may well be the most important aspect of Japan's three-fold approach to addressing trade friction. Even complete liberalization of Japanese markets should result only in modest increases of imports from the United States. This is so because the income elasticity of imports of Japan (0.8) is quite low relative to that of the United States (3.4). Hence, with the same GNP growth, U.S. imports are four times as large as Japanese imports.

Even this brief analysis strongly suggests that structural factors such as different income elasticities of imports play a key role in Japan's huge current account surplus. Both a sense of crisis and a perceived need for radical change prompted Prime Minister Nakasone to commission, in October 1985, the Advisory Group on Economic Structural Adjustment for International Harmony – the Maekawa Committee – to make recommendations for Japanese economic structural adjustment. The group's report to Prime Minister Nakasone was released on April 7, 1986.

The Maekawa Committee report will have a profound impact on Japanese industrial performance and trade pattern. Having served as one of the seventeen members of the Maekawa Committee, I would like to comment not only on the substantive recommendations made by that committee but also on the rationale behind those recommendations.

The Maekawa report was written on the assumption that Japan cannot and should not continue to accumulate such huge trade surpluses as it has in the recent past (reaching 3.6% of GNP in 1985). Japan now stands at a "historical turning point" for re-orienting both its economic policy and way of life. Slashing the surplus should be a national policy goal of high priority. This was our fundamental message to the Japanese people, and it was an announcement of drastic policy changes to the world. The Maekawa Committee sought to motivate and enlighten not only public and private sector leaders but all of our citizens in meeting the formidable challenges of economic reorganization.

The committee's first recommendation is that Japan must turn from export-dependent growth to domestic demand-powered economic expansion. To achieve this goal, expansion of housing investment is crucial, both because housing investment generates expansion along several industrial lines and because there is a strong social need for improved housing conditions. Recognizing that housing investment is restrained by high investment costs and limited disposable income, more lenient tax incentives, deregulation of construction, more lenient land use restrictions, and fiscal "pump priming" are recommended.

The second recommendation concerns the revitalization of Japanese industry. In particular, policy initiatives should be undertaken to promote a shift out of declining industries and to encourage direct overseas investment. As an example of the recommended shift out of declining industries, the report states that "coal mining policy should be reviewed" and that Japan should drastically reduce domestic production of coal, replacing it with imports.

While the Japanese coal industry is unquestionably economically depressed, some districts depend almost entirely on coal production for survival. This recommendation is, therefore, an extremely bold one, reflecting the committee's strong determination to promote industrial reorganization. Furthermore, we recommend that industrial structure adjustment programs under the Depressed Industries Law be accelerated, even though this law is due to expire in 1988.

With regard to direct overseas investment, the committee recommends that Japanese companies should contribute more to the local economies in which they operate. This could take the form of, for example, providing local employment opportunities. Furthermore, regarding investment in developing countries, the committee recommends greater transfer of technology and management skills to promote industrial development and increase the export capabilities of the host country. This may also contribute to alleviating the debt problems faced by some developing countries.

At the same time, foreign companies should also be encouraged to invest in Japan. This will contribute to internationalizing Japan's economic structure and will reduce the distance between foreign suppliers and Japanese consumers, facilitating the effective introduction of foreign companies into the Japanese distribution system.

The third recommendation is that exchange rate stability be pursued. Compatible, coordinated macroeconomic policies among trading nations are important in this regard. With compatible policies, the need for drastic and upsetting exchange rate readjustment is alleviated.

Last but not least, the report states that Japan should play a more active role in promoting the well being of the entire international community. To date, Japan's contributions have been mostly economic, but today active contribution is called for in the fields of science, technology, and culture.

The tasks ahead are not easy for any of us. Current account imbalances will not disappear quickly and without sacrifices on all sides. Like Japan, the American economy faces severe savings and trade imbalances. Furthermore, economic restructuring is needed not only in Japan and the United States but in Europe as well. Although Japan accounts for one-third of the U.S. global deficit, the U.S. international trade and payment position is not solely a bilateral problem vis-à-vis Japan.

Structural adjustments require time, however, and frequently encounter substantial political resistance. Tenacious efforts and extraordinary vigor are necessary to meet these challenges, and such efforts should be made with a view to their long-run effects. In light of the increasingly interdependent nature of the world's economies, comprehensive approaches and cooperative actions are particularly appropriate. Quick fixes and stopgap efforts will not solve the problem of trade friction. Japanese efforts will be most effective if coupled with similar efforts on the part of the United States and Europe.

Sharing common objectives, the United States, Japan, and Europe should effectively meet the formidable challenges of restructuring. What we need now is the resolve to proceed with policies aimed at achieving long-run benefits for us all in the face of political opposition. We stand at a crossroads. The actions taken today will greatly affect the world economy in the coming decades.

CHAPTER 3

Is the Japan problem over?

PAUL KRUGMAN

For most of the U.S. public, trade relations with Japan are the dominant issue of international economic policy. International debt is the problem of the bankers and may even serve them right; agricultural trade and the European Economic Community (EEC) is a farmers' problem; but the Japanese issue touches not only our sense of national pride but also our jobs. The future growth of world trade depends more on how the United States comes to perceive its trade with Japan than on any other issue.

The question of how to manage U.S.–Japanese trade relations comes on at least two levels. The first level is one of ascertaining the facts. Does Japan take unfair advantage of our open market while closing its own? Many, perhaps most, Americans believe this, though few economists would agree. I will take it as a working assumption in this chapter that the perception of Japan as a villain is at least 95% wrong. Even a brief review of the evidence explodes most of the myths that continue to circulate in U.S. discussion. While there is room to criticize Japan, the idea that Japan is pursuing beggar-my-neighbor policies on a grand scale is essentially preposterous. Nonetheless, many influential Americans believe it.

This difference in perception gives rise to the second level of the question: How should those who view U.S.–Japanese trade as mutually beneficial protect that trade from the political frictions menacing it? If you think that Japan, while not without flaws, is no worse an international economic citizen than the United States, should you preach this wisdom, in the full knowledge that much of Congress will dismiss you as a fool? Or should you advocate policies that throw the wolves a bone or two in the hope that this will appease them?

In practice, there are well-intentioned economists and policymakers along a broad spectrum of responses to this dilemma. At one end, academic economists such as Gary Saxonhouse (1983, 1985), think tanks such as the Institute for International Economics (Bergsten and

16

Cline 1985), and government agencies such as the Council of Economic Advisers (1983) have strongly argued Japan's case. The implicit political judgment of this group has been that the most effective strategy is to speak the truth and hold the line as best one can.

In the middle are the trade negotiators of the United States, especially the office of the U.S. Trade Representative (USTR). The staff at USTR knows, and will privately admit, that the trade policies of Japan are not the main source of trade frictions. They stress the importance of the *process* of trade negotiation, however. When Congress is on the attack against Japan's trade surplus, an immediate response that does not conflict with the U.S. historic commitment to the principle of free trade is to demand that Japan take action to remove some of its remaining trade restrictions. This may not do much to reduce the surplus – nor does USTR expect it to – but creating the appearance of meaningful action may help buy a temporary respite from political pressure.

Finally, there are some economists and others who view the attempt to maintain any sort of free trade between the United States and Japan as a lost cause politically. These observers may not accept the popular view that Japan is taking advantage of the United States. They believe, however, that this public perception, reinforced by structural features of U.S.–Japanese trade that give the perception credibility, is too strong to meet head on. Instead, the response must be a controlled degree of protection, sufficient to appease U.S. sentiment at minimum cost to the world economy. In this camp are Lester Thurow (1985), who advocates a cap on the U.S.–Japanese bilateral trade imbalance, and William Branson (1986), who advocates a flat tariff to protect U.S. manufacturing.

Clearly, one's choice among these political stances depends in part on a judgment about the way the political system works. It also depends, however, on a forecast of the future political climate. Will the fundamental sources of U.S.–Japanese trade friction remain unchanged, so that the pressure continues unabated? Or will the situation turn around, so that the trading system can be saved if we can hold out until the cavalry comes? If the latter is true, proposals of the Thurow variety are very bad ideas. They will destroy the institutional system of relatively free trade unnecessarily, when sticking to our principles would have been enough.

What I will argue in this chapter is that there is a very good chance that we are about to see a dramatic change in the fundamental background to U.S.–Japanese trade relations. I will argue that the main source of friction does not lie in such deep issues as the differences between U.S. and Japanese institutions and social structures. It lies instead in the huge manufacturing trade surplus and rapid export growth that Japan experienced from 1973 to the present. These proximate sources of trade friction in turn had their origin primarily in the more fundamental factors of oil price increases and a shift of Japan into current account surplus, with oil, not the current account shift, the more important of the two.

In little more than a year, both of these factors have experienced dramatic reversals. It has been widely recognized that the fall in the dollar will lead to an improved U.S. trade picture. It is also the case that falling oil prices tend, by strengthening the yen, to reduce Japan's surplus in manufactures – a point well understood by economists, if less appreciated among businessmen and politicians. What has been lacking so far, however, is a quantitative assessment of how much difference the recent changes can make. What we will see is that a simple numerical analysis suggests that recent changes will in fact have massive effects on the situation. Quite suddenly, it has become plausible to suppose that over the next 5 years we will see the growth of Japanese exports slow to less than 1% per year. If we can keep our tempers for a little longer, an era in which the United States learns again that trade is a mutual affair may well be about to begin. The implication is that now is the time to hold the fort against protectionism; the cavalry is on its way.

The sources of growing trade friction, 1973 to 1984

In the early 1970s a reasonable forecast for the future of U.S.–Japanese trade relations might have been quite optimistic. The realignment of the dollar–yen rate from 1970 to 1973 was visibly reducing the large Japanese trade surpluses that had emerged when the Bretton Woods system of fixed exchange rates ended. As far as most observers could judge, Japan's economy was experiencing considerable liberalization, as the government's control over both foreign transactions and domestic credit markets was loosened. There was every reason to expect Japan's role in the international economic system to become normalized, similar to that of other densely populated industrial countries such as Germany.

Instead, trade relations between the United States and Japan have grown increasingly strained. Many in the United States argue that this is because the apparent liberalization of Japan's economy was never real; that Japanese government and business practices continued to differ from those of the United States in a way that worked to the U.S. disadvantage. Defenders of Japan like myself argue instead that these accusations are being used to rationalize anti-Japanese sentiment that

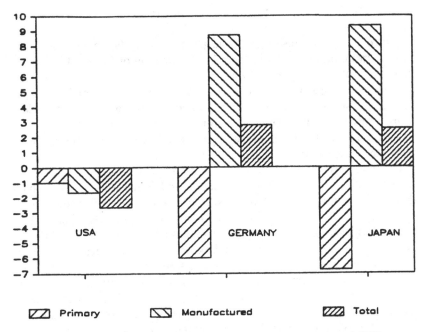

Figure 3.1. Trade balance by type of good, percentage of GNP.

has nothing to do with the alleged unfair practices. The true sources of trade friction, it may be argued, lie instead in two facts that have little to do with Japan's trade policy. The first fact is that during the 1970s and the first half of the 1980s the world economic environment changed in such a way that Japan developed a "structural" surplus in its trade in manufactures and its bilateral trade with the United States. The second reason, closely related to the first, is that structural change led to a rapid pace of Japanese export growth, arousing opposition from foreign import-competing sectors. One might also suppose that the growth and success of Japan's economy was in itself a source of tension: As we will see, a case can be made that this was of surprisingly little importance as compared with the rise in oil prices and the shift of Japan into current account surplus.

The structure of Japanese trade

The key facts about Japanese trade structure, and the reasons why U.S. firms inevitably feel that they lose far more often than they win in competition with Japanese rivals, can be seen clearly by looking at a simple graph. Figure 3.1 shows comparative trade structure by type of commodity for the United States, Japan, and (as a useful control) West Germany.

Figure 3.1 illustrates three basic points. First, Japan runs a huge surplus in manufactured goods trade. The feeling of foreign firms that they are not on a level playing field is simply the obverse of this dominant fact. Second, most of this trade surplus in manufactures is necessary for Japan to pay its huge *deficit* in primary product trade. Third, this trade pattern is not unique to Japan: Germany's trade structure is, at this level of aggregation, quite similar, although the absolute numbers are smaller.

The comparison with Germany is an important one. Economists schooled in general equilibrium theory find it natural to assert that there is an automatic mechanism whereby a shift toward trade deficit in one area will lead to offsetting shifts toward surplus elsewhere. This not only rationalizes most of Japan's manufactures trade surplus, but it also leads economists to deny any link between overall trade balances and protection. Politicians and businessmen have never been convinced by this argument and tend to view the application of such arguments in this case as an apologetic for Japan. The fact that Germany, although rarely accused of unfair trade practices, shows a similar pattern of trade should help strengthen the economists' case. As the figure shows, in their tendency to run manufacturing surpluses to pay for primary deficits, Germany and Japan are virtually identical twins.

In a purely accounting sense, almost three-quarters of Japan's manufactures surplus in 1984 went to pay for a deficit in primary products. The remaining surplus was virtually the same in Germany and Japan, suggesting that the cause of the trade surplus was something common to both rather than special to Japan. The natural explanation, of course, is that it was the United States, with its budget deficit and resulting overvalued dollar, that was responsible. That is, the German and Japanese surpluses should both be viewed as caused by the U.S. deficit.

This view should in fact be qualified somewhat. Germany's current account surplus as a share of GNP in 1984 was only 1.0%, compared with Japan's 2.8%. The difference was Germany's large deficit on invisibles, reflecting, in particular, remittances by guest workers. If we take Germany as a reference point, then we may say that there is in effect a component to the Japanese manufacturing surplus that reflects Japan's unusually large export of capital. This structural surplus component presumably reflects Japan's high savings rate, which makes Japan a natural exporter of capital. The point remains, however, that this structural surplus component is a small fraction of the total Japanese manufacturing surplus.

We may thus imagine a hypothetical accounting for the sources of Japan's trade surplus in manufactured goods, dividing it into three parts: a "primary products deficit" component, reflecting Japan's need to pay for imported raw materials; a "structural surplus" component, reflecting Japan's position as a natural capital exporter; and an "overvalued dollar" component, reflecting the temporary strength of the U.S. dollar in 1984. The first of these components is defined simply as Japan's deficit in primary products. The division between the other two is more difficult to ascertain. Later in this chapter it will be assumed as a base case that the overvalued dollar component of Japan's current account was $15 billion in 1984, or 1.25% of GNP. This was derived as follows. First, all of the $100 billion U.S. current account deficit in 1984 is assumed to represent a temporary dollar overvaluation. (It could be argued that some of this U.S. deficit is structural; however, it should be remembered that the rise in the U.S. deficit is of very recent vintage and was not tied to any substantial shift in either U.S. investment or private saving rates.) Second, it is assumed that if that deficit were eliminated, $15 billion of the shift would come from a reduction in Japan's current account surplus, reflecting Japan's roughly 15% share of the GNP of market economies outside the United States. These assumptions are rough-and-ready, but the essential point seems clear: The Japanese structural surplus on current account is not the main source of the surplus in manufactures.

The relationship between resources and trade also leaves its mark on Japan's pattern of regional trade. In 1984 more than half of Japan's trade surplus with non-oil-exporting countries was the counterpart of a deficit with oil-exporting countries. Thus, Japan's heavy dependence on imported oil can be viewed as the prime cause of its large surplus in trade with industrial countries, including the United States.

Given these figures, it is not surprising that Japanese trade gives rise to friction. But there are still some puzzles. In particular, if Japan and Germany look so similar, why does Japanese trade create so much more friction? Let us consider several possible explanations.

1. Current accounts: Germany's current account surplus is indeed much smaller than Japan's. However, the difference is essentially workers' remittances. It is hard to see why the fact that part of Germany's trade surplus goes to families in Turkey or Yugoslavia should make foreign competitors less upset about losing markets.

2. Scale: Germany is smaller than Japan, and its trade surplus, though slightly larger relative to GNP, is only about half as large in

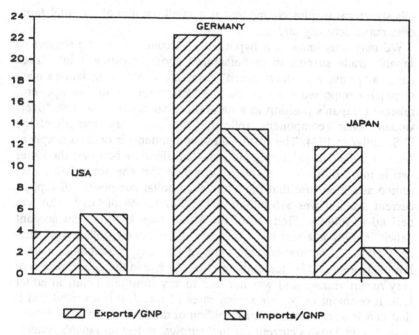

Figure 3.2. Manufactures trade as percentage of GNP.

absolute terms. But Japan certainly experiences much more than twice
as much grief in international trade negotiations. It is hard to believe
that there is a critical mass of manufactures trade surplus somewhere
between $50 and $115 billion.

3. Imports: Japan achieves its surplus with smaller imports *and* exports of manufactures than Germany. Figure 3.2 illustrates the point.
The question is whether Japan's small manufactures imports, aside
from providing a debating point for anti-Japanese rhetoric, actually
contribute to trade tension. Equivalently, if Japan's trade pattern
looked like Germany's, would tension be reduced? It is hard to believe
that it would. Indeed, it is hard to believe that it would even be
possible politically to accommodate Japan's exports if its economy
were as open as Germany's.

4. Cultural gap/racism: Germans look like us, talk a language not
too different from ours, and share a common cultural history; Japanese
do not. Thus, when experts tell us that Germany is not cheating, we
believe them, while we are always ready to believe that Japanese society works in mysterious and inscrutable ways. Unfortunately, there is
almost certainly a component of this kind of xenophobia in the U.S.

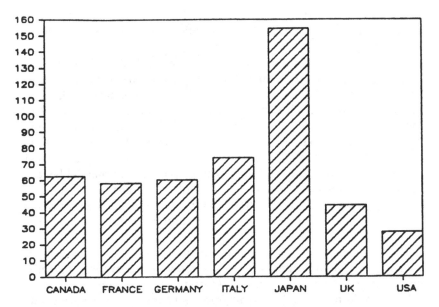

Figure 3.3. Percentage increase in export volume, 1973–1984.

hostility to Japan. It is possible that this will turn out to be the dominant sentiment and that reasoned argument will eventually fail. One can only hope that this is not the case.

So far our proposed explanations of the special friction with Japan seem either of doubtful force or too depressing to accept. There is, however, a further possible explanation that will turn out to yield substantial grounds for hope. This is the view that the cause of Japanese–U.S. trade friction was not so much the current state of that trade as the dynamics – that the rapid growth of Japanese exports, rather than their level, was the problem.

Japanese export growth

Figure 3.3 illustrates a key fact that may help explain the hostility to Japan even more than the features of trade structure we have considered so far. This is the high rate of growth of Japan's exports, which is unique among industrial countries. From 1973 to 1984 Japan's export volume increased by 154% – two and one-half times as much as Germany's.

There are good reasons for expecting rapid growth of exports to be at least as serious a cause of trade friction as the current structure of trade. Both a consideration of the rational interest of potentially protectionist groups and what we know about politics suggest that a rising share of imports will create more opposition than a stable share, however high.

Consider first the rational self-interest of workers and firms. It is surely a reasonable approximation to regard factors of production as sector specific in the short run but mobile between sectors in the long run. What this means is that any sudden shift in the trade pattern will impose capital losses on those factors stuck in the import-competing industries. If the changed trade pattern is retained long enough, however, the factors of production will exit the industry, and the political pressure for protection will abate. There will still be potential beneficiaries from protection that would redistribute income between broad factors of production along Stolper–Samuelson lines, but the pressures arising from these more diffuse interest groups should be much less severe.

The argument that new import competition creates more opposition than old is just the other side of the frequent observation that prolonged protection creates a vested interest in its own continuance. It is a familiar proposition that an import quota imposed for balance-of-payments reasons can give birth to a domestic industry that can prevent the quota's removal; correspondingly, a shift in comparative advantage that is allowed to happen long enough will lead to an exit of the firms and workers that oppose it.

To the rational self-interest argument we may add an empirical observation about the relationship between economics and politics. This is that in electoral politics, at least, the success of incumbents depends more on whether things have been getting better recently than on how good they are in absolute terms. Econometric estimates of voting behavior suggest that it is the recent change in the unemployment rate, not its level, that determines electoral outcomes. By analogy, we can suggest that trade tension depends more on whether foreign competition is perceived as getting more severe than on comparison with some unchanging norm of fair trade.

Suppose we accept that the rate of growth of Japanese exports was at least as important as the current situation at any point in time as a factor in creating trade tension. Then the next question is the source of that rapid export growth. What we want to know is whether the export growth was an inevitable accompaniment to the rapid growth of Japan's economy or whether it had more special and reversible causes.

To understand the sources of rapid export growth in Japan, it is useful to develop an accounting framework that relates four variables: export growth, import growth, the terms of trade, and the trade balance.

Table 3.1. *Japanese trade performance, 1973–1984 (annual rates of change)*[a]

	Exports	Imports	Difference
Volumes	8.5	1.6	6.8
Prices	4.2	8.6	−4.4
Trade balance[b]	NA	NA	−2.2

[a]NA = not available.
[b]Calculated as average annual change in ratio of exports to imports.

First, let us begin with an identity:

$$B = P_x Q_x - P_M Q_M, \tag{1}$$

where B = trade balance,
P_x = export price,
Q_x = export volume,
P_M = import price, and
Q_M = import volume.

If we totally differentiate equation (1), we get

$$dB = Q_x \, dP_x - Q_M \, dP_M + P_x \, dQ_x - P_M \, dQ_M. \tag{2}$$

Equation (2) can be simplified if we make the assumption that initially trade is balanced: $P_x Q_x = P_M Q_M$ (since this was not strictly true for Japan over the period, this will be a source of some slippage in our accounting). The rewritten formula is

$$q_x - q_M = -(p_x - p_M) + b, \tag{3}$$

where the lowercase letters signify rates of growth, and

$$b = dB/P_x Q_x,$$

that is, the change in the trade balance as a fraction of the initial value of exports.

What equation (3) tells us is that the discrepancy between export and import growth rates can be divided in an accounting sense between the rise in import prices relative to export – the terms of trade loss – and the shift of the trade balance into surplus.

Now let us consider the case of Japan. Over the entire period 1973–84 the average annual changes in the terms of equation (3) are shown in Table 3.1. We note immediately that Japanese export growth was much more rapid than the growth of the Japanese economy as a whole – 8.5% versus 3.7% for gross domestic product (GDP). At the same time, import growth, at 1.6% annually, was much less than economic growth. This immediately tells us that Japan's rapid export growth was not fundamentally connected to her general economic growth: If exports and imports had both grown at the same rate as GDP, Japan's export growth would have been less than half of what it was. We can also see that the huge discrepancy between export and import growth rates is primarily accounted for by the worsening of Japan's terms of trade and only secondarily by the move toward trade surplus.

So far no mechanism has been introduced to make this accounting identity into a causal story. If we put the observations here together with the information on trade structure above, however, the story seems very clear. During the post-1973 period, Japan suffered a sharp terms-of-trade worsening due to increases in oil prices. At the same time, there was some movement of Japan into structural current account surplus, as investment demand fell off and savings remained high. All this was reinforced by the overvalued dollar, pushing Japan further into trade surplus. The cause of trade friction was not simply the fact of Japan's extreme trade structure, with its huge surpluses in manufactured goods. It was the fact that this trade structure was still emerging, through a surge in Japanese exports, that made for rising tension.

But if this emphasis on the rate of change is right, it has very upbeat implications. It implies that much of the trade friction of the past decade has been the result, not of enduring features of U.S.–Japanese trade, but of the process of adjustment to a changed world economic environment. Even if that environment were to remain stable, we could expect some reduction of tension as the adjustment was completed. In fact, the news is better still: Since early 1985 we have seen a substantial reversal of both the rise in oil prices and the overvaluation of the dollar. Is the stage now set for a real easing of tensions?

Prospects for U.S.–Japanese trade friction

In the last few months both the value of the dollar and the price of oil have fallen sharply. The dollar–yen rate has fallen to record lows; the real price of oil, incredibly, is at least temporarily down to 1973 levels. It is still too soon to know where these prices will eventually settle. If any large part of the change proves to be durable, however, we are now getting exactly the reverse of the shocks that accounted for rising trade friction in the seventies and eighties.

There is no uncertainty about the qualitative direction of effect of a declining dollar and a declining oil price. The decline of the dollar may be viewed as a new unwillingness by international investors to provide the United States with a large surplus on capital account. As the U.S. capital account surplus declines, so must its current account deficit. At least part of that decline will show up as reduced Japanese trade surpluses and export volume. At the same time, the decline in the price of oil will produce a decline in Japan's primary commodity deficit, which will eventually be offset by a corresponding decline in its manufacturing surplus.

What we need to know, however, is how important this relief will be in quantitative terms. Are the recent declines in oil and the dollar enough to make a crucial difference? To answer this, we need at least a rough model. What I will do is build on the accounting framework developed above to make a first-pass answer to the question of magnitudes. The results suggest that the reduction in trade friction should be major indeed.

A simple model

To make as compact as possible a model of the future of Japanese trade, I will make two simplifying assumptions. First is that Japan's terms of trade will be taken as exogenous – that is, any effects arising from exchange rate changes will be ruled out. Since the yen may be expected to be stronger in the future than it was in the past, this assumption actually weakens my case.

Second, I will treat the Japanese balance of trade as exogenous, simply assuming plausible values rather than explicitly deriving them jointly with the exchange rate. In fact, I will substitute out the exchange rate and deal directly with reduced form expressions for trade flows as functions of the terms of trade and the trade balance. The main justification for this procedure is that it makes life easy. It may also be argued, however, that we know more about the determinants of long-run current accounts than we do about the process of exchange rate adjustment that gets us there.

Let us begin, then, with an equation for the growth of exports. I will assume that the growth rate depends on the rate of change of some measure of the real exchange rate and on a trend term reflecting the growth of the economy as a whole:

$$q_x = e_x r + y, \tag{4}$$

where e_x is the elasticity of exports with respect to the exchange rate, r is the rate of real depreciation, and y is the trend component.

We have a similar equation on the import side, where I assume that the trend component is the same; that is, at a constant real exchange rate imports and exports would grow at the same rate:

$$q_M = -e_M r + y. \tag{5}$$

We can now use equations (3), (4), and (5) to solve for the growth rates of both imports and exports as functions of terms of trade and the trade balance. We first note that

$$q_x - q_M = (e_x + e_M)r.$$

But from (3) this implies that the rate of real depreciation is:

$$r = (p_M - p_x + b)/(e_x + e_M).$$

This gives us our equations for volume growth:

$$q_x = y + s_x[p_M - p_x + b], \tag{6}$$

$$q_M = y + s_M[p_M - p_x + b], \tag{7}$$

where $s_x = e_x/(e_x + e_M)$ and $s_M = -e_m/(e_x + e_M)$.

What equations (6) and (7) say, in words, is that there is assumed to be an underlying rate of trade growth common to exports and imports. Shifts in either the terms of trade or the trade balance relative to exports will cause a divergence between export and import growth rates; this divergence will always be divided between higher export growth and lower import growth in the same proportions.

Our next step is to quantify these volume equations. We begin by choosing a plausible value for y. Over the period 1973–84 the Japanese economy grew in real terms at an annual rate of 3.7%. It seems reasonable to suppose that other things being equal, Japan's trade would have grown a little faster than GNP. I will assume a growth rate y of 4.0% annually.

This now allows us to go directly to s_x and s_M. From 1973 to 1984, export volume grew at 8.5% per year, an excess of 4.5 percentage points over our assumed y. Import volume grew at 1.6%, 2.4 percentage points less than y. The divergence in export and import growth was 6.8%. So in the past, we have $s_x = 4.5/6.8 = 0.65$, and similarly $s_M = 2.4/6.8 = 0.35$. Given any shock to Japan's external situation, whether from the terms of trade or the capital account, we can expect 65% to be reflected in export volume and 35% in import volume.

What we have now done is to create a small envelope whose back is well-suited to quick calculations. We now ask what this model tells us about the implications of recent international events for Japan's trade.

Recent shocks and Japan's export growth

In assessing the prospects for Japan's trade, we need estimates of how much correction is currently taking place. Two questions arise: how much will the decline in the overvalued dollar reduce Japan's current account surplus, and how much will oil prices fall?

Earlier I suggested as a plausible guess that an elimination of the U.S. current deficit would be associated with a decline in Japan's surplus of $15 billion from its 1984 level, or 1.25% of GNP. Since Japan's current surplus in 1984 was 2.8%, this implies a remaining structural surplus of 1.55% of GNP – not a small number. I will make a 1.25% decline in Japan's current surplus the central case. For comparison, however, the case of a 0.5% decline and a 2% decline will also be considered.

Oil prices are still in considerable flux. At the time of this writing they were dropping into single digit numbers. There seems to be no alternative except to consider a wide range of possibilities. Using 1984 as a baseline, I will consider the cases of 20, 40, and 60% declines, with 40% the central case.

To examine the consequences of these alternative scenarios, we first convert these assumptions into trade balance changes as a fraction of exports. In 1984 the average of Japan's exports and imports was $146 billion, so a trade balance reduction of $15 billion would have corresponded to 10.3%. Also, in 1984 fuels accounted for 45% of Japan's imports, so a 40% decline in energy prices would correspond to a terms-of-trade improvement of 18%. Thus in the central case the shock term $(p_M - p_x + b)$ in the export growth equation is set equal to −28.3. The same calculation is made for each combination of oil price fall and current account adjustment.

Now the adjustment will not come all at once, and in any case we are not only interested in the very near term. Furthermore, the framework is lacking in realistic dynamics. We can, however, use the approach to ask what the *average* rate of export growth over some specified future period is. I arbitrarily take a 5-year time horizon, treating the shock as if it were spread evenly over that period.

Tables 3.2 and 3.3 show the results of the assumed shocks for Japanese export and import growth over the next 5 years. Since most of the response is supposed to come on the export side, it is the export table

Table 3.2. *Five-year growth rates of exports under alternative scenarios*

Decline in oil price (%)	Decline in Japanese current account surplus (% of GNP)		
	0.5	1.25	2.0
20	2.3	1.5	0.7
40	1.1	0.3	−0.5
60	0.0	−0.8	−1.6

Table 3.3. *Five-year Japanese import growth under alternative scenarios*

Decline in oil prices (%)	Decline in current account surplus (% of GNP)		
	0.5	1.25	2.0
20	4.9	5.4	5.8
40	5.5	6.0	6.4
60	6.2	6.6	7.0

that is more striking. If Japan's current account surplus falls to 1.55% of GNP – well above its average during the 1970s – and oil prices remain 40% below their 1984 level, we can expect to see virtually zero growth in Japanese export volume over the next 5 years.

Clearly, such a cessation of Japanese export growth would bring about a dramatic reduction of trade friction. In fact, it will probably seem to most readers to be too good to be true. It is important to recognize, therefore, that there is nothing outlandish about this calculation. We have simply applied to the future of Japan's trade the logic that many observers have applied to its past. Oil price increases and a move toward current account surplus led to a pace of Japanese export expansion during 1973–1984 greatly in excess of GNP growth. Even a stabilization of oil prices and the current account would have implied a considerable subsequent slowdown. The fact that oil prices have once again fallen, and the likelihood of at least some reduction in Japan's surplus, mean that for the medium-term future Japan's exports must grow considerably more slowly than its GNP.

How high the yen?

The mechanism implicit in our reduced-form equations (6) and (7) involves exchange rate appreciation. I have tried, however, to avoid making the predictions about trade volumes contingent on an exchange rate forecast. Instead, the problem has been stated in terms of the link between fundamentals, the price of oil and the structural current surplus, and the trade outcome. The reason for stating the problem this way is to place the emphasis on the trade adjustment that must eventually happen rather than on the unpredictable details of the exchange rate path that gets us there.

Nonetheless, it is clear that the trade adjustment described here implies a very strong yen compared with that of 1984. It is an irresistible temptation to speculate about the level of the yen necessary to effect the shift in trade structure implied by tables 3.2 and 3.3.

The nominal value of the yen has of course been touching record levels in recent weeks. This apparent strength needs, however, to be discounted for at least three, and possibly four, reasons. First, there is the obvious point of differential inflation rates, with Japan having substantially lower inflation since 1980 than the United States. Second, there is the Kravis–Balassa effect: rapid Japanese productivity growth is disproportionately concentrated in tradeables, imparting a substantial bias to real exchange rate measures based on aggregate prices (see Kravis 1956, Balassa 1964). Third, there is the shift in the real exchange rate implied by the fall in oil prices, perhaps offset by a shift of Japan into structural current account surplus. Finally, and most speculatively, there is the question of "hysteresis" in the trade pattern, in which reversing the dollar's rise need not reverse all of its effects.

Inflation and productivity

The inflation and productivity issues can best be treated together. Suppose that, in standard fashion, we try to guess at the equilibrium value of a currency by calcuating a purchasing power par on some historical baseline. Our usual problem is finding a baseline; in the Japanese case, however, this problem is dwarfed by the problem of divergence in price indices. Richard Marston (1986) has recently emphasized the point that rapid Japanese productivity growth is concentrated primarily in its manufacturing sector. This unbalanced productivity growth means that a Japanese–U.S. purchasing power parity

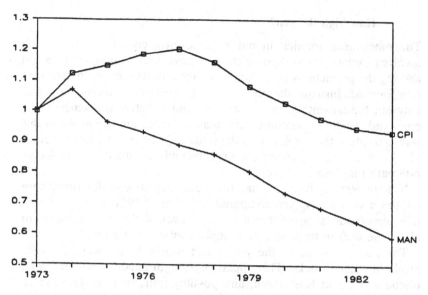

Figure 3.4. Alternative PPP measures, 1973–1983.

(PPP) calculated for prices of manufactured goods falls steadily relative to one calculated using more aggregate indexes, such as consumer price indexes (CPIs). Figure 3.4 shows the extent of this divergence. Using an arbitrary 1973 base, it compares the ratio of the Japanese CPI to its U.S. counterpart to the ratio of the Japanese manufacturing value-added deflator (MAN) to its U.S. counterpart. Incredibly, the divergence between the manufacturing price relative and the CPI price relative grew at an average annual rate of 4.4% over the 1973–1983 period.

To make a guess at the equilibrium yen, we need first to decide which of these price indexes to use. It seems clear that manufactures is the right choice, since what we want is the "battlefield" sector in which the United States and Japan compete. Also, we need to choose a baseline. Somewhat arbitrarily, I will take the geometric average manufacturing real exchange rate over the period 1973–1979 as the base. Finally, to bring the estimate up to date I assume that the manufacturing PPP has continued to fall relative to the ratio of CPIs at the same rate as during the 1973–1983 period, that is, 4.4% per year, and extrapolate using actual consumer price inflation. The result is shown in Figure 3.5: A seemingly innocuous procedure leads us to a purchasing power parity yen of less than 140.

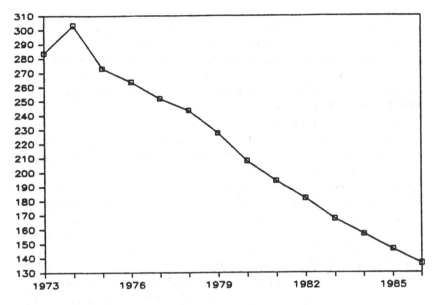

Figure 3.5. PPP value of yen, 1973–1979 base.

Oil prices and the current account

Ideally, we would like to correct the PPP estimate by an adjustment for the two offsetting factors of a rise in Japan's structural current account surplus and the decline in oil prices. During the 1970s Japan ran only small surpluses in its current account; with the liberalization of capital markets it now seems likely that Japan will run persistent current account surpluses. This factor will tend to weaken the yen. On the other hand, the decline in oil prices reduces the manufacturing surplus associated with any given current account and thus implies a stronger yen. It is useful to think of these effects as percentages of trade: Each 10% fall in the price of oil reduces the needed non-oil surplus by 4.5% of the average of imports and exports, while each percentage point of GNP added to the current account surplus adds 8.4%. If our baseline case of a 40% fall in oil prices and a 1.55% structural surplus were right, the net effect would be to strengthen the equilibrium yen.

Hysteresis

There is a widespread belief among businesspeople, shared by some economists, that the markets lost by the United States from a sustained strong dollar cannot be recaptured simply by restoring the dollar to its former level. A model in which temporary overvaluation can cause permanent loss of market share may be referred to as one characterized by hysteresis. A purely hysterical view of the trade balance would say that the exchange rate determines not the *level* of that balance but instead its rate of change. Hysteresis in the trade pattern can be justified theoretically by invoking the role of economies of scale, especially dynamic economies such as the learning curve.

There is no hard evidence at this point on the importance of hysteresis in practice. My own view is that there is substantial circumstantial evidence for hysteresis in the observed fact that countries such as Japan, that have had to expand their exports rapidly over time, have not had to have persistently declining relative export prices. Estimated trade flow equations reflect this either by finding that fast-growing countries, by coincidence, have low income elasticities of import demand and face high elasticities of export demand, or by including domestic capacity in the export equation. A possible alternative explanation is that fast-growing countries are able to buy steadily rising market shares simply by having a low, rather than a declining, relative price.

If there is in fact substantial hysteresis in international trade, the implication is not that the United States can never win its markets back. Instead, it is that for the United States to win back its markets, the dollar must go through a period of undervaluation comparable to its previous overvaluation. While I am not in a position to quantify this effect, it seems to point to an even higher yen than the previous numbers would suggest.

Financial markets and short-run exchange rate determination

This chapter has made a point of staying clear of the attempt to model the short-run determination of the exchange rate in financial markets. It could, for instance, be the case that even though the yen must eventually rise above 140, it is temporarily being kept low by the differential in real interest rates between the United States and Japan. Long-term government bonds are continuing to pay about 3.3 percentage points more in the United States than in Japan, a difference that exceeds conventional measures of the expected inflation differential.

We have just seen, however, that the biased nature of productivity growth in Japan implies that there should be a secular appreciation of the real exchange rate of the yen against the dollar, at least when the rate is measured using aggregate price indexes. For relative purchasing power parity in manufactures to have been maintained in the 1973–1983 period, the real yen as calculated using CPIs would have had to appreciate 4.4% annually. This suggests that the apparently higher real interest rate in the United States results from the choice of an inappropriate measure of inflation. If we use manufacturing value-added deflators, we would almost surely find that the real interest rate is higher in Japan. So there is no good reason for the real yen not to rise to the levels that Japanese trade adjustment must eventually require. Apparently financial markets either do not agree or do not understand this.

Our discussion of the value of the yen rests on shakier ground than the earlier discussion of Japanese trade adjustment. Certainly, after the last 5 years, nobody can have much confidence in any exchange rate forecast. What the numbers appear to say, however, is that the adjustment of Japan's trade to a reduced current account surplus and lower oil prices should be accompanied by an extremely strong yen. Somewhat startlingly, I have no difficulty in convincing myself that a yen above 140 is entirely reasonable.

Summary and conclusions

This chapter has offered something that is unusual in discussions of U.S.–Japanese trade relations: an optimistic outlook. The calculations on which this optimism is based will probably seem startling. Let us then finish the discussion by reviewing the argument, to see why the numbers suggested are not at all outlandish.

The key political assumption here is that U.S.–Japanese trade tension in fact owes little to Japanese trade and business practices. The accusations about these practices in the United States, I argue, are rationalizations for protectionist demands that would be there in any case. If the Ministry for International Trade and Industry (MITI) did not exist, the Americans would have to invent it.

The source of trade friction lies instead in the structure of Japanese trade, in the huge Japanese surplus in manufactures and especially in the rapid pace of growth of Japan's exports. The surplus in manufactures is primarily the counterpart of a huge deficit in raw materials, and part of the rest can be attributed to the overvalued dollar. The rapid growth in Japan's exports was *not* an inevitable counterpart of her much slower economic growth. Instead, it was driven mostly by the deterioration of Japan's terms of trade as oil prices rose and partly by a shift of Japan into current account surplus – of which, again, part can be attributed to the overvalued dollar.

Some relief from the frictions caused by rapidly growing Japanese exports would have come even if oil prices and the U.S. current account deficit had merely stabilized: Japan's export growth would have dropped down to something like her GNP growth once the adjustment was over. However, we have suddenly been given a much stronger dose of medicine, with oil prices plunging and the dollar dropping to levels that should reduce the current account deficit sharply. If we accept the story about what happened in the 1973–1984 period, we must also accept that the story will now run in reverse: For some time to come, Japan's exports will grow much more slowly than her GNP. The precise numbers given in this chapter are only speculative and illustrative, but they convey a message that is not too sensitive to the details.

The inevitable counterpart of this message is that we are entering an era of an extremely strong yen. The guess at the equilibrium yen is even more speculative than the analysis of export growth, but again the point seems clear: The sharp appreciation of the yen since 1985 has not overshot, and there is probably still a considerable way to go.

It is generally a bad strategy to be too optimistic in policy papers. Thus I will do my best to end on a pessimistic note. There will clearly be strong internal pressures on Japan's government to block the trade adjustment predicted here. The result could be an attempt to hold the yen down through massive intervention and even a return to activist trade policies. These pressures should be resisted, lest they manage to keep alive trade friction that should otherwise be fading away of its own accord.

References

Balassa, B. (1964). "The Purchasing-Power Parity: a Reappraisal," *Journal of Political Economy*, **72**, 534–559.

Bergsten, C. F., and Cline, R. (1985). *The U.S.–Japan Trade Problem*, Washington, DC, Institute for International Economics.

Branson, W. (1986). "The Dollar and the International Monetary System," testimony presented at the Joint Economic Committee, February 1986.

Council of Economic Advisers (1985). *Economic Report of the President for 1983*, Washington, DC, U.S. Government Printing Office.

Kravis, I. B. (1956). "Wages and Foreign Trade," *Review of Economics and Statistics*, February, pp. 14–30.

Marston, R. (1986). "Real Exchange Rates and Productivity Growth in the United States and Japan," presented at AEI Conference on Real-Financial Linkages, February 1986.

Saxonhouse, G. R. (1983). "Tampering with Comparative Advantage in Japan?" statement submitted to the U.S. International Trade Commission.
(1985). "What's Wrong with Japanese Trade Structure," Research Seminar in International Economics Discussion Paper No. 166, University of Michigan.
Thurow, L. C. (1985). "A Time to Dismantle the World Economy," *The Economist*, November 9, 1985.

Discussion

SHUNICHI TSUTSUI

On the issue of the U.S.–Japanese trade problem, there are many arguments that unfair trade practices and industrial policies, markets, and even cultural differences on the Japanese side are the real causes of the problem. Instead, Krugman emphasizes the following two points. First, Krugman reminds us of the fact that Japan's trade structure is almost identical to that of West Germany if we allow for the difference in real GNP between the two countries. That is, Japan's trade pattern as a percentage of GNP is nothing unique to Japan. In this sense, Krugman argues convincingly that the essence of what is called Japan's trade problem is not based on many commonly held views such as Japan's unfair trade practices, closed markets, and so forth.

Second, Krugman argues that Japan's trade problem has been brought about by "environmental" changes. He thinks that these environmental changes primarily consist of higher oil prices and the stronger U.S. dollar. Over the past 10 years, these changes have been the real culprits driving today's so-called trade problem. Now, however, the tide has turned: Oil prices are lower and the dollar is much weaker. As a result, Krugman predicts that Japan's trade problem will be greatly alleviated.

While I completely agree with Krugman with respect to his first argument, I have some reservations concerning his second argument. I cannot be as optimistic as Krugman about the resolution of Japan's trade problem.

To begin with, Krugman stresses the importance of Japan's export growth rate over the past 10 years as a major cause of Japan's trade problem, especially with the United States. According to his argument, an extremely rapid growth in Japan's exports is largely responsible for generating fear and hostility toward Japan, but the absolute level of trade surplus is not. Of course, he does not say that Japan's high export growth rate is the sole cause of Japan's trade problem. But it is apparent throughout the chapter that he believes the slowdown of Japan's export growth rate will definitely improve the situation. One of the major results in this chapter concerns estimates of Japan's export growth rate 5 years from now under various scenarios. Among them, the central scenario is this: Oil prices fall by 40%, the overvalued dollar is corrected. Under this scenario, Krugman derives virtually zero growth in Japan's export rate. According to his definition of the sources of Japan's trade problem, this amounts to saying that Japan's problem will disappear. However, I think that this argument is overly simplified because there is a good possibility that the level of Japan's trade surplus may still remain very high even though Japan's export growth rate decreases substantially. Thus, it seems quite questionable to simply say that the slowdown of Japan's growth rate means the end of the trade problem. A persistent, large Japanese trade surplus *level* has to cause problems.

Furthermore, as Krugman admits, the estimates that support his optimistic results are far from complete and have several problems. To understand this more clearly, let me rewrite his reduced form equation for Japan's export growth rate:

$$q_x = y + s_x(p_M - p_x + b), \tag{1}$$

where q_x, p_x, p_M, and b are growth rates of the volume of exports, export price, import price, and trade balance, respectively, s_x is a coefficient to be determined, and y is a trend component. The value of s_x is determined from past observations of the above-mentioned variables:

$$s_x = (q_x^* - y)/(p_M^* - p_x^* + b^*) = (q_x^* - y)/(q_x^* - q_M^*). \tag{2}$$

Note that the asterisk denotes the value of the past observation. To derive the second part of equation (2), we use the identity: $q_x - q_M = -p_x + p_M + b$. It is clear from equation (2) that the determinants of s_x are q_x^*, q_M^*, and y. In the chapter, Krugman uses the average values for q_x and q_M over the time period from 1973 to 1984. As for y, Krugman bases its estimate on the average growth rate of real GNP over the same period.

The problems with these estimates are as follows.

1. To get his estimates, Krugman uses only one time period: 1973–84. However, in this time period, there are two distinctively different subperiods: one from 1973 to 1979, the other from 1980 to 1984. Of course, 1979 is the year of the second oil crisis. In addition, from 1973

to 1979, the dollar was undervalued, while from 1980 to 1984, the dollar was overvalued. In Japan, we observe a significant change in the growth rate of real GNP in these two subperiods. Thus, it seems very likely that the division of the two time periods can end up with two very different estimates of y and s_X. Consequently, the results based on these estimates can also be very different.

2. We have to be much more careful about the estimate of y. As a value of y, Krugman assumes that it is slightly higher than the average real GNP growth rate of 3.7% (i.e., he assigns 4.0% for y). I do not see any convincing explanation for this assumption, even though the value of y is crucial to deriving such optimistic results as Krugman's. For example, if one chooses 6.0% for y instead of 4.0%, then the corresponding estimate of s_X changes drastically from 0.65 to 0.37. Therefore, even under Krugman's central scenario, Japan's export growth rate will never be close to zero in 5 years. In other words, the effectiveness and ineffectiveness of the environmental changes greatly depend on the value of y. So a more careful discussion of its determination is warranted.

3. Krugman assumes a 5-year adjustment period after the environmental changes. The length of this adjustment period is also deeply related to the results. More study has to be done on this as well.

4. In equation (1), it is assumed that the trade is balanced originally, that is, $Q_x P_x = Q_M P_M$. However, at this time, this assumption is clearly unrealistic. The reduced form must be revised to take into account the present imbalance because this probably has a strong bearing on the results.

Certainly, I agree with Krugman that the environmental changes he examines are major factors in Japan's trade problem. However, the issue is much more complex and wider in scope (i.e., it appears that the issue includes not only macroeconomic elements but also microeconomic elements). To clarify this point, consider the following question: Why is it that other industrialized countries (with the possible exception of West Germany) do not have such a trade problem? Despite the fact that the environmental change affects not only Japan but also most of the industrialized countries, why is it that only Japan is subject to the problem? In answer to these questions, one might say that Japan's y and s_X are different from others; hence Japan has the trade problem. But this kind of answer prompts us to ask *why* Japan's y and s_X are different from others. Much of Japan's trade problem results from this difference. Thus, until we completely understand the mechanism generating these differences in y and s_X, the problem of Japan's trade imbalance will persist.

Discussion

HARRY P. BOWEN

An accepted proposition is that most people dislike sudden change. In his chapter, Krugman uses this proposition as a basis for understanding the sources of trade friction between Japan and the United States. Specifically, he argues that the extent of trade friction is an increasing function of the rate of growth of trade and not its level. The economics underlying the importance of the rate of growth is that the more rapid are changes in trade, the larger (and perhaps less anticipated) are the short-run income losses suffered by the productive factors working in a country's import-competing sector.

To support his proposition, Krugman compares the trade structures of Japan and Germany and asks why, if these countries appear so similar in terms of their trade structure, has Germany not been subjected to the protectionists' outcry that has been directed at Japan. As noted, the answer to this question is obtained by examining the difference in the rate of growth of each country's exports. Although I agree that the difference in growth rates is important, it is not the whole story. Also important is that Japan's share of total U.S. imports exceeds Germany's share. In particular, at the mid-point of Krugman's period of analysis (1978), Japan held 14% of the U.S. import market while Germany held 5.8%. Therefore, I would argue that both a higher rate of export growth and being a relatively large player in the U.S. market is what makes Japan different from Germany when it comes to arousing U.S. protectionist sentiment.

Accepting, however, that a high rate of growth of trade increases trade friction, the chapter examines the sources of past growth in Japan's current account over the period 1973–1984. Using simple accounting relationships, Krugman finds the growth of Japan's trade surplus over this period to be primarily associated with a terms-of-trade deterioration that the author ascribes to an increase in the price of oil. Considering only exports, Krugman finds that less than one-half of Japan's export growth is explained by Japan's overall economic growth; Japan's real GDP increased 3.7% per year while its export volume increased 8.5% per year, leaving an unexplained gap of 4.8% per annum.

Although not discussed in the chapter, the accounting framework implies that the gap of 4.8% corresponds to an increase in Japan's average propensity to export out of GDP (9% in 1973), that is, an increase in Japan's export orientation. What accounts for this shift in export orientation? One answer is that it represents the outcome of a conscious "industrial policy." However, existing evidence on the impact of whatever industrial policies Japan has pursued suggests this explanation should be dismissed. Instead, it is likely that the increase in export orientation is the outcome of natural market forces.

On the basis of his growth accounting, Krugman concludes that oil price increases and an "overvalued dollar" were primarily responsible for Japan's rapid export growth and the increase in its trade surplus. And if so, Krugman continues, then recent declines in oil prices and in the value of the dollar should be expected to reduce Japan's export growth and its trade surplus. Given this, Krugman develops projections of the expected impact on Japanese export growth under alternative assumptions about the price of oil and the value of the dollar.

The base case projection assumes a current dollar overvaluation (vis-à-vis all currencies) equal to the change that would be required to eliminate the *entire* U.S. current account deficit. The assumed elimination of the U.S. current account deficit is then translated into a decrease in Japan's current account surplus of around $15 billion. Combining the assumed dollar depreciation with the assumption that oil prices remain 40% below past levels, Krugman projects that Japanese export growth over the next 5 years will fall to almost zero. While the projection seems optimistic, even his worst-case scenario (minor dollar depreciation and oil prices 20% below past levels) projects Japan's export growth to slow to about 2% over the next 5 years. For Krugman, these projections suggest an end to the Japanese problem.

How plausible are these projections? Before offering a judgment, some further analysis of the possible sources of Japan's export growth is warranted. In particular, the role of oil price changes in promoting Japanese export growth needs to be clarified.

If the effects of growth on exports are ignored, a terms-of-trade deterioration is normally expected to reduce both exports *and* imports. Why, then, did the oil price shocks and resulting deterioration in Japan's terms of trade lead to an increase in Japan's exports as suggested by the chapter? The answer to this question is Japan's special dependence on imported oil. Specifically, this dependence implies that (1) oil accounts for a major fraction of Japan's import bundle and (2) Japan's (short-run) demand for oil is inelastic. The first point implies that any change in the price of oil would have a relatively large effect on Japan's terms of trade. The second point means that the short-run effect of a terms-of-trade deterioration would be a decrease in imports but an increase in exports.

Although Japan's dependence on imported oil implies that an oil price increase would increase exports, an oil price increase is not the only source of either a terms-of-trade deterioration or an export expansion. For Japan, a factor of certainly equal importance is the high

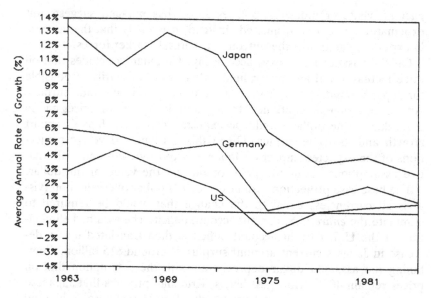

Figure 3.6. Growth rates of capital per worker.

rate of productivity growth concentrated in its export sector. In addition, most would acknowledge that the 1970s involved a noticeable shift in world demand toward Japanese goods, partly reflecting changed perceptions about the quality of Japanese goods.

The importance of increases in productivity and in world demand in generating Japan's export expansion is best understood by noting that Japan's long-run demand for oil, and for imports in general, is expected to be elastic. Thus, without increases in productivity and in world demand, the long-run effect of an oil price increase and subsequent terms-of-trade deterioration would be a reduction in exports.

Since a sustained increase in exports results from increases in factors such as productivity and demand, a decline in oil prices need not reduce Japan's trade surplus and export growth by the extent suggested in the chapter. Although declining oil prices would tend to reduce exports; particularly in the short run, this effect could be offset in the long run by increases in productivity and in world demand. Of course, the magnitude of the offset is an empirical question whose answer would require a study far beyond the scope of this discussion.

Nonetheless, an idea of both the past importance of productivity changes and their possible future impact on Japan's growth can be obtained by examining Figure 3.6. The figure shows annual rates of growth in the overall capital–labor ratio of Japan, Germany, and the United States from 1963 to 1982. The trends in these growth rates provide an indication of the changes in each country's labor productivity (ignoring the productivity-enhancing effects of technological change).

Note first that the growth rate data suggest an explanation for the worldwide increase in trade frictions over the past two decades. Namely, Japan's higher rate of productivity growth implies it has received an increasing share of world income. The role that the implied redistribution of world income has played in generating trade frictions is simply the counterpart to the sector-specific income losses underlying Krugman's thesis. In this context, note also that the suggested change in Germany's share of world income has largely paralleled that of the United States and thus offers another explanation for the difference between Japan and Germany in generating trade frictions vis-à-vis the United States.

Japan's significantly higher rate of capital accumulation and implied growth in productivity suggests these factors figured prominently in its export growth. At a minimum, Japan's high rate of capital accumulation reinforced the short-run effect of oil price increases on its terms of trade and thus on export growth, and it is also likely to have played a major role in sustaining Japan's export expansion. Overall, the data suggest an explanation for Krugman's finding of a strong relationship between Japan's export growth and a deterioration in its terms of trade.

Finally, the data indicate that Japan's rate of capital accumulation is converging toward that of the United States and Germany. This suggests that the growth and attendant economic adjustment (dislocation?) that characterized the 1970s would be expected to diminish in the 1980s. And thus one might expect a future reduction in trade frictions even if oil prices failed to decline.

The foregoing suggests that while Japanese productivity increases would offset the effect of oil price reductions on export growth, the magnitude of the offset is likely to be smaller in the 1980s than it was in the 1970s. Given this, it is not unrealistic to expect that the recent declines in the price of oil could reduce Japanese export growth, at least in the short run, by the amount suggested by Krugman's analysis.

A factor not discussed above but that would contribute to slower export growth is an appreciation of the yen. Krugman viewed the exchange rate issue as one of an "overvalued" dollar and based his projections on an expected dollar depreciation. To support the prospect of a dollar depreciation, Krugman calculated PPP values of the yen vis-à-vis the dollar based on manufacturing value added. Based on these PPP values, Krugman concluded that a yen value of 140 per dollar is not unlikely.

While the PPP calculation does suggest a stronger yen, a compelling argument against a major dollar depreciation, at least in the medium run, continues to be the relatively low U.S. savings rate coupled with the budget financing requirements of the U.S. government. Recall that the chapter's base case calculation assumes a dollar overvaluation equal to the change that would be required to eliminate the *entire* U.S. current account. Of course, the counterpart to this assumption is a major reduction in the U.S. capital account surplus. This raises the question of what alternative sources would be available for financing the U.S. budget deficit, or more importantly, what price (i.e., interest rate) would be required to call forth the needed financing. Of course, the subsequent rise in the interest rate would imply a change in the capital account that is counter to the initial effect of the dollar depreciation.

Another argument against a significant dollar depreciation is that the increase in Japan's real income resulting from any decrease in oil prices might simply be used to increase purchases of U.S. government debt. Thus, as Krugman admits, any medium-term forecast of the exchange rate must carry with it a relatively large standard error.

The above discussion has called attention to factors that suggest the chapter's projections of a significant decline in Japan's export growth and trade surplus due to falling oil prices and a dollar depreciation should not be taken too seriously. However, any questions about the adequacy of the projections should not undercut Krugman's insight into the potential for a fall in oil prices to retard Japanese export growth and also his recognition of the important relationship that exists between the rate of growth of trade and trade friction. Finally, whatever the magnitude of the effects, Krugman's indication that recent economic events can be expected to ease U.S.–Japanese trade frictions is cause for optimism.

CHAPTER 4

The Japanese–U.S. trade friction: some perspectives from the Japanese business community

MASAYA MIYOSHI

Introduction

The allegation that Japan's economic and trade behavior is unfair seems fairly widespread in the United States. This assessment, I think, stems at least in part from an American tendency to seek quick solutions and to get irritated when the situation fails to develop as they see fit. And when this happens, Americans all too quickly point an accusing finger at Japan.

Such accusations are particularly puzzling in the absence of any consensus as to what constitutes "unfair" trade practices. It is useful, therefore, to examine exactly what Americans mean by "unfair" trade practices. Three possible definitions come to mind. First, the General Agreement on Tariffs and Trade (GATT) and other international rules constitute one yardstick to measure whether or not someone is in violation of the rules of the game.

Informed Americans, however, know that average tariff rates are low in Japan by international standards and other barriers are also considerably reduced and will dismiss unfair trade allegations as measured by this yardstick as simple misunderstanding.

The second yardstick is the principle of reciprocity. The principle of reciprocity requires that the same market conditions enjoyed by Japanese products and services in the American market be provided to American products and services in the Japanese market. Should Japan be considered an unfair trading partner by this measure, substantial trade friction would readily develop. In deciding the right and wrong of such an assertion, it is therefore most important that both sides exercise pragmatic judgment based on concrete examples.

The third yardstick concerns the presence of bilateral trade imbalances. The typical argument runs as follows: The U.S. trade imbalance with Japan is already enormous. And if the situation is left unredressed, the imbalance will likely increase. Furthermore, unless the

45

trade imbalance is decreased, the United States will take little stock in Japan's claim that it is an honest trading partner. This argument illustrates a conflict in values between the United States, which attaches more importance to outcomes, and Japan, which regards intentions as more important.

Even more crucial than this difference in value judgment is the fact that this type of argument stems from irritation on the part of Americans caused by the loss of U.S. competitiveness vis-à-vis Japan in a number of key industrial sectors. This irritation is exacerbated by the perception of many Americans that the size of Japanese development assistance and defense expenditures are not commensurate with Japan's economic capabilities. Indeed, there are those Americans who wonder which country, the United States or Japan, really won the war in the Pacific.

Most Japanese do not understand the fundamental reasons behind American accusations of unfair trade practices in the third category. In coping with trade friction, however, it is important that Japan enhance its understanding in this area. What appears on the surface to be a conviction by America that Japan engages in unfair trade practices may often be nothing more than a knee-jerk American response to a loss of competitiveness.

Undeniably, the U.S.–Japanese trade imbalance plays an important role in the trade friction between the two nations. What then are the prospects for improving this trade imbalance? Many Japanese are much more optimistic about long-run solutions to this imbalance than short-run solutions.

On the other hand, many Americans seem to expect quick results through sharp appreciation of the yen, Japanese government measures to stimulate domestic demand, and increased access to Japanese markets. And if increased access and measures to stimulate demand prove ineffective, many Americans would cry for further appreciation of the yen, for example, to 150 yen to the dollar or even 130 yen. To those of us who know that structural factors are responsible for a significant part of the trade imbalance between the United States and Japan, such expectations of a "quick fix" are uninformed and unrealistic.

Any effort that attempts to improve the trade imbalance entirely through yen appreciation and ignores policy measures to deal with the structural causes of the trade imbalance is in fact "burning the house to roast the pig." The cure will be worse than the disease.

To some extent, progress has been made in redressing structural causes of the trade imbalance in recent years. Japanese business and industry are well aware of the changes that need to occur. However, more time is required before these changes can produce tangible effects. Whether or not such tangible effects will come soon enough to prevent protectionist arguments from heating up again in the U.S. Congress is an open question.

Redressing the trade imbalance

In dealing effectively with the considerable problems posed by the present trade imbalance and the resulting trade friction, it is first necessary that Japan and the United States reach an agreement as to its actual cause and not simply point accusing fingers at each other. In this section, I would like to discuss what appear to be the major causes of the trade imbalance between Japan and the U.S.

Exchange rate misalignment

The weak yen clearly played an important role in the huge Japanese–U.S. trade imbalance and the resulting trade friction. In the aftermath of the G5 meeting in September of 1985, however, the yen has appreciated dramatically. Appreciation of the yen will certainly mitigate U.S. trade imbalances with Japan. However, the extent of the reduction will probably not be large. This is so because the trade imbalance is not entirely an exchange rate phenomenon but also reflects important structural factors, such as the differential savings rate between Japan and the United States and the higher income elasticity of Japanese exports tc the United States. It is important that both countries recognize these facts and not embark on an exchange rate readjustment "binge."

Market accessibility

The Japanese market is just as open as any other market in the industrialized world if differences in social customs and legal and administrative systems are taken into account. Trade without friction requires, however, some standardization of trade barriers among trading nations. Seen from this perspective, there are various existing barriers to imports that should be eliminated as quickly as possible. However, even if these barriers are removed, Japanese imports from the United States will probably not increase that much unless government and people make concerted efforts to bring about such an increase. Again, it will take time before tangible results occur.

Macroeconomic policy

It is generally acknowledged that an important cause of the Japanese–U.S. trade imbalance is the savings shortage and expansionary fiscal policy in the United States and the savings surplus and lack of expansionary fiscal stimulus in Japan. Clearly, these factors matter a great deal. But even these important factors cannot be (though indeed they have been) overemphasized.

Even if Japan adopted expansionary fiscal policies without regard for the large deficits and high inflation rates that might result and succeeded in raising her GNP by 10 percent (more than three times the present rate), the U.S. trade imbalance with Japan would probably not be drastically reduced. Recently, studies by various Japanese research institutions support this argument, finding that the Japanese income elasticity of exports from the United States is quite low.

Primary commodity prices

In the years immediately after the first oil crisis, the price of primary commodities soared, with the result that Japanese imports from the United States expanded and the U.S. imbalance with Japan decreased sharply. We are now experiencing exactly the opposite phenomenon. Falling oil and other primary commodity prices translate into cheaper Japanese exports. Current estimates indicate that several billion dollars of the Japanese–U.S. trade imbalance is due to the effect of declining primary commodity prices. Should they increase substantially, reduction of the trade imbalance could be expected. However, such prospects are not in sight for the near future.

Product variety and improvements

Japan has done much to maintain the high income elasticity of her exports to the United States. New products have come out one after another, and the product mix has become ever more sophisticated. As a result, Japanese exports to the United States have continued to expand rapidly. On the other hand, U.S. exports to Japan have centered largely on agricultural products and other primary commodities where income elasticities tend to be low.

Thus, the differential income elasticities in Japan and the United States are not entirely due to different tastes toward one another's goods. That is, lower income elasticities of imports in Japan are not simply due to inherent Japanese aversion to U.S. products. Rather, the income elasticity differential is also the result of different degrees of marketing and innovation efforts as well as the nature of the goods traded.

While the causes of the trade imbalance are complex and perhaps seemingly insurmountable, changes that will improve the situation are taking place. A sharp increase in Japanese direct investment in the United States in recent years deserves special mention. A major part of this Japanese investment is expected to contribute to import substitution. Furthermore, the correction of the strong dollar is expected to help American business recover some measure of its international competitiveness, encouraging plant and equipment investment and expanding U.S. exports to Japan in due course.

CHAPTER 5

Industrial policy in Japan: overview and evaluation

KOTARO SUZUMURA
MASAHIRO OKUNO-FUJIWARA

Throughout the post-war period, the Japanese government has invoked a fairly sophisticated system of interventionist economic policy to promote steady growth, technological innovations, and international competitiveness. Such policy initiatives have benefited from cooperative response by the private sector. Given the remarkable post-war accomplishments of the Japanese economy, rapid economic growth in the 1960s and, thereafter, a smooth adjustment to international competition in the face of frequent and often unforeseeable external shocks, it is natural that the so-called Japanese industrial policy has become the focus of international concern.

The purpose of this chapter is to present a brief overview and a concise evaluation of Japanese industrial policy. Since there already exist sizable contributions in English on what Japanese industrial policy is all about, how it evolved and transformed itself through time, and how it is affecting the international competitiveness of the other countries,[1] we will focus here on a theoretical evaluation of Japanese industrial policy, citing concrete historical instances only for illustrative purposes.

The chapter is divided into four sections. In Section I, several basic

This chapter partly summarizes our joint research on Japanese industrial policy conducted under the auspices of the Tokyo Center for Economic Research, which is itself financially supported by the 21st Century Foundation. Previous research reports, parts of which have made use of in preparing the present chapter, include Komiya, Okuno, and Suzumura (16), Okuno-Fujiwara (24), Okuno-Fujiwara and Suzumura (26–28), and Suzumura and Kiyono (35).
[1] Representative works include Adams and Ichimura (1), Hosomi and Okumura (12), Johnson (13), Komiya (15), Okita (23), Pugel (30), Rapp (31), Saxonhouse (32), Trezise (36), Uekusa and Ide (38), and Ueno (39). Needless to say, these works differ substantially from each other in their views on the meaning and efficacy of industrial policy. Concerning our detailed historical as well as theoretical analysis of Japanese industrial policy, which forms the background of this chapter, the reader is referred to Komiya, Okuno, and Suzumura (16), an English translation of which is forthcoming in 1986 from Academic Press. In addition to the above literature, which deals specifically with Japanese industrial policy, Hindley (11) and Krugman (17) are also of interest.

concepts important for an economic analysis of industrial policy are introduced. Section II presents a brief historical account of Japanese industrial policy. Section III turns from description to evaluation. In particular, we study three important aspects of Japanese industrial policy, namely, welfare criteria for industry selection, regulatory activities to keep "excessive competition" under control, and informational activities by the government. Concluding remarks are in Section IV.

I. Industrial policy: some basics

A definition

For all the concern about industrial policy, it is rather perplexing that a standard definition of the concept has never been well established. As a result, arguments for or against a country's industrial policy may be addressing entirely different issues.

In the 1970s, for example, Kaizuka (14) observed that "at least as far as I could verify, it is surprisingly the case that the term industrial policy has never been unambiguously defined." The elusive nature of industrial policy was echoed by Hindley (11) in the 1980s: "The term 'industrial policy' has an entirely spurious sound of precision. Over the past ten or fifteen years, the term has become a portmanteau catchword for that broad range of governmental actions which directly affect the structure of production in an economy. From a political point of view, this very lack of precision in definition is a major attraction of support for industrial policy" (pp. 277–8).

In view of these well-taken critical remarks, we should begin with a workable definition of industrial policy. Throughout this chapter, we mean by industrial policy "the totality of governmental policies undertaken to change the allocation of resources among industries from what it would be otherwise, or to intervene in the industrial organization within a certain individual industry, with an intention to enhance the country's economic welfare if and when unrestricted functioning of the competitive market mechanism is found to fail in achieving that end" (27, p. 31).[2]

---

[2] This definition was also used in our research project on Japanese industrial policy reported in Komiya, Okuno, and Suzumura (16). It is admittedly rather narrow. For one thing, it excludes policies that are meant to pursue "non-economic" objectives, e.g., self-sufficiency and the like. It also excludes, e.g., an optimal tariff policy that would enhance a country's economic welfare in the absence of market failure at the sacrifice of other countries. Nevertheless, the policies covered by our definition are widely acceptable, whereas other policies are much harder to rationalize from a theoretical viewpoint.

Policy objectives

Two features of our definition of industrial policy, which is admittedly abstract, deserve emphasis. First, it is explicitly maintained that industrial policy is concerned with complementing rather than substituting for the competitive market mechanism if and when the autonomous functioning of the latter somehow fails. Second, the raison d'être of industrial policy is geared toward enhancing the country's economic welfare.

To lend concreteness to these abstract concepts, we must identify causes and types of market failures, on the one hand, and criteria on which to evaluate the country's economic welfare, on the other. The latter problem is complicated by the fact that, more often than not, there are conflicting interests within the country, each of which should be considered in talking about the country's economic welfare. Depending on the choice made by the government as to whose welfare is at the top of its priority list, there are several alternative routes one may take in pursuing the country's industrial policy, although no democratic government seems to be so crude as to make its priority rule explicit. Instead, more down-to-earth policy objectives such as industrial rationalization, self-sufficiency, sustained growth, international competitiveness, amenity of life, and the like are referred to. Nevertheless, the implications of these policy objectives for welfare distribution are often easily identifiable.

Policy implementability

In order for the country's industrial policy to be at all implementable, two basic conditions must be satisfied.

First, the government must be endowed with effective policy instruments. Generally speaking, the instrument or policy measures of industrial policy may be classified according to the following criteria:[3]

1. Whether or not the policy measure is discriminatory. What we call *discriminatory measures* are those that provide favorable treatment to a particular firm (or group of firms) within a specified industry, whereas *non-discriminatory measures* are those that apply to all firms within the industry.

2. Whether the measure is incentive compatible or regulatory. *Incentive-compatible measures* work by providing pecuniary or non-pecuniary rewards to private firms, whereas *regulatory measures* in-

---

[3] See Okuno-Fujiwara and Suzumura (27, pp. 3–4).

volve explicit legal stipulations and/or administrative persuasion and guidance.

Note that the sustainability and efficacy of each type of industrial policy is determined, at least in part, by its domestic and/or international implications. This leads us to the second basic condition for implementability, namely, domestic and international compliance.

In implementing an industrial policy (which may well favor some firms or industries at the sacrifice of others) in a democratic society, at least implicit public agreement on the policy objectives (with their de facto distributional implications) is a prerequisite for it to be sustainable. Also, more or less willing compliance by private firms is indispensable for the efficacy of intangible policy initiatives such as organizing cooperative research-and-development projects, collecting, exchanging and disseminating crucial industrial information that is typically not acquired on the basis of purely private incentives, and providing administrative guidance. With regard to international compliance, it should be noted that a country's degree of economic development may well limit its implementable industrial policies. In less developed economies, a country's pursuit of a protectionist industrial promotion policy in order to protect its infant industries may be more or less internationally accepted. However, such a policy will almost certainly become a target of harsh international criticism when implemented in mature economies.[4]

With these rudimentary concepts for studying industrial policy in hand, we turn now to a brief account of Japanese industrial policy.

II.   Brief historical overview

Post-war economic reforms: promoting competition

During the occupation period (1945–52), a series of economic reforms aimed at "democratization" of Japan were performed under the order and strict control of the occupation authorities.[5] Although they can hardly be classified among Japanese industrial policies proper, these reforms undeniably shaped the competitive framework of the post-war Japanese economy. The major reforms consisted of the *zaibatsu* (family-dominated combines) dissolution, land reform, and labor democratization.

[4] This is emphatically *not* to say that *any* criticism by a foreign country is by itself proof of the illegitimacy of a country's industrial policy. What we are saying is that the country should be ready to argue rationally and persuasively for the legitimacy of its industrial policy, and should include reasonable boundaries on the limits of that policy.
[5] Factual details of these reforms are concisely explained in Nakamura (21, Chapter 2).

The first step in the zaibatsu dissolution was the breakup of its core, namely, the holding companies. In fact, this reform far exceeded the mere dissolution of the zaibatsu itself. Indeed, the clear focus of the reform was to eliminate concentration in production as well as in property ownership in general, which culminated in the Anti-Monopoly Law (April 1947) and the Elimination of Excessive Concentration of Economic Power Law (December 1947). Although the extent to which these laws succeeded in eliminating monopoly power is debatable, it seems to be unambiguously true that the zaibatsu dissolution, coupled with a policy of purging pre-war business leaders, facilitated the separation of property ownership from managerial control and set the stage for the keen interfirm competition that characterized the post-war Japanese economy.

No less important were the drastic land reform initiatives stipulating that the property rights of all absentee landlords and a large proportion of landlords residing in rural villages should be transferred to tenant farmers. This reform naturally motivated farmers to carry out land improvements on a large scale. The resulting increases in agricultural productivity and income raised domestic demand, thus supporting from the demand side the rapid economic growth to follow. As an important and somewhat ironic side effect, this radical land reform generated an overwhelmingly conservative political stance among the farmers, who became the very backbone of conservative party governments.

The labor reform symbolized by the Trade Union Law (December 1945), the Labor Relations Adjustment Law (September 1946), and the Labor Standards Law (April 1947), all of which were enacted in accordance with orders of the occupation authorities, established an institutional framework for democratic labor–management relations in Japan. The proportion of unionized workers rose dramatically, and pecuniary as well as non-pecuniary working conditions were greatly improved, which also served as a factor supporting the ensuing rapid economic growth from the demand side.

Reconstruction period: from rationalization to
economic independence

Immediately after the war, the legacy of war time economic controls strongly influenced the stance of industrial policy, resulting in the priority of production systems (1946–48).[6] This system was aimed at in-

---

[6] For more details on this phase of Japanese industrial policy, see Komiya, Okuno, and Suzumura (16, Chapter 1) and Tsuruta (37, Chapters 1 and 2).

dustrial rehabilitation by allocating government funds to industries of strategic importance for obtaining raw materials and foreign exchange. Coal being the primary energy source at that time, that industry that was critical for the development of coal mining, namely, the steel industry, received first priority. All imported oil was injected into the steel industry, with the increased steel production being invested into the coal industry. The increased coal production was in turn reinvested into the steel industry, and so on. To further promote the development of Japan's coal industry, the Reconstruction Finance Bank lent funds on a top-priority basis to the government. These funds were subsequently channeled into the coal industry. Similarly, the Bank of Japan lent funds directly to the coal industry on a top-priority basis. Meanwhile, food and subsistence commodities were rationed as much as possible.[7]

It is true that the priority production system enabled Japan to provide coal to other industries, thereby initiating the process of economic rehabilitation fairly quickly. Nevertheless, the resulting allocation of resources lacked any guarantee of economic efficiency. Indeed, the expansion of coal and steel production (as well as the production of other so-called stabilization belt goods including fertilizer, soda, and gas) were made possible only at very high costs, so that the government had to provide large-scale subsidies to fill the gap between high production costs and low official prices. Furthermore, the Reconstruction Finance Bank obtained funds by issuing bonds that were accepted by the Bank of Japan. Obviously, this mechanism of the priority production system exerted serious inflationary pressures.

A strong decree to curb inflation was issued by the occupation authorities in December 1948. In particular, new loans from the Reconstruction Finance Bank were suspended in 1949 in order to cut inflation. In April 1949, the occupation authorities also set the official exchange rate at the rate of 360 yen to the dollar, which lasted until 1971.[8] Given this exchange rate (which was felt to appreciate the yen too highly) and the high domestic production costs of basic commodi-

---

[7] One might wonder how such a policy, which puts extraordinary weight on the expansion of producer goods in the midst of starvation and destitution, could ever be implemented without invoking oppressive measures. Apart from the widespread eagerness for quick economic rehabilitation among people, one factor that might have been responsible seems to be the fact that the sacrifice, which was inevitable anyway, was not imposed by direct order, but by the indirect and impersonal mechanism of forced saving through inflation.

[8] Private foreign trade, which was state managed, was reopened in the summer of 1947. Until April 1949, however, there was no fixed exchange rate. Instead, there were complex exchange rates for each commodity traded.

ties, extensive measures were needed to promote more efficient resource utilization and to enhance the development of new industries. In response to this need, major steps were taken in December 1949. The Industrial Rationalization Council (which in 1964 became the Industrial Structure Council) was established as an advisory organ under the Ministry of International Trade and Industry (MITI) with the purpose of arriving at a consensus among the government, private firms, and labor regarding measures to be adopted in pursuing rationalization. The council permitted informal participation of private agents in governmental policy formation through the exchange of ideas between government officials and private agents before authorizing any major industrial policy.

Similarly, the Foreign Exchange and Trade Control Law and the Foreign Investment Law were enacted, which enabled government to collect foreign currencies, to impose quantitative import restrictions, and to bring the inflow and outflow of capital under control. Within the framework thus established, several attempts were made to rationalize industries. Unlike the priority production system, which promoted several industries of strategic importance without discriminating among firms within the nominated industry, the focus of industrial policy was now to favor technically superior firms within the nominated industry. Productivity increased by virtue of this rationalization policy, but at the cost of incurring deflation, with massive bankruptcy of inefficient firms and increased employment.

The Korean War, which broke out in June 1950, changed this gloomy scene quite drastically. Exports, production, profits, and employment all rose rapidly in textiles, chemicals, iron and steel, machinery, metals, and lumber; Foreign currency income from special procurements (the expenditure of the U.S. Army and military personnel) raised the ceiling set by the balance-of-payments constraint. More important (from a long-run perspective) was the expansionary effect of the Korean War on plant and equipment investment and technological innovation. Expanding heavy and chemical industries and technology transfers from the U.S. Army to meet the special procurements demand motivated many industries to import technology from abroad and to expand and renew their productive capacity. It was against this background that the prototype of industrial policy in post-war Japan took clear shape.

Unlike the priority production system that retained vestiges of directly interventionist pre-war controls, the major tools of industrial policy now became largely incentive oriented and advisory in nature. The Japan Development Bank, which assumed the assets and liabilities of the Reconstruction Finance Bank, supplied key industries with low-interest national funds for plant and equipment investment, while the Japan Export–Import Bank was in charge of promoting exports by providing funds to exporting firms. Special tax measures for the promotion of plant and equipment investment and exports were introduced. The Law for the Promotion of Industry Rationalization was enacted, which established a special accelerated depreciation system for important machinery in order to facilitate plant and equipment investment. We should also mention the 1953 revision of the Anti-Monopoly Law authorizing cartels in times of depression and for purposes of industrial reorganization. Finally, the Temporary Law on the Adjustment of Supply and Demand of Goods, which was a powerful law giving government the leverage to allocate important goods, lost effect in April 1952. From this time on rigorous domestic control of manufactured goods essentially disappeared in Japan. In this sense, the termination of these laws symbolized the end of the transition period from the directly controlled economy to the government-assisted, competitive market economy.

Over the latter half of the 1950s, some of the promoted industries, such as the automobile industry, had already established themselves as high-yield industries and no longer received preferential tax treatment or low-interest public loans. Other decreasing cost industries, including iron and steel and electricity, had successfully rationalized themselves, whereas rationalization of increasing cost industries such as coal mining turned out to be a failure. The emphasis of industry promotion policy shifted toward such new and promising industries as synthetic fiber, plastics, petroleum refining, petrochemicals, electronics, and general machinery. Other salient features of industry policy during this period were, first, increased efforts to import oil and a shift away from coal production (with adjustment assistance given to the coal industry) and, second, expansion of the industrial infrastructure. It should also be mentioned that protection of domestic producers through import restrictions was used extensively in promoting certain industries including automobiles and heavy electric equipments, whereas the imports of advanced foreign technology were greatly facilitated.

By the end of the 1950s, the era of rapid economic growth was about to begin. Newly promoted industries as well as established industries maintained high rates of expansion. One may be tempted to surmise that this "success" is sure-fire proof of the efficacy of industrial policy. Certainly such policies did not hurt, but it is still an open question whether industrial policy should be singled out as the most important factor. More important factors would seem to be individual entrepreneurship, smooth expansion of domestic as well as international markets, and adaptability to newly introduced technology from abroad.

Rapid economic growth: the heyday of industrial policy

Plant and equipment investment by private firms continued to grow rapidly with the added fuel of technological innovation.[9] Even the seemingly over-optimistic Income-Doubling Plan (published in December 1960) proved to underestimate the growth potential of the Japanese economy. Throughout this investment spurt, which government authorities made every effort to sustain,[10] the share of heavy and chemical industries in total production and subsequently in export composition increased steadily, introducing several irreversible changes into the Japanese economy. Shortages occurred in the Japanese labor market for the first time in its history, increasing incentives to pursue plant and equipment investments embodying labor-saving innovation. A wider gap developed between the manufacturing sector, characterized by large, technologically advanced firms, and the stagnant sectors consisting of agriculture and small- to medium-sized firms. In order to make up for this lopsided development, policies designed to modernize agriculture and small- to medium-sized firms were undertaken.

Increasing exports of Japanese industrial products, coupled with an extensive lifting of import restrictions in the European nations, raised foreign countries' demand for trade liberalization in Japan. In the 1960s, the Japanese government responded to this trend by deciding in principle to proceed with trade liberalization. As far as the proportion of liberalized commodities is concerned, liberalization seemed to be nearly complete by 1964. However, several important items were kept off the liberalized commodity list for as long as possible. For example, passenger cars were kept off this list until 1965, and in fact, several agricultural products are still off the list. On the other hand, in 1964

---

[9] See Komiya, Okuno, and Suzumura (16, Chapter 2), and Tsuruta (37, Chapters 4–6) for more details.

[10] Along with pursuing policies for the protection and promotion of industries, they also played an important role in providing a temporary shelter to private firms when they were confronted with a severe business downturn: "When it seemed that a business downturn was becoming rather severe, a helping hand would be extended by the government in the form of cartel assistance, tax reductions or exemptions, and industry-wide plant and equipment capacity expansion agreements . . . While a floor was being held under recession in these ways, business prosperity would begin to revive again. As firms became active once more, they were able to launch into their next set of plans. In this sense, the government's industrial policies functioned as a safety valve so that firms could boldly pursue aggressive programs within a secure environment." (21, p. 66).

Japan became an IMF Article VIII nation and also a member of OECD, which meant that liberalization of inward direct foreign investment could not be far off.[11]

It was with these prospects of internationalization in view that the authorities in charge of industrial policy undertook several measures to enhance the international competitiveness of Japanese industries. It should be recognized that MITI was going to lose most of its control over private firms with the liberalization of trade and capital flows. Indeed, the assignment of import quotas, the authorization of individual patent and know-how contracts, and the screening and authorization of joint ventures between foreign and Japanese companies, which served MITI as powerful measures for regulatory intervention, were all going to evaporate into thin air.

One of the major industrial policy objectives in the 1960s was MITI's desire to directly intervene in plant and equipment investment in such industries as iron and steel, synthetic fiber, petroleum refining, petrochemicals, and paper and pulp in order to avoid "excessive competition." If left unregulated, it was feared that excess capacity would be generated, to the detriment of international competitiveness.

Another interventionist goal was the specialization of production in pursuit of scale economies and the organization of industrial complexes under MITI's auspices. In order to secure controls enabling MITI to accomplish these objectives, MITI submitted a bill to the Diet for a Law on Temporary Measures for Designated Industries (March 1962), with the declared purpose of promoting and improving international competitiveness in the heavy and chemical industries by such measures as standardization, specialization of production, establishment of joint capital enterprises, organization of industrial complexes, rationalization of plant and equipment investment, mergers, the conversion of businesses to other fields of activity in line with the reorganization of industrial structure, and so forth. This appallingly interventionist bill, which, if passed, would have enabled MITI to exert almost complete control over industries, was in fact defeated by the opposition of financial institutions.

Although the 1960s is occasionally dubbed the heyday of industrial policy in Japan,[12] it may alternatively be viewed as an era of struggle between two competing approaches to industrial policy, namely, direct regulation versus the provision of advice and incentives, with the latter prevailing in the end. MITI expedited merger among private firms in

[11] The first step toward liberalization of inward direct foreign investment was taken in June 1967 and was completed by April 1973.
[12] See, e.g., Komiya, Okuno, and Suzumura (16, p. 55).

such manufacturing industries as chemicals, petroleum, and metals and machinery so as to exploit potential scale economies and to help strengthen international competitiveness. In March 1964 Mitsubishi Heavy Industries was established, Prince Motor merged with Nissan Motor in August 1966, and Nippon Steel Corporation was born in March 1970 with the amalgamation of Yawata Iron & Steel and Fuji Iron & Steel. These mergers, however, did not materialize by the regulatory decree of MITI. On the contrary, MITI's help was invoked only when such mergers were consistent with the pursuit of private incentives. Indeed, MITI's plan to intensify automobile production (June 1961), which was designed to limit new entry and to specialize production in pursuit of scale economies, failed to elicit compliance by private firms.[13] These and similar cases seem to suggest that the so-called voluntary compliance by private firms to the regulatory objectives could be obtained only when such objectives were largely consistent with private objectives. Even MITI could not force an unwilling horse to drink water.

This tendency toward predominance of private incentives over administrative discretion was enhanced by the disappearance of MITI's controls in the process of trade and capital flow liberalization described above. A new era of industrial policy was approaching in which MITI's role was to be indicative, advisory, and catalytic.

In the wake of rapid economic growth, environmental disruption and pollution became increasingly prevalent. This was viewed as an inevitable result of the reckless pursuit of rapid growth via heavy and chemical industrialization. Criticism against pollution grew vehement in the latter half of the 1960s, and in 1967 the Basic Environmental Pollution Prevention Law went into effect. By 1970, such anti-pollution acts as the Prevention of Noise Pollution Law, the Prevention of Air Pollution

---

[13] This failure may be attributed to the lack of MITI's regulatory power in the form of screening, authorization, and permission. However, even during the 1950s, when MITI's power over private firms was considered to be extremely potent, the government could not necessarily impose its will on private firms if it was going squarely against the dictates of private incentives. The case of Kawasaki Steel Corporation will suffice to exemplify this point: "A plan by Kawasaki Steel Corporation to enlarge a steel mill in Chiba prefecture was assessed by the government to be on an excessively large scale in relation to the government's estimate of future steel demand. But Kawasaki Steel did not accept the official forecast and carried out the investment as they originally intended. Fortunately the judgement of Kawasaki Steel proved to be right, thanks to a rapid expansion of steel consumption" (12, pp. 133–4). Likewise, in the 1950s, it was already maintained that the petrochemical industry, being a typical heavy equipment industry with a large degree of scale economies, was in need of intervention by industrial policy with a view to controlling new entry and fostering orderly investment by excluding "excessive competition." For all of MITI's power, those firms that meant to enter eventually did so, and intervention proved to be futile.

Law, and the Prevention of Water Pollution Law were promulgated. The salient feature of these acts is that they imposed strict responsibility on the polluter, revising the conventional idea of no indemnity due without proven malfeasance in the civil law. The *social* regulations thus introduced were quite severe and directly interventionist in nature, in sharp contrast to the *economic* regulations described above. Private firms were not required to install effective equipment to keep pollutants under control.

The oil crisis and beyond: from direct intervention to catalytic intermediation

The year 1973 will long be remembered as a watershed in the post-war Japanese economy.[14] In February of that year, the flexible exchange rate system was adopted, and in the following October, the first oil crisis broke out when the Arab oil-producing countries set on their strategy of partial oil embargo and announced a five-fold increase in the price of crude oil. Rampant inflation, sharp declines in growth rates, and a balance-of-payments deficit ensued. The impact of the oil crisis was quite severe, particularly because the Japanese economy had developed primarily on the basis of high-energy-consuming heavy and chemical industries, which were heavily dependent on imported crude oil. Extraordinary efforts in economizing energy use, backed up by the voluntary cooperation of laborers to tolerate temporary cuts in real wages, enabled the Japanese economy to absorb almost entirely the impact of the oil crisis within 3 years. However, the high-energy-consuming basic material industries including iron and steel, non-ferrous metals, chemicals (excluding drugs and medicines), paper and pulp, and lumber became structurally depressed industries. In their stead, industries such as automobiles and electronics, which were less dependent on imported raw materials and still left much room for further technological improvements, recorded rapid expansion, as did tertiary industries. In April 1979, when some of the structurally depressed industries were still struggling with excess capacity in the face of stagnant demands, large-scale increases in crude oil prices by OPEC (the second oil crisis) took place. Moreover, there were striking price increases for other imported raw materials as well. Having learned important lessons from the bitter experience of the first oil crisis, adjustment to the second was faster and more efficient, backed up by the

---

[14] For more details on this phase of industrial policy, see Komiya, Okuno, and Suzumura (16, Chapter 3), Tsuruta (37, Chapters 8 and 9), and Uekusa and Ide (38).

voluntary cooperation of laborers to put up with temporary decreases in real wages. In the meantime, except for relatively brief periods after the first and second oil crisis, the balance-of-payments surplus had been accumulating massively, greatly escalating trade friction.

In response to these events, industrial policy after the first oil crisis had three focuses: adjustment assistance to the structurally depressed industries, promoting R&D investment in high-technology industries, and dealing with trade friction. In coping with these focal tasks, the stance of authorities in charge of industrial policy was in sharp contrast to that during the era of rapid economic growth for two reasons. First, MITI's power had diminished still further. In 1980 an important judgment was made by the court to the effect that cartels are illegal even if formed under MITI's administrative guidance. In other words, industrial policy in general and administrative guidance in particular were explicitly made subordinate to the Anti-Monopoly Law. Second, interventionist and protectionist policies were losing international acceptance as well as domestic "voluntary" compliance. Criticism against the allegedly protectionist nature of Japanese industrial policy was becoming sharper than ever in view of the increasing importance of Japan as an international competitor. And private firms did not have much reason to comply with administrative guidance unless such compliance was mandatory and/or doing so was consistent with the firm's private motives. Thus, the character of industrial policy became mostly passive, indicative, and intermediary rather than active, interventionist, and regulatory.

Adjustment assistance to the stagnant industries suffering from massive excess capacity and competition by newly industrialized countries was formally sanctioned by the Law on Temporary Measures for Stabilization of Designated Depressed Industries, enacted in May 1978. This law designated several struggling industries as structurally depressed when they were found to be suffering from severe excess capacity with more than half of the firms in deficit. Assistance was provided in essentially two ways. First, the law authorized the establishment of joint credit funds to purchase scrapped facilities and to guarantee bank loans for the disposition of excess facilities. Second, the law authorized collective capacity reduction among all firms within the industry. The designated industries included aluminum refining, synthetic fiber, shipbuilding, linerboard, cotton, and other spinning and chemical fertilizers.

It is still an open question whether the admission of such assistance did not work to hinder, rather than foster, the inevitable adjustments by keeping less efficient firms alive and by prolonging the process of intraindustry rationalization. Nevertheless, collective capacity disposal had been nearly completed in most of the designated industries by 1982. In order to assist those designated industries whose adjustments were made more difficult by the outbreak of the second oil crisis, as well as additional industries that had more recently fallen into distress, the Law on Temporary Measures for Structural Improvement of Designated Industries was enacted in May 1983, which authorized business tie-ups and promoted specialization in production as well as the development of process innovation.

One feature of the Japanese adjustment assistance policy described above deserves emphasis. No recourse was ever taken to such protective measures as import restrictions, tariff impositions, or direct subsidies in assisting structurally depressed industries.

Regarding the promotion of R&D investment, it should first be noted that, quantitatively speaking, the private sector has been playing a much more important role in R&D activities in Japan than has the public sector. Indeed, the rapid increase of R&D expenditure in Japan is not mainly due to government expenditures but rather to private sector spending. According to the 1984 White Paper on Science and Technology, for example, the proportion of government-funded R&D expenditures among major industrialized countries is lowest in Japan. Furthermore, almost all of the government and/or non-profit research institutions are engaging, not in applied research for industrial use, but in basic research. Therefore, the impact of government's R&D promotion policy in high-technology industries is indirect and relatively small.

Nevertheless, involvement in private R&D activities did help to promote cooperation. Cooperative research and development in frontier technologies was promoted by giving favorable tax treatments and subsidies to private firms that organized an association for cooperative R&D activities.[15] The most visible and successful association was the Research Association on Very Large-Scale Integrated Circuits for Next Generation computers (VLSI), consisting of five computer companies (Fujitsu, Hitachi, Mitsubishi Electric, NEC, and Toshiba) that carried out their cooperative research activities from 1976 to 1979.

Judging from the research output of this association as measured, for example, by the number of patents obtained, the promotion of the

---

[15] The origin of the cooperative research associations in Japan can be traced back to the early 1950s. The Law on Research Association of Mining and Manufacturing Technology was passed in 1961, which was meant to avoid unnecessary duplication of funds and researchers, which would occur unless research activities were coordinated by government intermediation, and promoted cooperative research in frontier technologies by giving tax benefits.

VLSI Research Association was a great success. These efforts helped to fill a wide technology gap existing between Japan and the United States and to establish the basis for the development of the Japanese computer and semiconductor industry. However, the government-promoted cooperative R&D projects were far from perfect. There were, in fact, many occasions when the association failed to be productive in research activities and also many cases where members of the association failed to maintain, let alone enhance, their competitive position. An example is provided by the Research Association on Laser-Using Complex Manufacturing Systems (1977–83). This was one of the projects under the title of the Large-Scale National Research and Development Projects, to which MITI gave special priority in the late 1970s. Throughout this project, the machine tool industry had experienced rapid expansion, causing some leading producers of machining centers at the beginning of the project to increase their capacity at high cost, while smaller producers (who tended to take participation in this project more seriously) established themselves as the industry's technological leadership.

While the VLSI Research Association was on balance successful in its aims, this success was made possible only by a rare combination of favorable factors including the following: (a) the association was driven by the target of catching up to IBM within the designated time span; (b) the association had its own research institute where the exchange of information was efficiently performed; and (c) the association was endowed with adequate funds as well as a mature and experienced research staff. We should also note that the cooperative research association may have some undesirable implications from the viewpoint of competition. Such dangers do not seem to have materialized in Japan, at least thus far. For example, the research association may serve as a basis for cooperative cartel behavior in the product market. However, this potential danger does not seem to have developed in Japan, at least thus far.

More recently, government subsidies to R&D activities have shifted toward the development of high technologies, for example, electronics, new industrial materials, biotechnology, and energy, where private incentives alone are unlikely to generate enough research efforts.

The third focus of industrial policy, namely, dealing with trade friction, consisted of such measures as the elimination of residual import restrictions, the abolition or relaxation of tariff and non-tariff barriers, the simplification of customs procedures and import standards, and the use of "voluntary export restrictions." Although the response by the Japanese government to trade friction has often been quite slow and incremental in nature, it should be emphasized that the Japanese government has not taken recourse to measures such as protective tariffs or emergency import quotas in coping with the domestic problem of adjustment assistance to structurally depressed industries. On the other hand, accusations often made about non-tariff barriers or unfair trade practices in Japan should be carefully examined and redressed if found to be legitimate. Not all of these alleged non-tariff barriers are legitimate, however. For example, it would surely be invalid if one claims that the Japanese environmental standard is a non-tariff barrier on the grounds that it is too severe and is serving to prevent the penetration of foreign cars, for example, into Japanese markets. Certainly, any nation is within its rights to determine whatever level of environmental standard to enforce within its boundary for the sake of the safety and health of its people. On the other hand, there seem to be a variety of areas, including finance, retailing, and air services, where the principle of reciprocity does apply.

III. Evaluation

Welfare criteria for industry selection

One of the most important tangible measures of Japanese industrial policy was the government subsidy in the form of preferential tax treatment and special reserves, which were aimed at reducing the financial burden of large-scale plant and equipment investment and risky R&D activities. In trying to rationalize the provision of these subsidies among several favored industries to the exclusion of others, MITI allegedly applied some criteria in picking industries of strategic importance. Although the exact nature of these criteria varied from time to time, they are typified by the criteria that were often invoked during the period of rapid economic growth. These criteria are explained by MITI in the following quotation:[16, 17]

The industrial vision (announced by the Industrial Structure Research Council in 1964) placed increased emphasis on the sophistication of the industrial structure through more strengthening of the heavy and chemical industries than ever, in order to enhance the country's international competitiveness. In defining the optimal industrial structure of the future, two criteria were adopted: one was the rate of productivity growth, and the other, income elasticity. The

[16] This quotation is taken from the Industrial Structure Division, the Ministry of International Trade and Industry, "Industrial Policy–Japan–," which was presented at the PAP Special Group in the OECD Economic Policy Committee in October 1980.

[17] The origin of these criteria may be traced back to Shinohara (34), who aired them in the *Principle of Dynamic Comparative Costs*.

income elasticity criterion led to greater appreciation of the importance of developing export industries with high demand elasticity relative to world growth in real income. On the other hand, the productivity increase rate purported to examine the prospects for relative superiority on the basis of improved productivity. These criteria were in effect an application of a theory of comparative production with long term consideration on dynamic development of international trade.

For all their practical appeal (at least to the Japanese in the 1960s who were eager to catch up with the developed countries), it is rather doubtful if the so-called strategic industries were actually chosen in accordance with these criteria, namely, the *productivity improvement criterion* and the *income elasticity criterion.* To substantiate our doubts, we have only to note that, although heavy and chemical industries (like iron and steel, general machinery, heavy electrical equipment, and chemicals and petrochemicals), which were actually chosen and promoted, satisfied these criteria, there were many other industries (camera, bicycle, watch, tape recorder, magnetic tape, tourism, supermarkets, and restaurants) that were not promoted despite their clear "success" in passing these criteria.[18]

Furthermore, almost no theoretically satisfactory explanations were provided justifying these criteria in the first place. To be sure, the well-known infant industry argument and other arguments based on market failures were sometimes invoked to defend them. The productivity improvement and income elasticity criteria, however, seem to have little to do with dynamic external economies that are key elements of the infant industry argument. Against many criticisms of these criteria (and Japanese industrial policy in general) made by economists, MITI officials often tried to defend their stance by declaring that they were concerned with avoiding dynamic non-competitive (or "excessively competitive" in their terminology) situations, situations their critics had failed to take into account. Nevertheless, no theoretical foundations of these criteria based upon dynamic non-competitive situations were provided either. Moreover, in spite of its importance, the welfare implications of these criteria were never made explicit. Thus, it is still left unanswered whether these two criteria (and, for that matter, other criteria mentioned in other phases of industrial policy) are really relevant criteria for industry selection, especially from a welfare standpoint.

As a first step in filling this theoretical gap, Okuno-Fujiwara and

---

[18] This point was made by Komiya in Komiya, Okuno, and Suzumura (16, p. 8).

Suzumura (26) examined the welfare-theoretic criteria for justifiable industrial subsidies in an oligopolistic setting. The model they considered is a static closed general equilibrium model consisting of two sectors, competitive and oligopolistic. Production technology is characterized by scale economies in the oligopolistic sector and by constant returns to scale in the competitive sector. Note that, in this model, the introduction of a (small) subsidy, say, for production, will produce three effects. First, the subsidy will shift the (private) marginal cost curve of the oligopolistic industry down. Second, taxation required for subsidy expenditure will shift the demand curve down by virtue of the income effect. Third, since the relative price of the oligopolistically produced good declines, its demand increases. In such a setting, the welfare effects of the introduction of various tax subsidy schemes for the promotion of an oligopolistic, increasing returns-to-scale industry were systematically examined. The welfare criteria derived by Okuno-Fujiwara and Suzumura depend subtly on the possibility of firm entry into the oligopolistic industry, but they are *not* related in any recognizable way to the two criteria mentioned above. As far as we can infer on the basis of the Okuno-Fujiwara–Suzumura analysis, therefore, the welfare-theoretic foundation of the two criteria for industry selection is quite shaky, to say the least.

It is probably much closer to the truth that these criteria (and those corresponding criteria that were referred to in other phases) were nothing more than after-thought rationalizations of a "strategic" industry selection that was in fact made for other reasons. Whatever these other reasons might have been, one fact is very clear. Unless these reasons for industry selection were (at least implicitly) agreed on in the process of bargaining among conflicting interests (each interest group being represented by the government agency participating in the industrial policy design), the de facto compliance of private firms and taxpayers to Japanese industrial policy could not have been maintained throughout the post-war period. To analyze the nature of this bargaining process is an important further step in the economic analysis of Japanese industrial policy.

Regulatory activities: "excessive competition"

In post-war Japan, interfirm competition has been consistently keen. This competition has served as a major force in securing the embodiment of new technology through extensive plant and equipment investment by incumbent as well as entrant firms. In such a lively environment, the competitive forces working in the market should not be interrupted by regulatory authorities unless some identifiable dysfunctions of the market mechanism are observed. Nevertheless, government intervention within a specified industry has been resorted to in Japan, frequently in the name of keeping "excessive competition" among firms under control. However, "most of the articles arguing the damage caused by 'excessive competition' and the necessity for interventionist policy are unconvincing when examined from the viewpoint of economic theory. Furthermore, hardly anyone has ever cared to define clearly the meaning of 'excessive competition' " (16, p. 12). Indeed, to those who are accustomed to the standard theory of welfare economics and industrial organization, the very term *excessive competition* sounds quite dubious and almost self-contradictory.

To examine if indeed excessive competition may make theoretical sense in the first place, let us note that industries where such phenomena allegedly prevailed in Japan were characterized by the necessity of heavy plant and equipment for production, homogeneity of output, and oligopolistic competition.[19] Keeping this observation in mind, Okuno-Fujiwara and Suzumura (28) examined a model incorporating these three features and tried to determine whether or not such a model exhibits an intrinsic tendency toward excessive competition in a clearly defined sense. As an auxiliary step, we defined the concept of socially first-best (respectively, second-best) investment as that level of a firm's investment that maximizes total market surplus when government can regulate both the firm's output and investment optimally (respectively, government can regulate the firm's investment only, leaving the output decision to the firm). To gauge the market performance in terms of these measuring rods, Okuno-Fujiwara and Suzumura examined a model with a fixed number of firms where each firm can commit itself to cost-reducing fixed plant and equipment investment with a view to threatening the other firms. In this model, it was shown that (a) plant and equipment investment at the oligopolistic equilibrium is socially excessive in comparison with the first-best level if there exist at least two firms within the industry and (b) plant and equipment investment at the oligopolistic equilibrium is socially excessive in comparison with the second-best level as well if the number of firms within the industry exceeds a critical number that is determined by demand conditions. The intuition behind these results is fairly clear.

---

[19] Iron and steel, petroleum refining, petrochemicals, certain other chemicals, cement, and paper and pulp may be cited as concrete examples of such industries. See Komiya (15).

Since each firm can reduce its cost by committing itself to a larger fixed plant and more equipment, each and every firm will try to do so ahead of the others, with the result that each firm ends up making a socially excessive commitment.

One assumption of this model, that the number of firms is constant, may seem questionable. Indeed, one of the features of the neoclassical competitive paradigm is that the number of firms within an industry is determined endogenously by the entry and/or exit decision of firms in accordance with the profit incentive. Noting this fact, Suzumura and Kiyono (34) examined a homogeneous output Cournot oligopoly model with free entry. If left to themselves, potential competitors (respectively, incumbent firms) will enter into (respectively, exit from) this industry until the marginal firm earns zero profit. Let the number of firms existing in this long-run equilibrium be called the "equilibrium number of firms." Depending on the extent to which government can regulate the behavior of firms, two concepts of socially optimal number of firms may be relevant. These are the optimal number of firms corresponding respectively to the "first-best" solution and the "second-best" solution. In the first-best case, government is assumed to exert strong control on firms, forcing them to price at marginal cost, whereas in the second-best case, government takes firms' profit-maximizing behavior as given. Let us say that a number of firms is first-best optimal (respectively, second-best optimal) if it maximizes the first-best market surplus (respectively, the second-best market surplus). It was shown by Suzumura and Kiyono that (a) the equilibrium number of firms is socially excessive in that it exceeds the first-best number of firms as long as the latter exceeds unity and (b) the equilibrium number of firms is also socially excessive in that it exceeds the second-best number of firms as long as the latter exceeds unity. The thesis of excessive competition is again vindicated in this free entry model.

With these theoretical conclusions at hand, we must concede that "regulation by enlightened, but not omniscient, regulators could in principle achieve greater efficiency than deregulation" (29, p. 313). Does it follow, however, that the actual regulatory activities by the Japanese government with the expressed purpose of keeping "excessive competition" under control are legitimate and theoretically defensible? Our answer is emphatically negative.

Note that, for government regulation to be first best, it is necessary that government impose marginal-cost pricing on all firms, which presupposes that government can get hold of exact and detailed information concerning demand and cost conditions. The informational requirements of second-best regulation are lighter than that of first-best regulation but are still substantial. Due to lack of access to this information, which is basically internal to the firms, actual interventions by the Japanese government had to be based upon much cruder information. Indeed, actual regulation (in the form of allocating, e.g., import quotas or mandatory authorization of new productive facilities) was conducted mainly in accordance with the "share principle," which assigned priority to a firm according to its rank order in terms of a simple index of productive capacity or market share.[20]

For example, import quotas for crude oil were allocated in accordance with the rank order of refining capacity at a certain time. The effect of the use of such a rule of thumb on regulation was rather paradoxical. Instead of keeping "excessive competition" under control as intended, it aggravated the situation by motivating firms to expand their productive capacity beyond the level justified by the prevailing market conditions in the hope of securing favorable treatment by the government ahead of competing firms. Thus:[21]

That productive capacity has actually been used or referred to for administrative or allocative purposes in direct controls, administrative guidance, or cartelization, and that companies rightly or wrongly expect this to be repeated in the future, seem to be the real cause of the "excessive competition in investment." (15, p. 214)

Informational activities

Several economists have expressed the opinion that, among the many policy measures the Japanese government undertook as part of its industrial policy, those that explicitly and/or implicitly manipulated industrial information flows within the economy were the most, if not the only, successful measures. For example, according to Komiya (15, p. 221):

Whatever the demerits of the system of industrial policies in postwar Japan, it has been a very effective means of collecting, exchanging and propagating industrial information. Government officials, industry people, and men from governmental

[20] Quite apart from easy enforceability due to informational simplicity, the rule of thumb to the effect that one should "remunerate each in accordance with his/her past accomplishment" does have an intuitive appeal with an equitable flavor, so that it is rather difficult to argue against its application. It would seem that this was the reason why government officials took recourse to the share principle in their regulatory practice.

[21] See also, Komiya, Okuno, and Suzumura (16, pp. 13–14, 225, 226).

and private banks gather together and spend much time discussing problems of industries and exchanging information on new technologies and domestic and overseas market conditions. People at the top levels of the government, industries, and banking circles meet at councils, and junior men meet at their subcommittees or less formal meetings. Probably information related to the various industries is more abundant and easily obtainable in Japan than in most other countries. Viewed as a system of information collection and dissemination, Japan's system of industrial policies may have been among the most important factors in Japan's high rate of industrial growth, apart from the direct or indirect economic effects of individual policy measures.

In a slightly different context of industrial relations, Shimada (32) also claims:

Our review of the development of the *shunto* system above, especially after the oil crisis, suggests that a complex structure of information channels were constructed among organised labor, organised capital and the government through which information was exchanged and shared . . . as symbolically exemplified by the active role of *Sanrokon* (Triparite Round Table Conference on Industry and Labour issues) . . . it would be possible to interpret that Japanese wage increases have been more compatible with macro-economic conditions than European countries simply because the intensity and extent of information sharing in the process of wage negotiations has been much greater than for their European and American counterparts.

Although this statement seems persuasive and thought-provoking at first glance, it becomes much less convincing if one looks at it more carefully. In particular, the following arguments may be made against this statement.

1. If markets are perfectly competitive and there are no missing markets, the resulting res)urce allocation should already be Pareto efficient, and no improvement would be possible with information sharing or with the facilitation of information transmission.

2. Even if some markets are missing and/or some markets are not perfectly competitive, more information will not necessarily make resource allocation more efficient.

(3). Even if a mechanism of information sharing is created, it is not clear whether there is an incentive to share truthful information. And if there is no incentive to report truthful information, how would reported information (which may possibly be manipulated and incorrect) help improve resource allocation and economic efficiency?

In what follows, we would like to make some theoretical remarks relating to the above questions on the basis of our recent research results. It is *not* our intention to claim, however, that the following arguments are always practically viable and that there are no other possible reasons to support information-related policies. Instead, our intention is to stimulate interest in this still undercultivated area of economies with a view to increasing our understanding of the role of industrial policy.

There seem to be at least three major channels through which the government can potentially affect resource allocation within the private sector by explicitly or implicitly applying policy measures concerning information:

1. Government may be able to affect communication channels among private firms, thereby changing their strategic behaviors. In particular, government may be able to coordinate actions taken by private firms.

2. Government can acquire information itself and/or give extra incentives to collect information that would not be acquired otherwise by private firms.

3. Government may be able to design and implement information sharing mechanisms, which enhance incentives to increase information flows.

Let us examine each one of these channels in detail.

Action coordination: When markets exhibit some degree of monopoly power and/or incomplete information prevails, strategic behavior becomes essential. Compared to markets where all agents take prices as given, such an economy must be described by a game in which strategic actions are explicitly taken into consideration.

Recently, many examples have been found where an economy described by a game possesses multiple Nash equilibria, some of which Pareto dominate the others.[22] In such examples, the economy may be stuck with a Pareto-inferior equilibrium. We may call such a situation *coordination failure,* as inferior equilibrium is obtained due to a lack or coordination among players. Since the coordination failure occurs because of incomplete information, some mechanisms that improve pregame communication among players and/or create coordination in

---

[22] The games with these properties may be found in various places, e.g., Diamond (6), Heller (10), Okuno-Fujiwara (24), and Weitzman (43), all of which are neatly summarized in Cooper and John (5). According to their presentation, a necessary condition for this phenomenon to occur is the presence of strategic complementary. The fact that Nash equilibria may be Pareto ranked was first emphasized by Heller (10). Models of macroeconomic coordination failure, e.g., Diamond (6), and Marshallian or pecuniary externalities, e.g., Okuno-Fujiwara (24), may be subsumed in these models.

choosing proper strategic actions may help to achieve a Pareto-superior equilibrium.

Many arguments for the informational role of Japanese industrial policy seem to rely implicitly upon the idea of coordination failures. For example, several economists have argued that an important role played by the Japan Development Bank (JDB) was the so-called cow-bell effect of its loan decisions.[23] When the JDB decided to provide loans to a private firm, it worked as a signal to many private banks of the favorable prospects for that firm. As a result, the small loan the firm received from the JDB actually enabled it to satisfy much larger financial needs. The alleged reasons why private banks willingly followed the JDB's suit are two-fold. First, the JDB was thought superior to private banks in acquiring information about the growth potential of private firms. Second, the internal decision-making process within private banks was such that, more often than not, it was much easier to argue for providing loans to a firm once the JDB had decided to do so. In other words, the JDB loan decision may have acted as a coordination mechanism in that the act of giving the JDB loan may have coordinated private banks' own loan decisions.

Another example may be provided by government-promoted cooperative research associations. Technological information shares the feature of a public good in that, once produced, it may diffuse fairly easily to those who did not take part in its development. Due to this lack of appropriability, it is in principle desirable to form a joint research association, which also helps to avoid redundant simultaneous investment by private firms. However, a problem of free-riding within the association, namely, the lack of guarantee that firms within the association would provide sincere information and exert maximum effort, remains. In a situation like this, government may facilitate coordination by providing administrative persuasion and guidance, favorable tax treatments and subsidies, and personnel who can serve as neutral referees in resolving internal conflicts.

Serious problems still remain even with this potential role of government. There is no convincing criterion by which we may arrive at an equilibrium when the game possesses multiple equilibria, nor do we have a method to identify policy measures required to bring the economy out of coordination failure.

Information acquisition: Consider an economy where some markets

---

[23] See, e.g., Komiya, Okuno, and Suzumura (16, p. 206) and Tsuruta (37, p. 74).

are not perfectly competitive, so that prices do not convey all relevant information. In such an economy, where strategic behavior plays a crucial role, every agent needs information in addition to price information in order to select an optimal strategy. Since information acquisition is often costly, whether or not to engage in such an activity should be determined by weighing potential benefit against necessary cost ex ante. Note, however, that potential *private* benefit may be different from potential *social* benefit accruing from such an activity. For example, the information in question may concern the potential for new technologies, which, if successful, may reduce the price of output and increase consumers' as well as producers' surplus. Whenever social benefit outweighs private benefit, and information acquisition cost is not more when it is undertaken publicly rather than privately, public intervention in information acquisition activity may be socially beneficial. Indeed, as shown in Okuno-Fujiwara (24), there are cases where government should intervene into the private activities of information acquisition even if the information acquisition cost is the same for the government as for private agents.

Two qualifying remarks are in order. First, an important question remains as to whether government should directly engage in information acquisition activities or whether it should instead devote itself to providing incentives for private firms to do so. Second, in order for government's intervention into information acquisition activities to be socially justifiable, two conditions must be satisfied: (1) the expected total benefit from intervention must exceed its cost and (2) left to itself, the private agent must lack incentives to engage in information acquisition.[24]

Information sharing: Many, if not all, economic agents seem to possess information that is exclusively their own. If such private information can be successfully diffused to all concerned agents, economic welfare may well increase in the aggregate. The question we now pose is two-fold: (1) under what conditions will information sharing be welfare enhancing and (2) by what mechanism, if any, can we generate incentives for information sharing?

A partial answer to the first question is provided by the recent literature on information sharing.[25] Although the result seems to de-

---

[24] One is reminded in this context of the famous criteria of infant industry protection.
[25] See, among others, Clark (4), Gal-or (7, 8), Novshek and Sonnenschein (22) and Vives (41).

pend on whether the information in question concerns cost or demand parameters, on the one hand, and on whether interfirm competition is the Cournot quantity type or the Bertrand price type, on the other, there are identifiable cases where information sharing does indeed improve economic welfare.

The second question seems much more difficult to answer. The problem lies in the fact that, information being private, agents usually have incentives to convey false signals so as to harvest private gain. For example, a firm may tell competitors that its costs are low (when in fact they are high) so as to induce them to be less aggressive and to increase its own profit. There seems to be, however, at least three eligible mechanisms that may limit the firm's incentive to provide misinformation.

1. Reputation mechanism: If the information exchange process is repeatedly applied and if an act of false signalling is made publicly known ex post, the lying agent's reputation will be severely damaged. Therefore, any agent with a reasonably long time horizon will be motivated to comply with the information-sharing scheme by providing accurate information.

2. Binding contract mechanism: Suppose that private information is verifiable ex post and that firms can sign binding contracts ex ante to share information. In such a case, true information must always be disclosed as long as the expected profit of sharing information is not less than that of not sharing.

3. Self-unravelling mechanism: Even if binding contracts are not possible, verifiability alone may induce information unravelling for a fairly large class of games.[26] As an example, suppose that the relevant information concerns the firm's own cost and that the possibility of information sharing exists. A firm whose cost is the lowest possible has every incentive to reveal this private information, thereby discouraging other firms and securing higher profit. It follows that a firm that does *not* reveal that its cost is the lowest possible is in fact revealing that its cost is *not* the lowest possible. Knowing that the other firms may infer this much anyway, a firm whose cost is the second lowest possible has every incentive to reveal this private information truthfully, given verifiability and the possibility of information sharing.

With these possible mechanisms to provide incentives for information sharing at hand, let us now pose a question: Should government intervene to promote information sharing? Generally speaking, the

[26] See, among others, Grossman (9), Matthews and Postlewaite (18), Milgrom (19), Milgrom and Roberts (20), and Okuno-Fujiwara, Postlewaite, and Suzumura (25).

answer is negative. First, information sharing may be welfare decreasing rather than welfare enhancing. Second, even when information sharing is welfare enhancing, such sharing may be better organized by the private sector. Only when welfare-enhancing information sharing cannot be realized without public assistance can government intervention be justified.

By what truth-revealing mechanism should government intervene when such an act is justifiable? The answer seems to depend subtly on the nature of the information in question. Note, however, that government assistance does play an important role in supporting the viability of each mechanism mentioned above. In the case of the reputation mechanism, the ex post identifiability of true information is the key for its viability and such ex post verification may be more easily conducted and disseminated by government. In the case of a binding contract mechanism, enforcement of such contracts may be performed only by a government that can impose large penalties on those who breach. Finally, in the case of the self-unravelling mechanisms, government cost advantages in verifying information may serve to guarantee its efficient operation, although the role government plays in this mechanism is mainly catalytic.

IV.   Concluding remarks

In this chapter, we have tried to trace out the mainstream of post-war industrial policy in Japan and to make several welfare-theoretic remarks on some of its salient features.

The central message here is that competitive market forces should not be interfered with unless there exist clearly identified causes of market failure and that, even when intervention is warranted, it should be implemented so as to complement underlying private incentives. Both historically and theoretically, we have seen that policy interventions that are inconsistent with private incentives are often ineffective and unsustainable.

This chapter has left many problems unresolved. In this sense, what we have presented here may be regarded simply as the beginning stage of a rather large research agenda. Nevertheless, it is our hope that we have helped the reader form a balanced overview of the nature and role of Japanese industrial policy.

References

1. Adams, F. G., and S. Ichimura, "Industrial Policy in Japan," in *Industrial Policies for Growth and Competitiveness,* F. G. Adams and L. R. Klein (eds.), Lexington, MA, Lexington Books, 1983, pp. 307-23.
2. Aumann, R. J., "Subjectivity and Correlation in Randomized Strategies," *Journal of Mathematical Economics,* Vol. 1, 1974, pp. 67-96.
3. Bulow, J., J. Geanakoplos, and P. Klemperer, "Multimarket Oligopoly: Strategic Substitutes and Complements," *Journal of Political Economy,* Vol. 93, 1985, pp. 488-511.
4. Clark, R., "Collusion and the Incentive for Information Sharing," *Bell Journal of Economics,* Vol. 14, 1983, pp. 383-94.
5. Cooper, R., and A. John, "Coordinating Coordination Failures in Keynesian Models," Cowles Foundation Discussion Paper, Yale University Press, 1985.
6. Diamond, P., "Aggregate Demand Management in Search Equilibrium," *Journal of Political Economy,* Vol. 90, 1982, pp. 881-94.
7. Gal-or, E. "Information Sharing in Oligopoly," *Econometrica,* Vol. 53, 1985, pp. 329-43.
8. Gal-or, E., "Information Trasmission – Cournot and Bertrand Equilibria," *Review of Economic Studies,* Vol. 53, 1986, pp. 85-92.
9. Grossman, S., "The Informational Role of Walrasian and Private Disclosure and Product Quality," *Journal of Law and Economics,* Vol. 24, 1981, pp. 461-83.
10. Heller, W. P., "Coordination Failure with Complete Markets in a Simple Model of Effective Demand," mimeograph, Department of Economics, University of California at San Diego, 1984.
11. Hindley, B., "Empty Economics in the Case for Industrial Policy," *World Economy,* Vol. 7, 1984, pp. 277-94.
12. Hosomi, T., and A. Okumura, "Japanese Industrial Policy," in *National Industrial Strategies and the World Economy,* John Pinder (ed.), London, Croom Helm, 1982, pp. 123-57.
13. Johnson, C., *MITI and the Japanese Miracle,* Stanford, Stanford University Press, 1982.
14. Kaizuka, K., *Agenda for Economic Policy,* Tokyo, The University of Tokyo Press, 1973 (in Japanese).
15. Komiya, R., "Planning in Japan," in *Economic Planning: East and West,* Morris Bornstein (ed.), New York, Ballinger, 1975, pp. 189-227.
16. Komiya, R., M. Okuno, and K. Suzumura (eds.), *Industrial Policy in Japan,* Tokyo, The University of Tokyo Press, 1984 (in Japanese).
17. Krugman, P. R., "The U.S. Response to Foreign Industrial Targeting," *Brookings Papers on Economic Activity,* 1984, No. 2, pp. 77-121.
18. Matthews, S., and A. Postlewaite, "Quality Testing and Disclosure," *Rand Journal of Economics,* Vol. 16, 1985, pp. 328-40.

78   K. Suzumura and M. Okuno-Fujiwara

19. Milgrom, P., "Good News and Bad News: Representation Theorems and Applications," *Bell Journal of Economics,* Vol. 12, 1981, pp. 380–91.
20. Milgrom, P., and J. Roberts, "Reliance on the Information and Interested Parties: Does the Invisible Hand Operate in the Marketplace for Ideas?" mimeograph, Stanford University and Yale University, 1984.
21. Nakamura, T., *The Post Japanese Economy,* Tokyo, The University of Tokyo Press, 1981.
22. Novshek, W., and H. Sonnenschein, "Fulfilled Expectations Cournot Duopoly with Information Acquisition and Release," *Bell Journal of Economics,* Vol. 13, 1982, pp. 214–18.
23. Okita, Y., "Japan's Fiscal Incentives for Exports," in *The Japanese Economy in International Perspective,* Isaiah Frank (ed.), Baltimore, The Johns Hopkins University Press, 1975, pp. 207–30.
24. Okuno-Fujiwara, M., "Competition, Interdependence of Industries and Marshallian Externalities," Discussion Paper 85 F-I, Faculty of Economics, The University of Tokyo, 1985.
25. Okuno-Fujiwara, M., A. Postlewaite, and K. Suzumura, "Verifiability and Information Sharing," in preparation.
26. Okuno-Fujiwara, M., and K. Suzumura, "Welfare Criteria for Industrial Subsidies in an Oligopolistic Setting," Discussion Paper No. 118, The Institute of Economic Research, Hitotsubashi University, 1985.
27. Okuno-Fujiwara, M., and K. Suzumura, "Economic Analysis of Industrial Policy: A Conceptual Framework through the Japanese Experience," published in the PAFTAD Conference Proceeding on the Industrial Policies for Pacific Economic Growth, 1985.
28. Okuno-Fujiwara, M., and K. Suzumura, "Capacity Investment, Oligopolistic Competition and Economic Welfare," Discussion Paper No. 132, The Institute of Economic Research, Hitotsubashi University, 1986.
29. Panzer, J. C., "Regulation, Deregulation and Economic Efficiency: The Case of the CAB," *American Economic Review: Papers and Proceedings,* Vol. 70, 1980, pp. 311–15.
30. Pugel, T. A., "Japan's Industrial Policy: Instruments, Trends and Effects," *Journal of Comparative Economics,* Vol. 8, 1984, pp. 420–35.
31. Rapp, W. V., "Japan's Industrial Policy," in *The Japanese Economy in International Perspectives,* Isaiah Frank (ed.), Baltimore, The Johns Hopkins University Press, 1975, pp. 37–66.
32. Saxonhouse, G. R., "What Is All This About 'Industrial Targeting' in Japan?" *World Economy,* Vol. 6, 1983, pp. 253–73.
33. Shimada, H., "Wage Determination and Information Sharing: an Alternative Approach to Incomes Policy," *Journal of Industrial Relations,* Vol. 25, 1983, pp. 177–200.
34. Shinohara, M., "Industrial Structure and Investment Allocation," *The Economic Review,* Vol. 8, 1957, pp. 314–21 (in Japanese).
35. Suzumura, K., and K. Kiyono, "Entry Barriers and Economic Welfare," mimeograph, Hitotsubashi University, December 1985.

36. Trezise, P. H., "Industrial Policy in Japan," in *Industry Vitalization*, E. Dewar (ed.), New York, Pergamon, 1982, pp. 177-95.
37. Tsuruta, T., *Industrial Policy in the Postwar Japan*, Tokyo, Nihon Keizai-Shinbun-Sha, 1982 (in Japanese).
38. Uekusa, M., and H. Ide, "Industrial Policy in Japan," to be published in the PAFTAD Conference Proceedings on the Industrial Policies for Pacific Economic Growth, 1985.
39. Ueno, H., "The Conception and Evaluation of Japanese Industrial Policy," in *Industry and Business in Japan*, K. Sato (ed.), New York, M. E. Sharpe, 1980, pp. 376-434.
40. Vander Weide, J. H., and J. H. Zalkind, "Deregulation and Oligopolistic Price-Quality Rivalry," *American Economic Review*, Vol. 71, 1981, pp. 144-54.
41. Vives, X., "Duopoly Information Equilibrium: Cournot and Bertrand," *Journal of Economic Theory*, Vol. 34, 1984, pp. 71-94.
42. Wakasugi, R., *Economic Analysis of Technological Innovation, Research and Development*, Tokyo, Toyo Keizai Shinpo Sha, 1986 (in Japanese).
43. Weitzman, M., "Increasing Returns and the Foundations of Unemployment Theory," *Economic Journal*, Vol. 92, 1982, pp. 787-804.

Discussion

BARBARA GOODY KATZ

Suzumura and Okuno-Fujiwara present a theoretical evaluation of Japanese industrial policy. This is an extremely important as well as difficult task and differentiates their work from that of many others whose primary focus is either descriptive or comparative.

In their chapter they define industrial policy as all government interventions aimed at altering the resource allocation among firms or altering the market structure within industries where the intent is to produce a level of economic welfare that exceeds the level the competitive market would have generated in the absence of such intervention. This last phase is extremely important, and I will return to it later. Since industrial policy is defined only as complementary to a market economy, it is clear that it shares little with either central planning, whether decentralized and based on incentive mechanisms or not, or with economy-wide indicative planning. Central planning, of course, was initiated to supplant the "anarchy" of the market mechanism, not to be an adjunct to it. Thus, plan construction, plan implementation, and plan fulfillment, all traditional elements of a centrally planned economy, do not have their counterparts in Japanese industrial policy. Indicative planning was designed to facilitate continuous coordination throughout an economy of utilizing, rather than replacing, the market mechanism. To this end, enhanced information flows within industries were mandated, as were governmental incentives to steer the economy in prearranged directions. Indicative planning was designed to modify market forces ex ante so that ex post market failures would not arise. This obviously differs from the thrust of Japanese industrial policy, which attempts to address only those market failures that have, in fact, occurred. According to the definition of Suzumura and Okono-Fujiwara, perhaps the role of industrial policy is somewhat similar to the role of an adjunct professor who is hired only when it is realized that there is a class full of students and no faculty member to teach it. That is, one does not, as a matter of policy, staff all classes with adjunct professors, but when a staffing problem presents itself, often hiring an adjunct professor can provide a solution. In this manner, the adjunct professor is complementary to the full-time faculty member.

After providing a historical background, Suzumura and Okono-Fujiwara evaluate industrial policy along three main dimensions:

1. choosing the industries to treat specially;
2. dealing with excessive competition; and
3. affecting, acquiring, and distributing information.

Overall, they come to a negative assessment of industrial policy. Indeed, they state that the market should be left alone except in specific cases where a precise market failure can be documented, and then only incentive-type policies should be utilized.

The negative conclusions concerning industrial policy appear to have been generated in the following manner. Suzumura and Okono-Fujiwara formally incorporated various aspects of industrial policy into theoretical models and then assessed the welfare implications of their models. In the case of selecting the industries to favor, they reference a model that has a competitive as well as an oligopolistic sector. They find no evidence that the welfare effects of a subsidy in that model depend at all on the criteria chosen by MITI to single out industries: productivity improvement and high income elasticity. In the case of excessive competition, they do cite theoretical models that show that excessive competition can occur in the context of heavy investment in plant and equipment, a homogeneous product, and oligopolistic competition. But they then ask, "can industrial policy offer an improvement?" and answer a resounding no. Their negative response is based on the conclusion, drawn from their model, that it would be necessary for the government somehow to legislate that all firms set price equal to marginal cost. That, at least in theory, this should not be a problem follows from the work of Oskar Lange, to which I will later refer. In the case of information, Suzumura and Okuno-Fujiwara discuss the coordination failure problem, the social costs and benefits of the government's acquisition of information, and the problems of eliciting truthful information in the context of information sharing. They conclude that the government would be in a poor position to choose among the possible multiple equilibria spawned by coordination failure, and even if the government were able to promote information sharing, there is no presumption that this would increase welfare. In fact, their presumption is to the contrary. Only in regard to the acquisition of information is there a hint that the government's role might be non-negative.

It is perhaps noteworthy to recollect that it was precisely to counter vast informational requirements that 50 years ago the Polish economist Oskar Lange introduced his model of market socialism (see Lange 1936; 1937). In that model the central planning board was to instruct all firms to set price equal to marginal cost and produce the profit-maximizing level of output. Through a trial-and-error approach, equilibrium was to be achieved.

Lange's model was part of the famous "socialist controversy," begun in the 1920s, in which Ludwig von Mises, Friedrich Hayek, Lionel Robbins, Fred M. Taylor, and others also participated. An earlier seminal contribution by Enrico Barone, in which he built on ideas of Vilfredo Pareto and demonstrated that rational resource allocation was possible in a socialist economy, was also integral to the debate. For a review of the debate see Lippincott (1964) and Bergson (1966).

At the heart of the debate over the actual as well as the theoretical possibilities of socialism was whether incentive mechanisms and other levers could be constructed to prompt the socialist enterprise to respond in certain desired ways. The tension between socialism and capitalism in theory, and socialism and capitalism in practice, was acute in this debate. Nonetheless, in reviewing the debate, Professor Abram Bergson could argue that "one must distinguish between blueprints of economic systems operating in hypothetical worlds and rival economic systems in the real world. . . . We must compare ideals with ideals or facts with facts. Participants in both sides of the debate have erred in failing to observe this elementary rule" (Bergson 1966, p. 236).

Unfortunately, Suzumura and Okuno-Fujiwara have made the same error in their present chapter. The thrust is that industrial policy, as practiced by Japan, is not welfare enhancing. But I am prompted to ask, as compared to what? Compared to the theory of perfect competition or compared to the mixed market economies that exist in the world? At this point it is useful to recall the definition of industrial policy given in the beginning of the chapter: "The totality of governmental policies . . . with an intention to enhance the country's economic welfare if and when unrestricted functioning of the *competitive market* mechanism is found to fail in achieving that end" (emphasis added). It is precisely the characterization of the "competitive market" in this definition that is at issue. Certainly in the absence of market failures and under suitable assumptions about the behavior of consumers, firms, resource markets, long-run profits, and individually clearing markets, competitive markets are sufficient for Pareto-optimal resource allocations. However, western mixed market economies as we know them are surely not sufficient for Pareto-optimal resource allocations. It follows, then, that it is not appropriate to downgrade an actual economy employing industrial policy due to its inability to produce efficient resource allocations. Neither with nor without industrial policy is it likely that such an ideal could be obtained. The appropriate comparison is either at the ideal or at the actual level. That is, one might ask two distinct questions: whether a mixed market economy assisted by industrial policy is able to achieve results superior to those of a mixed market economy without an industrial policy or whether a general equilibrium model that incorporates an interventionist industrial policy is able to produce the Pareto optimality that, of course, we know can be generated under suitable conditions in a general equilibrium model of a competitive economy.

Distinguishing between actual and idealized performance leads to a rather straightforward question that should be of interest to all of us: Was industrial policy responsible for the "Japanese miracle?" Suzumura and Okuno-Fujiwara allude to this question early in the chapter, but their approach does not allow for its resolution. Nor do I know of any evidence currently available that would resolve this question. Thus, until comprehensive counterfactual histories become available, I expect it to remain unsolved.

Although I do not believe that the present chapter has offered a solution to the question of the relationship of Japanese industrial policy to the Japanese miracle, I found it to be stimulating and valuable. Suzumura and Okuno-Fujiwara have shown that industrial policy can be formally introduced into traditional microeconomic models, and they have suggested three basic areas in which additional research might proceed. While I quarreled with what I took to be their mixing and matching of hypothetical ideals and actual economies, I am reminded here of a statement by A. K. Sen: "a society or an economy can be pareto optimal and still be perfectly disgusting" (Sen 1970, p.

22). Obviously in the realm of actual economies, where resource allocations are unlikely to even be Pareto optimal, the levels of satisfaction that these resource allocations provide are clearly a matter of the greatest concern.

References

A. Bergson, "Socialist Economics," in *Essays in Normative Economics* (Cambridge, MA: Harvard University Press, Belknap Press, 1966), pp. 193–236.

O. Lange, "On the Economic Theory of Socialism," *Review of Economic Studies* **4**, No. 1 (October 1936), pp. 53–71, and No. 2 (February 1937), pp. 123–142; reprinted in Oskar Lange and Fred M. Taylor, *On the Economic Theory of Socialism* (New York: McGraw Hill, 1964).

Benjamin E. Lippincott, "Introduction," in O. Lange and F. Taylor (eds.), *On The Economic Theory of Socialism* (New York: McGraw-Hill, 1964). pp. 1–38.

A. K. Sen, *Collective Choice and Social Welfare* (San Francisco: Holden-Day, 1970).

Discussion

M. THERESE FLAHERTY

The discussions of trade friction between the United States and Japan have had important political and emotional, as well as economic, dimensions. As the U.S. trade deficit increased, the U.S. public became less concerned with identifying root causes and promoting international cooperation. They increasingly focused on implementing immediate remedies.

In response, we economists offer at least two independent, and apparently unrelated, explanations of the trade deficit. One from microeconomists focuses on institutions. Briefly, trade protection along with government-sponsored industrial policies is thought to have allowed technology-intensive infant industries to develop to world excellence in Japan, to keep Japanese technical expertise at home, and to give Japanese companies the advantage of a base market in which to earn the capital required to penetrate export markets. (In Chapter 11 Pugel considers these issues in the semiconductor industry.) The second explanation from macroeconomists focuses on the trade flows and the purchasing power parity (or disparity) of the Japanese yen and the U.S. dollar. Marston (Discussion to Chapter 9) and Krugman (Chapter 3) lay the blame for the U.S. trade deficit on large government budget deficits and Japan's relatively rapid productivity growth in the manufactured goods sector. They never mention industrial policy, trade protection, or companies.

In contrast to these two explanations for the trade deficit, Suzumura and Okuno-Fujiwara present both a stylized history of the industrial development and industrial policy of Japan and a summary of several mathematical models of issues highlighted in the history. Such combined work is not usual in the policy arena, but it can be valuable in the trade discussions.

The stylized history identifies what Suzumura and Okuno-Fujiwara believe are important institutional aspects of Japanese industrial experience. Its separation from their economic theory interpretation of the policy record allows scholars to discuss the industrial history and the assumptions of the models separately from the logic of the models. The separation should also promote a less emotional discussion of the trade issues and the related industrial policy history of Japan. One case in point is an ongoing discussion I have had with Suzumura and Okuno-Fujiwara about the importance of the Japanese government's protectionist trade and investment policies. It appears as an implicit assumption in the models and with a lower profile than I would have expected in an early version of the history. The occurrence of protectionist policy is a historical fact. But judgment about its necessity for the effectiveness of other industrial policies affects the decision about its emphasis in the history. Our discussion could clearly distinguish between the historical incident and the role of protection in Japanese industrial policy by focusing on the models and the history in turn. The discussion resulted in a question for a future mathematical model: was trade protection necessary for the success of other Japanese industrial policies?

Unlike stylized history, mathematical models can seem simplistic and alien to policymakers discussing the complicated trade friction issues. However, this chapter illustrates the significant, albeit limited, contributions mathematical models can make to the trade friction discussion. They can, for example, establish that particular policies were sufficient to have particular effects on the Japanese and U.S. economies. They can help to separate allegations that might stem from emotional or political sources from salient policy issues. They can provide warnings to policymakers interested in emulating the Japanese experience that there may be positive or negative interactions among policies, which may otherwise appear to be independent and to have only positive effects.

For example, the provocative conclusion of one of the models that Suzumura and Okuno-Fujiwara describe in their paper is that industrial policy was not responsible for the Japanese success in restructuring industries that were "too competitive." Their model demonstrates that the capacity restricting policies MITI followed (basing capacity reductions on a firm's share of current industry capacity) would have had the effect of motivating companies to overbuild capacity before the reduction policies went into effect. (This results from each oligopolists's incentive not to be the company with the lowest capacity during the restructuring program.) Thus, Suzumura and Okuna-Fujiwara's result should warn industrial policymakers in Japan and elsewhere that such policies to reduce or limit capacity may have undesirable effects.

The model is, as Suzumura and Okuno-Fujiwara are aware, limited in its conclusion. It does not preclude such policies from having other, useful effects: it simply does not explore them. The exploration of such policies for Japanese sunset industries – where government restructuring policies appear to have been unusually successful – might identify both other pitfalls and some critical positive aspects of such policies.

Mathematical models, such as the ones Suzumura and Okuno-Fujiwara describe here, can also be used to explore connections between the micro- and macroeconomic explanations of the trade deficit. In particular, a model could address the question of how Japanese industrial policy has managed to foster stable competitive oligopolies in which firms compete fiercely and increase their productivity rapidly. This fact of Japanese industrial development is inconsistent with one basic presumption of industrial organization economics: that oligopolies with stable membership tend to collude and stagnate. From a technical standpoint this would entail incorporating dynamics into the model and so would require more complex models than the static models Suzumura and Okuno-Fujiwara describe here. But the macro- and microexplanations of the trade deficit suggest that this question relates to one of the basic issues facing the United States and other countries in their dealings with Japan.

PART II

Macroeconomic policy

CHAPTER 6

The U.S. and Japanese economies in the remaining Reagan years

PAUL A. SAMUELSON

One of mankind's oldest myths, long antedating Tchaikovsky's ballet or Grimm's fairy tales, is the legend of the sleeping beauty who is awakened back to life by the kiss of a prince charming. What we are not told is whether, after the princess is brought back to life, the couple really did live happily ever after.

Were there no quarrels? Did the wife come to outstrip the husband in earning power? What kept their balance of payments in equilibrium? The tale ends just when the real-world problems begin.

It is not too fanciful to think of 1945 Japan as the helpless sleeping beauty. The MacArthur occupation authority is cast in the role of the prince charming. In doing so, no prejudgment is being made about how the credit should be divided for bringing about the postwar Japanese miracle. After all, even in the folk story, it is possible that the princess was already awakening of her own accord and that the prince was merely a lucky passerby who happened to appear on the scene at the critical moment.

The takeoff of the Japanese economy after 1945 might even be considered a rerun of the sleeping beauty legend. The first would have to be Commodore Perry's opening up of Japan just prior to the Meijii Restoration. Admittedly, the 1950–75 takeoff does have to be regarded as something of a miracle. However, those who are familiar with Japan's progress from about 1860 to 1905 ought to have been somewhat prepared for the postwar spurt. A miracle is more surprising the first time it happens than the second time around!

My intention here is to survey and analyze macroeconomic developments involving Japan and the United States for the remaining years of the Reagan administration. Such a large topic can never be finally resolved. However, we can sample some of my tentative findings and hypotheses.

That I shall raise more questions than I can answer requires no apology. For in an inexact science like political economics, posing the right questions to investigate and ponder over is an important part of the battle.

A success story

Americans are often alarmed to find that we have a large adverse balance of payments on the current account. This is a dramatic reversal from the 1950s, when the rest of the world complained resentfully of a chronic "dollar shortage."

The time interval from the dollar shortage to the present is precisely the epoch of the postwar Japanese miracle. In 1950, Japan was a poor oriental country with life expectancy still not much more than 50 years. It is no wonder that retirement in Japan was then set at an early age.

At best, we can estimate the 1950 per capita real income of Japan as 17% – or about one-sixth – of that in the United States. However, things then changed dramatically.

By 1955, Japan's living standard was almost one-fourth that of the United States. By 1960, it reached one-third. Sometime between 1965 and 1970, Japan went past one-half of the U.S. level, having already surpassed the Soviet per capita level along the way. After 1970, it left Great Britain behind. By the time of the 1973 OPEC crisis, Japan reached two-thirds of the American level of living.

Where does Japan now stand? I suspect that most people have an exaggerated estimate of Japanese productivity. Sometimes Americans think that each Japanese worker is 7 feet tall. Moreover, Japanese management is supposed to have secret weapons of compromise and consensus agreement and to possess mysterious procedures that ensure perfect quality control.

At White House meetings I have heard American businessmen and trade unionists complain that the Japanese work too hard, in the manner of Benjamin Franklin and Max Weber they save too much, and to top off the indictment they are just too smart.

The statistical facts do not quite bear this out. As of 1985, Japanese productivity level still trails U.S. productivity. Calling U.S. per capita real income 100 in 1985, Japan's per capita income is estimated to be somewhere around 75. This puts her perceptibly below Canada, Norway, West Germany, France, Sweden, Switzerland, and Denmark.

The life expectancies of the Japanese are now in the high seventies, making theirs second to none. In addition, by the end of the century, Japan may well be at the top of the list in per capita real income, provided it continues to enjoy annual growth rates that are on average 2% higher than those of the United States. The largest economies in the year 2000 in terms of *total* rather than *per capita* real GNP will still be the United States first and the USSR and Japan next, without much difference between the second- and third-place nations. Since the Soviet population is more than double that of Japan, its total GNP is about the same. For all of China's population size, even if the post-Mao economic reforms work out well, China will still not come close in total economic weight to the Big Three. Even if we include all of Western Europe in a common market bloc, China will still trail the Big Four.

Not a zero-sum game

I do not care for the sports page way of looking at economic rivalries. Since 1870, when Bismarck unified Germany, England and third-party observers could envisage a rival that eventually would threaten the hegemony of the British Empire.

The German GNP grew faster than that of Britain. Science in the Wilhelmine universities spawned the successful German chemistry and electricity industries. As far as economics is concerned, this could have been a fruitful competition and rivalry. German progress did not have to be bought at the price of British progress, any more than nineteenth-century American progress had to be at the expense of the British Empire's standard of welfare.

Otto von Bismarck has much to answer for in history. Provoking two wars, against Austria and France, Bismarck bequeathed to the vain Wilhelm II an unstable legacy. World War I was the bitter fruit of Bismarckian adventurism, and Hitler's World War II was part of the total bill.

None of this served an economic purpose or followed inevitably from economic causation.

This basic truth needs to be emphasized in our own time. From 1950 to 1975 the mixed economies of Western Europe and the Far East gained on the United States. In 1945 the 6% of world population who are Americans enjoyed almost half the global GNP. By 1980 this had dropped to only a quarter of global GNP.

Foreign gain was not American loss. Rather, it was part of the acceleration of global real output that occurred in the third-quarter of the twentieth century and was widely shared both by developing and industrialized regions. This step-up in global GNP was also shared by North America: in terms of U.S. history over two centuries, 1946–73 were years of generous real growth – albeit West Germany, Japan, and the Common Market were gaining on us.

Attention should be directed to the remarkable fact that Japan's post-1950 prosperity owed nothing to military expenditures. Early in this century, Lenin, Hobson, and Rosa Luxembourg propounded a theory of imperialism that has much appeal in Marxian circles. According to their thesis, advancing economies like Germany and Japan must necessarily run out of purchasing power as their masses receive too little effective income to maintain full employment. Only by imperialistic adventures in colonies and war can the metropolitan center keep itself going.

So much for science fiction. What are the mid-century facts in this age after Keynes? Japan has about the lowest ratio of military personnel to total population of any nation. Indeed, if we adjust for relative wealth, Japan joins with Switzerland and Canada in having *negative* ratios! Japan today, six-sevenths of the way through the twentieth century, displays the precise reverse of the Bismarck pattern of Germany at the comparable point in the nineteenth century.

This demonstration is good for the world. It is good for Japan. At the future date when Japan gets tempted to bring its military might in line with its economic might, let us hope Tokyo and Washington will be reminded of the salutary truth that economic welfare no longer has to depend on political power.

The present crisis in U.S.–Japanese relations

To recapitulate, the sober truth is the reverse of the proposition that Japan's growth robs America's growth as I wrote earlier:

Since 1950 the typical American has had a rise in real income of about 93 percent. A respectable fraction of this gain came from technical progress abroad (the cost cutting lobbyists complain about). Our purchases from abroad give us the benefit of the services of foreign workers and resources; at the same time that this is a bargain to us, it raises the real wage rates of workers abroad as a wider circle of consumers bid for their services. Examine a 1950 Sears catalog and the equipment in a 1950 hospital; do the same for 1985, and realize that much of *our* real gains do stem from cheaper imports. (Samuelson 1985b)

Although Japan is not mentioned in the above paragraph, more than any other country it deserves credit for the growth in the U.S. standard of living associated with cheaper imports. This is not to say that the problems of American manufacturing industries faced with new foreign competition should be overlooked, and I shall address this serious matter below. What I do want to stress is the other side of the coin. Good policy for both countries should preserve the mutual-benefit aspects while trying to minimize or contain the traditional burdens.

Pure theory of trade

Over the years I have written numerous articles on the economics of the Pacific Basin and its challenge to Europe and North America (Samuelson 1972, 1981, 1985a). The thrust of this work is that there are two truths that need underlining.

1. The living standard of American workers and capitalists on the average increases when Japan or Korea makes technological advances in producing goods that are characteristically exported to the United States.

2. However, it is an oversimplification to argue that free trade *always* entails a boost in America's well being. When Pacific economies make technical advances in goods for which the United States was previously the low-cost producer, this dynamic change in comparative advantage most definitely will subtract from America's surplus from trade and thus from average real U.S. incomes. Those Americans hurt are not merely the workers and factory owners in the export industries that have lost viability, but most U.S. incomes may have to come down to clear markets in the new equilibrium. That can imply a slowdown in the trend of mean real wage rates or even can entail an outright decline.

I should add that the necessary drop in European real wage rates can be as great or greater than the implied drop in American wages. There is perhaps some evidence that post-1973 European real wage rates have been even more resistant than those of the United States. This may help explain why the United States has been able to create more than 30 million new jobs in the last decade, while Western Europe has barely been able to maintain the same number of jobs.

When non-economists learn that dynamic free trade can reduce American living standards, they have one natural reaction: Avoid free-trade's hurt by putting quotas and tariffs against the low-cost foreign imports.

Economists expert in the analysis of international trade cannot agree. Their system deduces that in addition to the harm innovation under free trade brings, there will also be harm from the protectionist measures. It is true that some old high-paying jobs can be maintained by subsidy; however, the accompanying spread of the new market-clearing real wages will average out to a lower overall standard of American earnings. What holds for production labor can also hold for capital or for U.S. natural resources. That is why experts advise: Don't react to a decline in effective productivity brought about by innovation abroad by gratuitously shooting yourself in the foot.

Qualifications

That in a nutshell is basic trade theory. Are there no exceptions and qualifications? There are two possibilities, but they do not stand up as significant under quantitative measurements.

The first argument is that if American firms have a lot of unexploited monopoly power, then some cleverly allocated modest tariffs might force foreign buyers to pay more for the products the United States alone can supply. Note that this does not suggest tariffs where lobbyists and senators are most eager to put them – namely on auto, steel, shoe, and textile industries, where the United States no longer has competitive viability much less unexploited monopoly power.

There is a new second argument associated with the name of Henry Rosovsky of Harvard University. Schumpeterian innovators, he points out, typically make large temporary profits in the time period when rivals have not learned to imitate their productivity. However, the Japanese are alleged to collusively rob American entrepreneurs of these Schumpeterian rents from innovation by erecting "unfair" trade barriers. Professor Rosovsky (1985) in effect counsels "an eye-for-an-eye" approach. He suggests that the United States should put on quotas as a bargaining chip to force Japan to play the free trade game fairly.

If we study the Rosovsky point, we shall ultimately find that it belongs with the earlier point alleging that America does have some monopoly power in the sense that what it legislates can effectively alter the terms of trade for exports relative to the prices paid for imports.

Does America have great power over its international terms of trade? Under pure-competition theory, where rivals and potential rivals exist in many regions, the answer is, only within narrow limits.

Under realistic workable competition, where Fortune 500 companies here and abroad learn by doing and where economies of large-scale production are important, one cannot be so dogmatically negative.

However, what is actually being proposed by the protectionists? They have no way of calculating the maximal-terms-of-trade "scientific tariff" of the advanced textbooks. They in fact are not proposing tariffs or quotas for new infant industries and processes. Either they favor across-the-board surcharges on all Japanese exports or all Pacific Basin exports or they favor ad hoc quota relief for old industries that have long been losing market share – textiles, shoes, steel, autos, sugar, and so forth.

Almost all economic experts here and abroad doubt that quotas on typical American manufactured goods can succeed as a bootstrap operation for raising or preserving real U.S. real income. Well-known exceptions are Lord Kaldor of the U.K. Labor Party, who believes that U.K. protection will actually raise U.K. incomes, and Miyohei Shinohara, a Japanese economist who believes that MITI-like industrial policy can succeed in dynamically altering a nation's comparative advantages. Both on the liberal left and the American labor movement and at that West Point of American capitalism – the Harvard Business School – there is a similar belief by Professor Bruce Scott and others (1985) that replacing free trade has a useful role as part of a new American industrial policy.

Fair trade versus free trade

The economic theory of the seminar room and the learned treatises seem to be in another world from discussions in Congress and the newspapers. When imports from the Pacific Basin eliminate American manufacturing jobs, that is assumed axiomatically to be an economic tragedy.

Most businesspeople and politicians are ashamed not to pay lip service to free trade. Senator Danforth of Missouri, whose position was described in the *Wall Street Journal* on December 2, 1985, is a typical example. He is concerned when his constituents lose jobs in the shoe industry. Senator Danforth is not against free trade, but he believes that the Japanese, while pretending to believe in free trade, in fact engage in unfair trade. They protect formally against imports of meat and citrus. Informally, they block bids by our telecommunication industries. They dump goods into our markets at below true costs. An elaborate system of reciprocity among Japanese corporations effectively excludes our exports from getting into the Japanese markets.

The net result is to make Danforth favor U.S. protectionism. Until the Japanese change their ways, as attested by a marked reduction in our bilateral trade deficit with Japan, people like Danforth would favor surcharges, tariffs, and quotas targeted against Japan and similar Pacific Basin nations. Such people also lend a friendly ear to proposals for "a new industrial policy."

In various statements Lester Thurow and Michael Piore of MIT express concern with what they see as a decimation of middle-class workers and a sapping of the vigor of the trade union movement. Regretfully, they favor some interference with free trade. The more liberal of our two parties, the Democrats, at present are more protectionist than conservative Republicans such as President Reagan.

There is some truth to the charge that Japan does impede some imports. It is a pity that nagging by friends such as myself gets almost nowhere in persuading Japan to open its markets out of self-interest. The Senator Danforths of the world would soon learn that the elimination of *all* unfair trade practices would still leave a large U.S. deficit on current account and trade.

Calling the bluff of protectionists would not convert them to free traders. The mayors of cities such as Pittsburgh and Detroit and the Congressional delegations from manufacturing regions would still want to protect jobs from cost-cutting importers.

I will therefore move to a discussion of the basic economic causation of America's overvalued dollar.

Exchange rate trends

Two basic forces affect the value of the dollar. The first is successful innovations abroad and the second is the interaction of U.S. and foreign macroeconomic policies. We will examine the role of these forces and the appropriate responses. First, successful innovation and investment by Pacific Basin countries brings down their manufacturing costs and leads to a balance-of-payments problem for an advanced country like the United States, with its reduced pace of productivity progress and its modest rate of private saving. Under floating exchange rates, a declining dollar could be expected even if macroeconomic policy were optimal or tolerably good.

Second, United States macro policy in the Reagan years has been disastrous from the standpoint of the balance of trade. The single most important factor raising real interest rates here and attracting demand for dollars on capital account is our colossal fiscal deficit. Right-leaning supply siders deny that "crowding out" of investment is possible. Neoclassical and post-Keynesian economics recognizes truth in the story that public fiscal thriftlessness compounds our low private thriftiness. Favorable tax incentives for investment – investment credits, fast depreciation, and so forth – reinforce the rise in market-clearing real interest rates. Financing the public debt competes with domestic investment needs for Americans' savings. The eagerness of foreign investors to cycle back their balance-of-payments surpluses perpetuates the overvaluation of the dollar on current account just as it alleviates the crowding-out process here. Some of the crowding out of investment that takes place is in Asian and European domestic investments.

Robert Mundell long ago pointed out the therapy for such unbalance. America should raise taxes and cut expenditures to increase its national saving and reduce its real interest rates. Japan and Germany should do the opposite, pursuing a looser fiscal policy and a tighter monetary policy.

Enlarged saving in the United States and reduced saving abroad will result in less capital inflow into America. This means a downward floating dollar and greater competitiveness in global markets of American producers. It is easy to diagnose these basic problems, but it is hard to implement the appropriate therapies.

Let us now examine recent exchange rate trends.

The dollar has been floating downward relative to the yen and the mark since February 1985. After September 22, 1985, when the Group of Five met in New York to agree on official exchange-market interventions to help the dollar depreciate further, good progress has been made in reducing the degree of the dollar's overvaluation.

Some economists dogmatically deny that a few tens of billions of dollars of stabilization operations can have any perceptible effect on markets that involve hundreds of billions of dollars of gross transactions. Economists, myself included, suspect that when conditions are right for the dollar to fall spontaneously, the authorities have a window of opportunity at just that time. Their limited efforts can then speed up and accentuate the depreciation that is in accord with economic fundamentals.

Still, I must confess to being pleasantly surprised by the degree and persistence of the dollar weakness during the winter of 1985–86. Much of the credit, one suspects, is due to determined Japanese cooperation.

The *Bundesbank* and the German government have been less enthusiastically cooperative. In private, Chancellor Kohl and his colleagues are quite pleased with Germany's economic pattern. They are unwilling to risk their stability just because the tiresome Americans keep urging them to fire up their locomotive.

West Germany and the Common Market have less to fear from American resentments than do the Japanese. American public and Congressional opinion is resentful of the flood of imports from the Pacific Basin. Most economists, both in the United States and in Japan, have been urging that the most effective tactic against nascent American protectionism would be depreciation of the dollar exchange rate. The Japanese authorities have been persuaded to give this therapy a good hard try.

Repeatedly I have suggested that a powerful reinforcement to interventionist operations would be informal capital controls designed to impede the automatic flow into dollar assets of the trade surpluses accruing to Japanese firms and investors.

Some of the success in raising the yen relative to the dollar was due to strong moral suasion exercised by Japanese authorities on banks, insurance companies, corporations, and institutional investors. Their message was: "We intend to appreciate the yen beyond 200 to the dollar. We shall act creditably to do so. We warn you that if you persist in putting funds back into dollar assets, you may end up getting your fingers burned."

I have no proof that this was the *modus operandi* in the background. But it does seem plausible. In any case, some such forces need to be invoked to explain why relatively modest intervention operations were able to achieve such quantitative results.

If the goal of dollar depreciation has been so agreeably realized, cannot Japanese and American observers now breathe more easily? Has not protectionism been contained? Is it not reasonable to look ahead toward a substantial reduction in the U.S.–Japanese bilateral trade deficit? Reckoning up the costs of the stabilization interventions, can we not conclude now that Japan is behind us in that the game was well worth its costs?

I warn against comfortable affirmative answers to these questions. The victory is not won. The game is not over.

Those Japanese investors who were deterred from buying dollars because they feared the yen would fall even further may regain the courage to invest in Wall Street securities once they are confident that the yen has reached a plateau. Successful intervention may have to be more than a one-time, once-and-for-all operation.

My pessimism will be reinforced if the Federal Reserve tightens up on credit, ending the decline in U.S. interest rates and even initiating a rise. The Nakasone government's engineered rise in Tokyo interest rates definitely helped the yen to appreciate. Against this must be reckoned Washington's disappointment that Prime Minister Nakasone has stalwartly refused to embark on vigorous fiscal policy stimulus. Surely Japanese economists understand the important logic of Columbia University Robert Mundell, whose argument was noted earlier.

In summary, the political fever for protectionism against Japan is a degree lower in 1986 than it was in mid-1985.

However, as I appraise the econometrics of the 1985–90 outlook for the United States and its trading partners, the U.S. deficit on current account will not heal itself by 1990. Even with a proper mix of macro policies here and abroad, improvements will be slow in coming. Therefore, I place the rational odds of a protectionist blow-off in America at no less than 1:2. Such an eventuality would be an economic tragedy – a tragedy for Japan and Asia as well as for America.

References

Rosovsky, H. "Trade, Japan and the Year 2000," *New York Times,* September 6, 1985, p. A 23.

Samuelson, Paul A. "International Trade for a Rich Country," Lecture before the Swedish-American Chamber of Commerce, New York City, May 10, 1972. Stockholm: Federation of Swedish Industries pamphlet, 1972.

"To Protect Manufacturing?" Zeitschrift fur die gesamte Staats-wissenschaft (ZgS) *Journal of Institutional and Theoretical Economics* (A Symposium), **137**, 407–14 (1981).

"Analytics of Free-Trade or Protectionist Response by America to Japan's Growth Spurt," in T. Shishido and R. Sato (Eds.), *Economic Policy and Development: New Perspectives,* Auburn House Publishing Company, Dover, MA, 1985a.

New York Times, September 15, 1985b.

Scott, B., ed. *U.S. Competitiveness In the World Economy,* Harvard Business School Press, Boston, MA, 1985.

CHAPTER 7

U.S. macroeconomic policy and trade relations with Japan

HERBERT STEIN

I am pleased to have this opportunity to discuss a subject that is close to all of the conference participants. This report comes at the end of a day and a half of talk about tensions between the United States and Japan concerning economic matters, and I suppose my message, if it could be summed up in a few words, is "not to worry." I have not participated in recent official discussions of economic relations between United States and Japan, but I did participate, on earlier occasions, in discussions of issues of great tension. One was the first Nixon shock, when we closed the gold window, and allowed the dollar to drop. This disconcerted the Japanese to some considerable degree. A second was the shock in 1973 when the Nixon administration embargoed the export of soybeans.

There are several lessons from those events and, perhaps, from what is going on now. One is that the tension, insofar as it is not focused in particular sectors that are affected but is felt by the country at large, is largely a result of misunderstanding. This seems to be true here in the United States and is also, supposedly, true in Japan. Partly, the misunderstanding is about motivation; there is a feeling that one or the other country is guilty of a hostile act toward the other. At least in the case of the United States, we were mainly guilty of neglect when we went to Camp David in 1971 and closed the gold window. Nobody was there from the State Department or from the National Security Council, and there was nobody there really to think about how the Japanese would react. Similarly, when the export of soybeans was stopped, there was not much thinking about how it would affect Japan. But at least there was no plot.

I recall an incident that occurred when I attended a meeting of the OECD, the Organization for Economic Corporation and Development, in Paris in 1973. The Japanese delegate said that the United States had relaxed price controls in order to unleash a wave of inflation that would provide a cover for devaluation of the dollar. That seemed like a very devious approach, more devious than we were capable of, and it probably would not have been very sensible. However, it reflects the attitude that countries have about other countries and that people in general have about their own government. In both instances, it is often thought that there is a lot more planning and plotting going on than is actually the case. What is really going on is a lot of stumbling around. People give governments more credit for thoughtful malice than is really justified.

The other misunderstanding is about how badly countries are hurt. People in the United States exaggerate the extent to which they are being hurt by the present trade relations with Japan or the rest of the world. In the case of the soybean embargo, the people who were mainly hurt were the American farmers, not the Japanese. The American farmers were hurt because the action provoked the development of soybean production in Brazil and elsewhere that lasted for a long time and is still going on.

Despite the concern that exists when these tensions occur, they basically do not seem to affect political relations among countries that have good political reasons for being friends. We are always bickering with our NATO allies and with Japan about economic matters and seem to be in a state of tension and hostility. But our fundamental, political, and strategic military security relations have not been adversely affected by any of this. This is very important and it shows a good sense of priorities on the part of all the countries involved. It takes an awful lot of VCR business to be worth as much as one good ally.

U.S. macroeconomic policy in the 1980s

We now turn to the macroeconomic policies in the United States that have important bearing on economic relations between it and Japan. To do so, we start with a review of the history of U.S. policy in the 1980s and end with the subject of trade friction.

In 1980, there were a number of obvious problems in the country, but it is interesting to point out some things that were not problems in 1980. It is important to go back to 1980 because President Reagan made such a big hit by asking people, "Are you better off than you were four years ago?" and everybody assumed that the answer was no. But if one looked at the statistics, instead of election rhetoric, he would have been hard put to answer no. Output had been rising at about the average post-war rate, during the preceding 4 years. Real per capita disposable income, which is probably the best measure of the economic welfare of the people in general, had also been rising at about the average rate in the preceding 4 years. Employment had been rising very rapidly, total employment in the United States had increased 10 million in the 4 years from 1976 to 1980, and unemployment had fallen. Unemployment was down to 7%, whereas it had been 7.6% in 1976. But despite these signs of fairly good economic performance, there was the general belief in the country that we needed some sharp change in our economic policy.

There were several reasons for that. The first was inflation. Inflation was the obvious trauma affecting the American people, the item Americans put at the top of their list of concerns when inflation was running about 11% per annum. Also, there was a great feeling in the country that we were overtaxed. Federal revenues had risen from 17.5% of GNP to 19.5% between 1976 and 1980. This increase in taxes was in a form that was most visible to taxpayers, the personal income tax and the Social Security tax. Within that category of taxes it was the middle class that was most hard hit. In a sense, we were getting a middle class revolt in 1980. There was also great concern about government spending. Government spending was up somewhat as a percentage of GNP, and there was a great feeling in the country of resentment (a middle class resentment) about the idea that taxpayers were being taxed heavily to pay benefits to people who were not needy. There was a general impression of unfairness, highlighted by the notion of the welfare queen, who got welfare on seven or eight different checks and rode around in a Cadillac, a rather unrepresentative picture. At the same time, there occurred another, and more serious, development on the expenditure side of the budget that was not so commonly noted. Defense spending had fallen to a very low level – something like 5% of GNP. Finally in a list of problems not very much noted, except by economists, the most serious one was that the rate of growth of productivity had fallen dramatically to a very low level.

To summarize the situation at the beginning of the Reagan administration, the United States faced inflation, which was too high, taxes that were perceived to be too high, some non-defense expenditures that were perceived to be too high, defense expenditures that were too low, and productivity growth that was too low. The administration then embarked on a program that was designed to deal, or rather that was claimed to deal, with most of these problems.

The program had three major elements. First, there would be a gradual slowdown of money growth and stability thereafter. That was to be the main instrument for dealing with the most important problem, the high rate of inflation. Second, there would be a big tax cut. And finally, there would be a big increase in defense expenditures.

There were two obvious and serious questions about this program, questions that became more obvious later, although a number of economists were aware of these problems at the time. One was how this program would avoid a big rise in unemployment in the course of getting the inflation rate down. For the previous 15 years or so, the fear of unemployment had deterred the government from following an adequately vigorous policy to get the inflation rate down. So the question was whether it would be possible to get the inflation rate down from 11 or 12%, at which it had been running, without going through a period of serious unemployment. The second big question about this program was how to avoid a big increase in the deficit, which would depress investment and slow down the growth of productivity. In view of what happened subsequently, it is interesting that one question that was not raised about this program was what would be its effect on foreign trade. That is a reflection of the general provincialism of American economic thinking – that we could imagine going through this big revolution in economic policy without thinking very much about what it would do to our foreign economic relations.

The Reagan administration had several answers to these questions. The first was that the announcement and initiation of a stable disinflationary monetary policy would change expectations about what the future course of inflation was, which would make people expect that the inflation rate was going to be slow; thus, the inflation rate could in fact diminish without much increase in unemployment. Second, it was expected that the tax changes proposed, plus deregulation of industry, which was also part of the program, would increase productivity very rapidly. The increase in productivity would help to reduce the rise of labor costs, and this would also help to bring the inflation rate down without unemployment.

The Reagan administration thought that the tax cut and deregulation would cause an exceptionally big rise of GNP with consequent gains in the revenue. This was the heyday of the Laffer curve – the argument that more revenue can be gotten from lower taxes than from higher taxes. This, of course, was a wonderful way of solving the budget problem, which was especially attractive to politicians. I do not know whether Japan ever suffered from the Laffer curve. However, its main locus is on the West Coast of the United States so let us hope it does not. Furthermore, the theory underlying the program was that with big cuts in non-defense expenditure and the increase in revenues, it would be possible both to eliminate the budget deficit and to finance the big increase in defense expenditure.

The outcome can be divided into two subjects. First is the area of aggregate demand and monetary policy and of inflation and unemployment, and second is the real world of the budget. Monetary policy turned out to be almost exactly the opposite of the initial Reagan plan. The rate of monetary growth fell very sharply in the latter part of 1981 and in the first half of 1982, and money growth then rebounded, partly in response to the depth of the recession in the United States and the difficulties in Mexico and other less developed countries. Since 1982, the money supply has risen sharply but irregularly.

All in all, the United States has had exceptionally rapid money growth in the last 5 years, possibly more rapid money growth than any 5-year period in our history, except in the Civil War. Nevertheless, we have gotten inflation down substantially. But we did not succeed in getting the inflation down without the deep recession that other governments had feared. We did have the deep recession. Perhaps one of the positive attributes of our policy in this period is that we did stick it out through this deep recession and come out on the other side with a recovery. The Reagan theory was that if its prescription had been followed, we would have had disinflation without a recession. This is still the position of the administration (see the 1986 Report of the Council of Economic Advisors). The report complains about monetary policy, claiming that if it had been more stable and gradual, we would have had the same results in getting the inflation down without the intervening recessions. This is a very uncertain, after-the-fact rationalization. What it assumes is that if the steady gradual policy had been adopted, there would have been a radical change in expectations. One must ask, naturally, why, after the experience of the previous 15 years, the private sector should suddenly come to believe that inflation was going to end radically and permanently. The only reason why the administration could have thought that, and this is a very common tendency of administrations, was that the public would be so charmed by this government, that they would think they had entered a new world and all the old precedents no longer applied.

We had a course of events that conformed to the traditional expectations of economists, that is, significant disinflation and a serious recession. The more interesting surprise was that we did not have a substantial recovery without a revival of the inflation. We were helped more recently by oil and earlier by exchange rate developments. However, we must give some credit to management of monetary policy by the Federal Reserve, which was either wise or lucky in being able to ease up on monetary expansion before the lid was blown off the recovery.

Now, I turn to the other half of this equation – the part that has more to do with the balance of payments and U.S.–Japanese economic relations–that is, policy and performance in the budget. Despite the initial projections of the administration that the deficit would be reduced to zero by 1984, we continue to have persistent and unprecedented deficits in the range of $200 billion. The reasons are fairly obvious. The Laffer curve did not work. Despite the fact that revenue-increasing measures were taken in 1982–84, revenue turned out to be much less than expected. This was because real output grew about one-third less than had been predicted and because less inflation provided less expansion of revenue from inflation than if inflation had continued. We did not get the big cuts in non-defense expenditures expected. In fact, the administration did not propose specific cuts in non-defense expenditures on a scale that would have eliminated the deficit or even gone far toward eliminating the deficit, and Congress did not approve the cuts asked for. Mainly as a consequence of the deficits, we got a big increase in the interest burden. In the early projections made by the administration, the interest burden by now should have been 1.5% of GNP; in fact, it is now running about 3.3% of GNP. Of course, this makes a big difference in the size of the deficit and the size of the budget. Congress did chip away at the Reagan defense program. It reduced the defense program enough to be worrisome from a national security standpoint but not enough to be successful in avoiding the emergence of big deficits. So the dominant fact of our fiscal life and maybe of our economic life has been these large budget deficits.

There were many warnings of catastrophic results from the deficits. There were warnings that we would get a revival of inflation and that we would abort the recovery and never be able to get back to a high level of employment. Neither of these things happened, and there never was any good reason to think that the deficit would either have to cause inflation or abort the recovery.

The most realistic expectation was that the deficits would crowd out private investment. The private savings that would otherwise have been available to finance investment in the United States would be absorbed in financing the deficits, and therefore we would have low levels of investment. The consequence of the low rate of investment would be a low rate of economic growth and a low rate of growth of productivity.

The big surprise, on this side, has been that we did have, despite the large deficits, a rather average performance of domestic investment. Net investment is now running at about the same fraction of GNP as it did in the 1970s and a little less than in the 1960s.

So, although we did not get the big surge of investment and productivity that had been hoped for, we did not get the big drop of investment expected to result from the deficit. So the investment rate has been surprisingly high. This brings us to the subject of this conference, because the reason we continue to have a fairly high rate of domestic investment, despite the deficits, is that we had an enormous inflow of capital from abroad. This replaced most of the savings that had been absorbed in financing our own budget deficits. In December 1981, we were facing a budget deficit of $100 billion, which at that time seemed to be a shockingly large figure. At a meeting about this at the American Enterprise Institute, William Niskanen, who was then a member of the Council of Economic Advisors, said: "Well, this would not really be so terrible because part of it would be financed by capital inflow." Many, including myself, said: "No, that could not happen." We had never had a balance-of-payments deficit of more than $12 billion before; thus, capital inflow could not make a big dent in a $100 billion budget deficit. Moreover, if we should happen to get this big inflow of capital, we would also get a big inflow of imports. We would have a big trade deficit, and certainly measures would be taken to protect the country against the big trade deficit. Therefore, we could not count on the capital inflow to offset the results of the budget deficit on domestic investment. Nevertheless, we were all wrong about that, save Niskanen, and I do not think that even he thought we would have a $150 billion capital inflow. But we did get the big capital inflow, partly because the tax measures taken tended to make investments in the United States very attractive and thus brought capital into the United States. Also, developments in less developed countries reduced our capital outflow because they no longer were attractive places to invest. Europe was not thriving, and so there was a tendency for funds to flow here, where the economy was more vigorous.

An inevitable consequence of the big capital inflow was the high dollar and the big trade deficits. If we have the big capital inflow, we also have the big trade deficits. And Japan was in a particularly good position to respond to this situation because Japan had a large capital supply. Japan has a very high savings rate relative to its own propensities to invest, and it was becoming increasingly competitive in many fields. So we have the picture of the big balance-of-payments deficit and big trade deficit, much of this connected with Japan.

Consequences of the trade deficit

And how did the United States react? Partly by nagging the Japanese to open their markets, and with some limited success. The United

States reacted with a wave of protectionism. By this I mean talk about protectionism but with very little actually put into effect. Congress likes to talk about the damage done by imports and to encourage protectionist language but it knows that to move radically in a protectionist direction would not be good for the United States. Members of Congress have the luxury of being able to talk vigorously about protectionism, realizing that, in the end, the president will save the country from the demands of Congress, which is what usually happens.

In any case, neither the opening of markets by the Japanese nor the closing of markets by the United States can remedy the balance-of-payments situation as long as the United States is running a big budget deficit, which absorbs so much of our savings and has left us with a deficit of savings relative to our own investment propensities.

What are we to make of this situation and the tension it has caused? It seems that I am not on the same wavelength as many other observers, because I do not see the problem they are trying to solve. The United States should not complain or worry about the balance-of-payments deficit it has with Japan and other countries.

The United States has adopted policies that generated domestic demand for goods and services in excess of its ability and willingness to produce. The fact that other countries were able to supply us with goods and services, that is, to allow a net flow of imports to the United States, permitted us to meet those demands we presumably wanted to meet. We wanted the big increase in domestic consumption. We wanted to maintain our level of investment. We wanted an increase in defense expenditure. Thus, we must want an increase in imports. I regard this as beneficial to us.

I wrote a piece in the *New York Times* on this subject. When I sent it to them, the headline I wrote was "Thank God for Japan." That was a little too strong for them, I guess. Maybe it was the reference to God. They changed the title to "Japan Fills the Gap," which is a somewhat more pedestrian way of describing the situation.

We benefit by the fact that if we are so profligate as to use up our savings in financing the budget deficit, there are other countries willing to save and lend to us, which implies the trade deficit. Also, we have greatly exaggerated the adverse effects of the trade deficit in the United States. There has been a common myth that the United States has lost over 3 million jobs as a result of the trade deficit. This is clearly not true. We have had an enormous increase of employment during the period in which the trade deficit has been rising. The increase of employment has been at about the same rate as it was during the period when the trade deficit was not rising. We have had an enormous increase in employment while the European countries, which did not have a trade deficit, had no increase in employment.

This is not just empirical observation; this is what the economic theory would tend to have you expect. There is no reason for a trade deficit to cause an increase or decrease in employment. A trade deficit changes the composition of unemployment but not necessarily its total amount.

The trade deficit has been hard on some industries and has reduced the rate of growth of employment in others, although it has not tended to increase unemployment very much. By now, in the industries that seemed to be most affected, the people who were disemployed and who lost jobs have either died, retired, or gone somewhere else. One does not find big pockets of unemployment around industries like textiles, which seem to have been most adversely affected.

It is important to note that if we did not have this capital inflow and this trade deficit, other industries would be adversely affected. If we did not have the capital inflow, interest rates would be higher in the United States, and the housing industry and other domestic investment industries would be weaker. So it is not the case of saying: "Look, even though the whole country has not been hurt, some industries have been hurt." Some industries would be hurt if we did not have the trade inflow.

U.S.–Japanese trade relations

Our emphasis in discussing economic policy with Japan seems to have shifted somewhat, and Japanese attitudes have shifted as well. There is less concern about the barriers to trade. This is not to say that barriers to trade are not important. They are important as they affect efficiency in both our countries, but they do not affect the trade deficit or the balance-of-payments deficits. We have now shifted from talking about particular trade impediments to discussing macro policy. We seem to be in the business of nagging the Japanese to spend more, to run bigger budget deficits, to save less, and to keep their money invested at home. The Japanese may not find this a somewhat attractive proposition, but the choice is theirs. The United States does not have any interest in this because we are beneficiaries of the supply of capital that we get from Japan or from other countries.

It is difficult to talk about "we" in the United States, just as there is a great difficulty in talking about "we" in Japan. A great deal depends on whether one is a saver or a consumer or a user or a supplier of capital. An American supplier of capital might have an interest in not

having the Japanese supply so much to us. Whereas an American user
of capital would want the Japanese to supply us with capital. If there is
a "national interest" of American workers, it is in getting a supply of
capital that will increase their productivity. American workers used to
complain of American capital being invested in Europe and depriving
us of the capital stock that would increase our productivity. That argument runs both ways.

We may be moving out of the period of tension for a number of
reasons. The most important is that we are incapable of focusing our
interest on this subject for very long. If one were in the integrated
circuit industry, the focus might be on this for quite a while. But for
the American on the street, interest in the balance of payments will
not last long and is passing.

Congress has much on its agenda this year. Dealing with the trade
imbalance with Japan will not have high priority during the rest of this
year, and if we can get by the political temptations of 1986, we will
have a chance to see some reduction in what many regard as a problem. The whole thing may simply go away.

We are on a course of reducing our budget deficits, which would tend
to reduce the balance-of-payments deficit. The new tax bill in the
United States will reduce the attractiveness of investment in the United
States. That will be, from what most people say, undesirable from the
standpoint of the American economy but it will reduce the inflow of
capital, and therefore, it will tend to reduce our trade imbalance.

The revival of the European economy, which seems to be underway,
may also increase the attractiveness of investment there. Thus, there is
a good probability that this problem will fade from attention, although
there will continue to be particular industries that are greatly concerned about it and the need for doing something about trade barriers
for the sake of efficiency will remain. In addition, we will embark on a
new round of multilateral trade negotiations, which will take this issue
away from the unilateral decisions by Congress and into a broader
orbit, where they can be considered in a more judicious and reciprocal
way. This can also be a way of relieving Congress of the feeling that it
has to do something rambunctious about it. There is a good chance
that a conference held in the near future will have as its theme "U.S.–
Japanese Harmony."

CHAPTER 8

New financial aspects of the U.S.–Japanese trade relationship

ROY C. SMITH

Emergence of economic gridlock

The U.S.–Japanese trade relationship is based on a number of deep-rooted economic, social, and political fundamentals that are extremely difficult to change. On the surface, however, the relationship can be affected by actual or threatened political actions and by changes in financial markets. Recently, for example, the yen rose 30% against the dollar in a little more than three months, and this rise took the urgency out of the effort in 1985 by the U.S. Congress to protect American industry and jobs from Japanese competition. But the basic fundamentals that underlie the U.S.–Japanese trade relationship continue, only partly affected by the sudden increase in the value of the yen. Japan is a manufacturing nation, and it must export its goods. America has been unable, or unwilling, to produce comparable goods at competitive prices so it imports Japanese goods. We have run an increasing trade deficit with Japan for a long time. Trade frictions have existed between us throughout this period – periodically reaching hysterical levels in the United States when all sorts of responsible citizens call for drastic action. There is an equivalent hysteria that develops in Japan as people there resent American interference in their affairs and constant charges of unfair trade practices. Then, after lots of storming about, the exchange rate changes or other temporary concessions are made and things cool off for a while, only to be repeated in a year or two. This has been our basic trade relationship with Japan in a nutshell. It has not changed very much for nearly 20 years.

However, a new factor entering the equation has changed the relationship considerably: Japan's emergence as a financial investor on a scale equal to that of its standing as a manufacturer.

A decade of low domestic growth, high export earnings, persistently high household savings, and progressive deregulation of financial institutions has created a Japan that is bursting with cash and has no place to put it. Cash can move fast, if permitted to do so, and its cash has moved into our economy, replenishing our own depleted savings, helping to fund the government's deficit, propping up the bond markets and financing new manufacturing investments in this country.

The flow of Japanese savings into U.S. dollar investments more than compensates for the outflow caused by the trade deficit, as big as it is. For the past several years this offsetting cash flow has prevented the yen from rising to a level that would, more or less, stabilize the trade balance. As a consequence of the too low value for the yen over these years, the trade deficit increased to its present level, which is more than five times what it was in 1980. Such a large deficit has put much more of American industry under severe competitive pressure, heightening trade frictions. However, we have become addicted to Japanese savings, just as the Japanese have become dependent on our markets for their exports.

Our historical economic relationship now has a financial counterpart, and this has changed the relationship profoundly. We are now entangled in a kind of gridlock that neither side can do much about. It is a gridlock in which neither of us can make progress in altering the fundamentals without injuring ourselves at the same time. The relationship has become very complex. This chapter is an attempt to analyze and understand this new condition of gridlock.

There are four main points to make:

1. The gridlock is based on fundamentals that have evolved over a long period of time.
2. The conditions we find ourselves in at present are as much the result of powerful economic forces inadvertently unleashed by the United States as they are the result of any diabolical Japanese plan to take over our economy.
3. For all its problems, the gridlock has its bright side.
4. The gridlock can be managed better than it has been; the tensions it generates can be reduced by accentuating some of its positive aspects.

Observations on the Japanese economy

To bring the present into perspective, I will begin with some of my own observations on Japanese economic development. My perspective as an investment banker emphasizes the financial side. Japan, as everyone knows, is an extraordinary economic nation. But just how extraordinary, I think, is lost on most people. Japan entered the modern world only in the late 1860s after an American naval officer, Commodore Matthew Perry, paid an unwelcome but friendly visit to islands that for the previous 250 years had lived in a kind of splendid, feudal isolation from the rest of the world. Perry's visit sparked political changes that resulted in the overthrow of the Shogunate and the restoration of Emperor Meiji, who led the country to open relations with the rest of the world and attempted to develop Japan along western lines. Following Perry's visit, an American consul-general was allowed in to attempt to negotiate Japan's first commercial treaty with a foreign country, which after some baffling and frustrating years he managed to do. Unfortunately, he then left, and Washington neither replaced him nor put the treaty to much use. European countries, led by Britain, which clearly saw the economic potential of Japan, followed and took over the guiding and teaching that modernization required. How later events might have unfolded if the United States had more fully developed its early special relationship with Japan, no one can say. The Japanese modeled themselves on the great European powers and in a comparatively short time developed substantial manufacturing and trading capabilities as well as political ambitions. Japan began to think of itself as a major power that ought to be able to participate along with the others in the exploitation of China, which intensified after the Boxer Rebellion of 1900. Japan wanted special trading relationships and colonies too—even then it was mindful of its dependence on imported raw materials.

Less than 40 years after Emperor Meiji was restored, Japan was able to stand up militarily against one of the great powers of the time, Tsarist Russia, and to defeat its entire Grand Fleet, in the stunning and rightly famous battle of Tsushima Straits in 1905. This event was in its own time no less surprising to the rest of the world than if today a country like Korea were to put half the French fleet on the bottom.

Events evolved into those of the thirties and forties, which are well known to all of us. Postwar Japan was physically and financially ruined. The yen, which traded at about 2 to the dollar before the war, was reconstituted at 360. Everyone who had anything before the war had lost it. But the Japanese did have the MacArthur governance, which was exceptionally enlightened in many ways. Many reforms were made, following American practices, but the principal reorganization of the country was left to the Japanese, who were fortunate to have some exceptional leaders to accomplish it.

The period from the end of the war until the outbreak of the Korean conflict was spent trying to remove the rubble and put new structures in place. The Zaibatsus were broken up and a new government and financial institutions set up to marshal savings into productive investments. Some (but not a lot of) economic aid was provided by the United States. The Korean War, however, provided a boom for the Japanese economy and helped Japan get back on its feet. Clearly the Japanese motivation to rebuild was enormous, and much of the strong societal bonds, cooperativeness, and work ethics that we see today can be traced to the harmonious adaptations the Japanese were forced to make for the first time to survive the early postwar period.

By the 1960s Japanese economic strategy had become one of export or die. Without foreign exchange reserves and needing to import raw materials, they had no choice but to manufacture items for foreign markets and, in doing so, develop the domestic economy. Ruthless centralized controls by the government were brought into play wherever the balance of payments went soft. Credit would be curtailed, a highly meaningful action in a country with huge debt-to-equity ratios, and the economy would cool off, reducing imports. It was rough on those who were displaced, but larger companies employed people for life and did not lay people off. Throughout the sixties, however, intelligent economic planning, firm controls, hard work, and determination paid off. Japan's real growth rate for 1961–70 averaged 11% per year. Its recovery indeed was a "miracle." In those years, however, Japan had two advantages it would not have after 1971. Its exchange rate was still fixed at the early postwar level of 360 yen to the dollar, which made Japanese exports very price competitive, and the relative price of oil and other imported raw materials was low.

Just as the Japanese began to accept the new exchange rate system that was imposed on them by the 1971 U.S. decision to float the dollar, and just as it started feeling like a fairly prosperous nation again, the "oil shock" of 1973 occurred, slamming them back into high inflation and high interest rates. It was hard to feel secure when they imported 90% of their oil and the price suddenly quintupled. The Japanese worked hard and stabilized their economy but were reminded once again that for a country with a high import bill, exports were essential.

In the decade following the introduction of floating exchange rates and the oil shock, the Japanese growth rate declined to 5.3% per year, or about half the rate of the preceding 10 years. A rising level of exports made up a significant part of this growth; the domestic sector of the Japanese economy only grew at about 3%, hardly a miraculous pace. Capital expenditures were not required at the same rate as in the sixties. Consumers were cautious and preferred to save rather than spend their money. Their anxieties had been heightened by the recognition that they were vulnerable to things like oil shocks, and most

Japanese are conservative with their money anyway. They live in a country in which land and housing prices are sky high, social welfare and pension systems are much less well developed than in the United States, and credit is generally harder to come by for those who want it. They save because they feel they have to, whether they do or not. The household savings rate in Japan is around 20% versus less than 5% for the United States.

This propensity on the part of the consumer to save is a problem for the Japanese government when it wants to take fiscal steps to stimulate the economy. It is difficult to induce consumer demand, which will then pull through the economy by increasing government spending. Instead, the traditional practice in Japan is for the government to try to increase domestic growth by increasing spending for public works and other projects. This helps but does not provide the same beneficial multiplier effects that are expected. Over a period of time government efforts to stimulate the economy through spending has led to the accumulation of large fiscal deficits without a commensurate increase in the growth rate. Indeed, the Japanese government deficit today, now 25% of the total budget, is somewhat larger than the U.S. deficit, which is 21% of its budget. The Japanese cumulative deficit, in relative terms, is significantly larger. The Japanese worry about the size of their deficit, just as we do, and most political and administration officials feel that the deficit is already as big as it ought to get and should be reduced. Feeling as they do, it is not surprising that the U.S. government encounters resistance to its suggestion that the Japanese try to stimulate domestic growth through further government fiscal actions.

Despite Japan's development of a strong export bias in the years following the war, Japan's exports today do not constitute that large a portion of its total GNP—only about 17% in 1984, which is up from 11% in 1970, but still a considerably lower percentage than for, say, Germany, France, Great Britain, and Italy, each of which exports more than 24% of its GNP. The United States exports only 7.5% of its GNP. The problem, of course, is that almost all Japanese exports are manufactured goods. In a country with an export bias and little else to export but manufactures, it is not surprising that this concentration developed. In managing their exports, the Japanese have shown unusual sophistication and intelligence. Their basic policy has been to secure export markets by manufacturing high-volume, high-value-added goods, such as consumer products, at as low a cost and with the highest quality they could manage.

One of the first tasks the Japanese undertook in the fifties and sixties was to learn how to manufacture things efficiently, through good process engineering, quality control, and management of production costs. To make consumer goods, companies do not have to concentrate on pure science and R&D, and the Japanese corporation did not do so. Their engineering energies were spent on the manufacturing process itself and on product design. The technology for this was not hard to come by or to improve if one spent the time on it. It was not hard for a country with a high literacy rate, a good technical education system, and a history of superior engineering skills going back at least to 1905 to master the science of manufacturing.

Quality control was an early concern of the Japanese, as the Japanese consumer was and is unusually quality minded, and a high manufacturing reject rate was costly and wasteful of precious raw materials. Ironically, the Japanese learned their modern quality control procedures from Americans hired as consultants after the war. With a highly disciplined and dedicated work force, they were able to apply and perfect these early lessons very successfully.

Managing production costs was handled in some unique ways. They would seek economies of scale by manufacturing larger quantities of goods than they knew they could sell in Japan. They would estimate world-wide demand for each item and the share of the world market they could target for themselves and then turn the ensuing output over to their domestic and overseas sales forces or to the giant trading companies whose job it was to distribute the goods. As long as they could sell the goods on the whole, for more than cost, they were ahead. The emphasis was on building up sales volume – through the stimulation of primary demand for their products and by seeking an increasing share of the market. If they did this well, profits would take care of themselves. Building up sales volume and market penetration were more important than current profits. Companies grew, many new jobs were created, the greater public was served, and prestige was enhanced. These remain important values to the Japanese company, but they were especially so in the postwar recovery period.

On the whole, the strategy of worldwide market development has worked very well. However, more than good strategy was needed to produce the results that were obtained. Japanese industry also had some help from the government and from their financial system. Most of this help has been more indirect than the theory of "Japan, Inc." would imply, but it was certainly useful. Japan's centralized economic system is very effective. There is a national industrial planning effort to keep Japan's manufactured goods moving up the technology curve, in which representatives of industry participate, and the product of which is well known and reasonably consistent. Which industries are to be fed with resources and which cut back are identified in advance. For years, now much liberalized, restrictions were placed on foreign competitors manufacturing in Japan. Vigorous competition among Japanese companies was encouraged. Social welfare programs provided by the government were few, so employees looked to their companies for their long-term welfare (in exchange for long-term employment) and were willing to accept comparatively low wages and to extend their loyalties to employers.

Also helping was the country's remarkable financial system. In the early days after the war, and for some time thereafter, Japanese industry was short of capital. This was dealt with in several ingenious ways. First, the banking system was set up under very tight controls by the Bank of Japan and the Ministry of Finance. The banks, both commercial banks and the long-term credit banks, were designed to be highly leveraged themselves and to extend as much credit to manufacturing companies as they could. Everything was very highly averaged, but bank supervision was extremely tight. The larger companies tended to belong to groups, some based on the old Zaibatsus, in which cross shareholdings and supplier–customer relationships were encouraged to provide a group economic support system. If a member company got into trouble, the group, together with its bank, would be called in to rescue it, with the government watching closely from the sidelines. The rescue of Mazda, which overextended itself in rotary engines in the seventies, was a classic case of the fire brigade in action. Because there was some assurance that the company would survive no matter what, larger enterprises were free to take greater risks than their American counterparts and their stockholders would have thought prudent. The ability to take these risks has greatly enhanced the competitiveness of Japanese manufacturers over the past 20 years.

The Japanese also rebuilt their capital markets in the fifties. A corporate bond market, which required all debts to be secured, developed to some extent, but not as fast as the bank debenture market, which enabled the powerful long-term credit banks to obtain funding for medium- and long-term industrial loans. The stock market rejuvenated very quickly. The principal stockholders of companies after the war were other group members and allied financial institutions. Their holdings were never traded; rather they were added to periodically as companies issued new shares through rights offerings. Most of the trading in stocks was done by individuals who paid no capital gains taxes and who had no other place to invest small amounts of money in speculative investments. The retail brokerage industry developed rapidly to supply the infrastructure for share dealings. Throughout the sixties and the seventies Japanese companies also issued large quantities of securities abroad, predominantly in the Euro-bond markets, and foreign investors became large holders of Japanese stocks. The growth in the Japanese economy and the influx of foreign funds into the stock market, together with increased investment by Japanese individuals and corporations, pushed stock prices steadily upward over quite a long period. At present the Nikkei Dow Jones average is more than four times what it was at the beginning of 1974. Our Dow Jones average is now a little more than twice what it was at the beginning of 1974. Japanese price–earnings ratios became very high compared to the United States and Europe. Even today, with our great bull market and shares being withdrawn from the market because of mergers, buyouts and repurchase programs, the average price–earnings ratio of a NYSE-listed stock is 15. In Japan the average price–earnings ratio of a Tokyo Stock Exchange share is 36.

For most of the past decade Japanese interest rates have been relatively low, reflecting the low inflation rate, its trade balance, and government regulation. For companies operating with large amounts of leverage, low interest rates, and high price–earnings ratios, the cost of capital is very low. For example, in the United States an A-rated company might have 40% of its capital structure in the form of debt, for which it has been paying about 6% after tax on average for several years. Sixty percent of the company's capital is represented by equity, which is traded in the market at an average price–earnings ratio of, say, 12. One crude indication of a company's cost of equity capital is obtained by taking the inverse of the price–earnings ratio (or earnings as a return on investment as measured by market value), or 8% in this case. In this example, the weighted debt and equity after-tax cost of capital for the American company would be 7.2%. Using the same method to calculate the cost of capital of a comparable Japanese company, which would instead have a debt-to-total-capital ratio of, say, 60% and a price–earnings ratio of 36, yields a weighted cost of capital of 3.2%.

This lower cost of capital makes a difference, a large one, in the comparative manufacturing costs for Japanese companies as contrasted with their western competitors. The Japanese use this advantage well, as they constantly invest in new capital equipment, which they depreciate rapidly, for both expansion and for improving their manufacturing efficiency. As a result, Japanese plant and equipment is among the youngest in the world and productivity among the highest. Further, their propensity to invest in plant improvements encourages them to lead the way to totally new manufacturing technologies, like robotics, which can produce quantum leaps in productivity improvements for the future.

Comparison to the U.S. economy

I would like to turn now to the United States and to highlight a few points about its economic activity since the war that bear on today's relations with the Japanese. Immediately after the war the United States was the only superpower – the most powerful economic organization ever – and arguably much more powerful than the gods ever intended it to be, as there was no competition. The situation was unnatural; it enabled us to accumulate enormous wealth, but it could not last forever. Two major forces had to be contended with, both of which required power sharing, which, it is not surprising, popular opinion in the United States has not appreciated. The first major force was the emergence of the Soviet Union as a rival superpower, which required us to make large expenditures for national defense. The second, a more benign factor, was the rebirth of the free world economy, which brought its own challenges and disputes. In the fifties and sixties, for example, our economic relations in Europe created great problems: Were we going to overwhelm or totally gobble up the economies of Germany, France, and Great Britain? In showering Europe with funds from investments, foreign aid, military expenditure, and tourism, were we over-inflating their economies with a glut of dollars? This glut, which organized itself into the Euro-dollar market, grew and usefully functioned as a deposit-taking and loan-making institution for financing trade and capital transactions. But central banks still accumulated more dollars than they wanted, so they sent the excess back to the United States to be exchanged for gold. The gold reserves of the United States were rapidly being drained from Fort Knox. The United States, in financing world recovery and competition, had developed a serious balance-of-payments problem. Something had to be done. The United States imposed controls on capital exports. The Special Drawing Rights (SDR) was created by the International Monetary Fund to take some of the pressure off the dollar as a reserve currency and to provide an alternative way to finance current account deficits. The United States closed the gold window halfway – central banks would be dealt with at the established price of $35 per ounce; but if the rest of the world wanted to make a market in gold it could – and it did. These steps helped but were not enough; in 1971 the whole fixed rate foreign exchange system broke apart. The United States would no longer redeem its currency for gold from anyone.

Holders of dollars would have to sell them in the market for gold or other currencies – the value of the dollar and all other currencies would no longer be fixed; from now on they would float in the foreign exchange markets. Immediately the dollar was devalued against all other currencies – the yen, for example, went from 360 to 303. From then on, imbalances in trading or capital flows would be adjusted by changing exchange rates, which would reflect market forces. Japan's slowing domestic growth after the oil shock and its vigorous export sector continued to produce a strong balance of payments, so the yen continued to strengthen. At the end of 1980 it stood at 202.

There was a growing Japanese trade surplus with the United States; but several factors seemed to keep it in proportion. The magnitude was manageable. In 1980, for example, the Japanese trade surplus with the United States was $9 billion; Japanese exports were concentrated on particular industries, but the concentration moved from textiles to steel to electronics to automobiles in the period from 1970 to 1980 and was then heading toward semiconductors. There were plenty of complaints from the affected industries, but mostly these were dealt with by temporary quota systems or by administrative tribunals that were set up to adjudicate dumping and other unfair trade charges. Also, Japan was a big buyer of commodities from the United States, which helped to offset the surplus, although it was stunned by the Nixon embargo on soybeans and other grain exports in 1973 and afterward began to look elsewhere for more reliable suppliers. Mainly, however, the U.S. trade deficit with Japan did not matter much because the value of the yen was reflecting it and overall stabilizing influences were in play; U.S. surpluses with the developing world offset the deficit with Japan. The overall trade deficit of the United States in 1980 was $36.4 billion.

All of this began to change in 1981, when a new president, with a strong popular mandate and a different set of economic policies came into office. In the ensuing five years, these policies have had many effects – some very salubrious, some not – but nothing has affected the magnitude of the numbers that define the U.S.–Japanese economic and financial relationship as much as these policies have. Whatever trendline the relationship between the two countries was on in 1980, the new policies were like a shot of adrenalin. In some respects the relationship has become distorted; but it has also resulted in the entanglement that I have called the gridlock. The adrenalin charge has now largely been spent, and market forces (especially in the foreign exchange market) are beginning again to counteract its effects, but the adrenalin accelerated the emergence on the international stage of Japan as an investor on a massive scale, and this has forged a permanent change in the nature of our relationship.

When President Reagan came into office, he had three principal goals: to reduce taxes so as to liberate the entrepreneurial spirit of America, to reduce the role of government as an expensive impediment to economic progress and personal freedom, and to reverse the decline that the United States had fallen into in international affairs and, in particular, to strengthen its national defenses vis-à-vis the Soviet Union. For the most part, President Reagan's popularity reflected the appeal of these fairly basic policies. To implement these policies, however, dramatic action was required: a large cut in federal spending, a big increase in defense spending, and a large tax reduction despite the fact that the budget would be thrown into the largest peacetime deficit ever. The deficit provided a lot of stimulus to the U.S economy. It reversed the slump of 1982 and created growth in the period 1983–85 at an average of 4.3% per year, far more than during any recent 3-year period. Inflation, however, did not rise; in fact, it declined sharply. This was partly because of the exceptionally high real interest rates in the economy that resulted from the deficit. The financial markets refused to provide long-term money to a system with such a high deficit except at interest rates that reflected a substantial premium over the long-term rate of inflation that the market rather cynically expected the deficit to produce in the long run.

Such high interest rates coupled with strong domestic growth and lowering inflation appealed greatly to the foreign exchange market, which on the whole endorsed President Reagan's policies. The dollar strengthened, foreign investment poured into the United States, and financing the deficit was not too hard with so much money coming in from abroad. Corporate profits improved; Detroit turned around; business really picked up. The securities markets bottomed out in 1982 and began a 4-year bull market that is still continuing. This helped to bring in even more foreign capital and boosted the dollar further. The yen fell from 202 in 1980 to 235 in 1982 to 251 by the end of 1985. The Japanese trade surplus with the United States exploded. The cheaper yen and the growing U.S. economy made exporting to the United States easy as well as necessary; Japanese domestic growth was down to about 2% in 1984, and other markets for Japanese exports were doing even worse. The Japanese surplus with the United States became $19 billion in 1982, $34 billion in 1984, and $50 billion in 1985.

Another change also took place: Japan's great surplus of savings began to flow into the United States, ultimately in such a large quantity as to virtually counter-effect the pressure in the foreign exchange markets caused by the extraordinary trade surplus. For years Japanese domestic savings had been accumulating. Now the foreign exchange proceeds of the surging export business were added to them. Japan did not need to retain the foreign exchange earnings; it already had a payments surplus. If the Japanese were to promote recycling of the funds back to the United States, then the yen would remain at its comparatively low level, ensuring that exports would continue, and this would prevent the Japanese domestic economy from sinking into a recession.

A recession in Japan would be very difficult socially and politically for Japan. There was no further room to increase Japan's fiscal deficit, already overextended in the opinion of many. Besides, at any evidence of a slowdown in Japan, the cautious Japanese would increase their savings even more to provide a cushion against the inevitable lay-off or wage reduction that was bound to hit the family. True, Americans complained that the export surplus could not be tolerated forever and that Congress would retaliate with protectionist measures if Japan did not do something. But what could the Japanese do? Open up domestic markets for foreign goods? They were open, but foreigners did not understand that the consumers were not buying and what they did buy was sold on the basis of intense competition between strong, efficient Japanese companies with long established, loyal customers. A foreign company would have no more success in the Japanese market than would, say, a well-known Japanese consumer products company like House Food Industrial in competing against Proctor & Gamble, Beatrice Foods, and General Foods in the United States. Besides, the quantities involved are absurd. America exports airplanes, military equipment, computers, and agricultural commodities to Japan. In 1985 these exports totaled about $12 billion to $15 billion. Japan had already bought as much of these as it could, and there was still a $50 billion difference.

Americans were not satisfied; they wanted some important concessions. "Well," they said, "if you can't do much to open up your commercial markets, how about opening up your financial markets?" "All right," said the Japanese, "if that's what you want." Financial deregulation, which had been occurring in Japan for the previous 10 years, accelerated. All sorts of new foreign securities were created that could be sold to Japanese institutional and individual investors. "Samurai Bonds" (yen-denominated issues in Tokyo by foreign governments and a few corporations) were joined by "Sushi Bonds" (non-yen issues in Europe by Japanese companies sold back to Japan) and "Shogun Bonds" (non-yen issues sold in Japan by foreigners). They also were encouraged to purchase U.S. Treasury and Agency securities, corporate and other Eurobonds and to increase their rather modest holdings of U.S. equities. Japanese life insurance and trust companies were urged to learn how to manage foreign portfolios and to take advantage of the new rule that permitted up to 10% of net assets to be invested abroad. They could form joint ventures with foreign portfolio managers to manage these investments if they wanted to. The capital outflow from Japan that resulted was incredible. In 1980 the Japanese net capital account showed an inflow of $2.3 billion; in 1982 it was an outflow of $15 billion; by 1985 the outflow had reached $65 billion. Japan became the world's hottest source of capital since OPEC. International securities firms flocked to Japan to open representative offices, branches, and trading desks and finally, this year, to become members of the Tokyo Stock Exchange. Japanese investors were key to structuring any kind of important financing anywhere in the world. By the end of 1985 they owned almost $30 billion of U.S. government securities, and their appetite or lack of it was crucial to each Treasury auction. The investment flow out of Japan was predominantly, but not exclusively, limited to portfolio investment. Direct investment, especially in the United States, also surged as Japanese banks increased their U.S. assets; new manufacturing facilities were built, and marketing and distribution investments in the United States were expanded. Japanese companies run out of Tokyo found in an increasing number of cases that the largest part of their business on a consolidated basis was centered, if not actually located, in the United States.

The U.S.–Japanese economic gridlock

So we now arrive, after a long journey, at the present. Here we encounter the gridlock. America cannot prevent a huge quantity of imports coming from Japan. There is no way that Japan can absorb additional imports equal to even a fraction of the present deficit, no matter how much Congress threatens, the Prime Minister promises, and others complain. We are, for the time being, locked into a continuation of the trade imbalance. If we take drastic action to eliminate the deficit, such as introducing punitive tariffs, we will severely injure our most important and loyal ally in the Pacific, undoubtedly injure a lot of other countries around the world much poorer than us, who depend on either the United States or the Japanese market for survival, and be in direct violation of all of our carefully structured trade and commercial treaties, which have long helped to prevent the world from protectionistic retrenchments whenever difficult times have appeared. We would also cut off the Japanese flow of funds into the United States and thereby injure ourselves.

Looked at from another side, Japan has no other market in the world for its products that equals the United States. Without the U.S. market, Japan's prosperity is endangered. Japan presently has the world's largest supply of excess savings and must find investment markets big enough to accommodate them. Investment returns in Japan are low. The United States has a huge deficit and pays high interest rates in order to finance it. If we do not import savings from Japan and elsewhere, interest rates would rise, probably very sharply, and growth would be reduced. Bankruptcies might follow in several sectors already dangerously stretched to the limits of their resources – the banking, savings and loan, and farming sectors are obviously among these. Withdrawal of Japanese funds from the United States would have a serious, adverse effect upon U.S. financial markets, which would greatly reduce the value of remaining Japanese investments. We need Japanese investments, but equally they need to make them and to keep them here.

Neither the Japanese nor the United States can greatly change either the trade or the financial situation for the time being. The magnitude of the numbers is just too big. To cut the recycling of money to strengthen the yen in order to accelerate the adjustment of the trade imbalance would create immediately painful consequences for both nations.

This is the gridlock that defines our new relationship. There are benefits, to be sure, but we cannot expose American industry to another five-fold increase in the trade deficit because of a yen–dollar rate that is subsidized by reinvestment flows. Nor can we slam the door on Japanese exports without ruining the Japanese economy and precipitating a retaliatory withdrawal of funds from the United States.

There may be some hope in the short run. It is doubtful whether the problems represented by the U.S. deficits – fiscal and trade – can continue to increase at the same pace as the last five years. Already adjustments are taking place; the dollar has fallen 31% against the yen since reaching the high point of the last cycle of 260 yen in September of 1985. At this writing (April 1986), it is at 180, near its all-time low against the yen, a very big change in seven months. At this level some economists have predicted a $10 billion reduction in the Japanese trade deficit with the United States, though perhaps not in 1986. The deficit may widen in 1986 as we experience the J curve effect of the weaker dollar. Also, the fiscal deficit of the United States appears to be stabilizing, perhaps even getting a bit smaller. A "hard landing" is still widely forecast for the United States, as it brings its deficit into line, but the sharp reduction in oil prices and interest rates has introduced an unexpected positive element into the equation. These factors have improved the outlook for growth in the United States as well as for the hard-to-motivate domestic sector of the Japanese economy. The basic economic problems remain, but they are easing; perhaps we have been granted a breathing spell, a time for Japanese and U.S. officials to rethink policy positions aimed at affecting the fundamental elements of the problem.

Long-term prospects

The problem of excessive Japanese imports into the United States will be influenced over the long run by three basic factors. First, absolute manufacturing costs in Japan will increase, which will make it harder to sell products in the United States at a relative price advantage. There is a shortage of land and a shortage of labor that will prevent Japan from indefinitely increasing manufacturing output to supply the whole world's markets, and new, expensive social programs are being introduced. American industry, on the other hand, has had a lot of success recently in lowering its manufacturing costs. Second, the Japanese domestic economy has been undergoing deregulation, most evidently in the financial sector, and this ought to loosen up the domestic market, permitting greater growth. Social changes are also taking place, and there ought to be some loosening up of the consumer too, who sooner or later will realize that he has oversaved. Credit is more available to assist consumption. New opportunities for entrepreneurial activities, especially in the service sectors of the economy, are also being developed, which help to redirect consumer activity. Third, Japanese companies are increasing their manufacturing activities in the United States, which directly affects the trade equation but also provides jobs and a transfer of sophisticated manufacturing technology to American workers. Most of the Japanese consumer electronics products are now manufactured in the United States; all of the automobile makers have committed themselves to large factories in the United States, and these factories have attracted others to be built by Japanese companies that supply tires and other auto parts to them. Most major Japanese manufacturers now realize that they have to do this or they will lose their position in the U.S. market, either from protectionist action or because they will not be able to sell products here at the same price advantage that they have enjoyed in the past. It is a difficult task for them to erect a large manufacturing plant in the United States, and it is not hard to see why it has taken so long for Japanese companies to undertake the task, especially when the short-run profits inherent in the export boom of the past five years were so attractive.

It is clear that the United States benefits by these longer-run trends. There are several things we can do, however, to accelerate them through policy actions. First, we can stop wasting time and energy on threatening the Japanese to "open their markets to our goods, or else." There is no way that such statements can produce more than lip service responses. Instead, we should press equally hard on the Japanese to increase manufacturing investments in the United States and to accelerate the pace of commercial deregulation in Japan. Mainly, we have to have a clear, focused understanding with the Japanese that these steps will help, they are what we want, and they must cooperate with us in seeing that such things work. I do not think that the new Yeutter initiatives to change the U.S. trade negotiating posture can provide the clear kind of understanding that we need, but some of the proposals made appear to be heading in a more constructive direction. If they work at it by focusing on realistic objectives, there is much our two governments can do to help.

A second thing we can do is to recognize that the yen has to float at a rate, relative to the dollar, that enables the fundamental changes to take place. The financial investment in the United States tends to prevent the yen from being strengthened as much as it otherwise should. Preventing portfolio investment in the United States per se is not a healthy step; and it is the anti-thesis of the deregulations we are trying to encourage. However, financial deregulation that increases portfolio investment in the United States ought to be slowed. It might have been a good idea, for example, to have delayed the recent deregulatory step that now permits Japanese life insurance companies to invest up to 25% of their assets in foreign securities, up from 10% previously.

Obviously, the Japanese have their own ideas about a long-term program to manage the yen–dollar rate. We need, however, to have an understanding that we will work together to set target yen–dollar rates to support what we are both otherwise trying to do and make sure that appropriate policy steps are taken on both sides to bring about the targeted rate levels, or at least not set them back.

A third thing we can do is to continue to encourage U.S. industry to make new investments to improve manufacturing efficiency and to upgrade plants and equipment. Somehow, abolishing investment tax credits and accelerated depreciation in the interests of tax reform do not seem to be steps in this direction.

A fourth thing we can do is to suggest to the Japanese that they recycle some of their excess billions into other countries, such as Mexico and Brazil, where the Japanese have substantial trading relations and where the money could help stabilize these countries. Japan could assist them in dealing with debt problems of recent years, which would help American banks sleep a bit easier and make a lot of friends in Latin America. Japanese investors could also work out some commercial or investment concessions, making the loans, in such a way as to be an excellent long-term investment for them. At present the United States does not have the money to help these countries, but their problems are very much our problems, and if the Japanese help, we would be indebted to them – but not at the cost of weakening the yen. There are many ways in which enlightened use of the Japanese savings surplus could be put to good effect without disrupting the free market aspects of financial deregulation that the Japanese have undertaken or the free market setting of the yen–dollar exchange rate needed to stabilize our trade situation with Japan over the long term.

A fifth thing we can do, as an incentive to the Japanese and as a favor to ourselves, would be to change our laws and permit the sale of Alaskan oil to Japan, which the Japanese could use to reduce their heavy dependence on Middle Eastern oil. We could replace Alaskan oil in the United States by purchasing Mexican oil in greater quantities. The effect of such a swap could increase our exports to Japan by about $8 billion to $10 billion, much of which could be used to help Mexico at a time when it needs our help.

If both Japan and the United States take the problem seriously, over a period of a few years much of the tension and friction can be resolved, and in so doing, the many positive aspects in their closely linked economic and financial relationships can be accentuated and preserved. This has to be an exceptional opportunity for both countries, which in the end are both stronger for their mutual interdependence.

CHAPTER 9

Japanese–U.S. current accounts and exchange rates before and after the G5 agreement

KAZUO UEDA

The world economy has been greatly influenced over the past 10 years by the monetary and fiscal policies of the industrialized nations. Looking back at U.S. economic policy in particular, we see that expansionary monetary policy kept inflation at a high level over the latter half of the 1970s. It was with the aim of curbing this inflation that tight monetary policy was brought into play over the period 1979–82. This restrictive monetary policy, which brought about recession not only in the U.S. but throughout the world, was clearly successful in the sense that it managed to reduce the rate of inflation.

With monetary policy being eased after 1982, large-scale expansionary fiscal policy, including various tax cuts, was implemented. This resulted in an increase in fiscal and trade deficits, high interest rates, and a strong dollar.

The rising fiscal and trade deficits, in turn, shifted economists' attention to studying the effects of fiscal policy in an open economy context. These studies suggest that the largest factor behind the U.S. current account deficit (or the Japanese current account surplus) is the increase in the U.S. fiscal deficit. As a result, it has become apparent that the U.S. fiscal deficit must be reduced and that Japan must pursue expansionary fiscal policy if the U.S.–Japanese trade imbalance is to decline.

In an attempt to resolve their trade imbalance, the United States and Japan held the historic G5 meeting. While the participants at that meeting recognized the need for the directions in fiscal policy outlined above, political realities suggested that the implementation of such policies would not be easy. The G5 meeting was an attempt to find a way to avoid such political constraints by once again resorting to monetary policy.

To assess the effectiveness of the G5 meeting, I analyze trends in interest rates, exchange rates, and the current account before and after the meeting. Such an examination will help determine to what extent monetary policy alone can redress U.S.–Japanese trade imbalances and to what extent changes in fiscal policy may be necessary.

The chapter is divided into three sections. Section I discusses the important relationships between investment/savings balances, fiscal policy, and the current account and explains the role of investment/ saving behavior and fiscal policy in determining Japan's current account surplus. Section II discusses trends in exchange rates and interest rates before and after the G5 agreement against a background of a persistent Japanese trade surplus (U.S. trade deficit). Finally, Section III discusses the outlook for U.S.–Japanese interest and exchange rates and current account imbalances.

I.   Fiscal policy and the current account

It is imperative to first understand the relationship of investment/ savings balances and fiscal policy to the current account in order to understand movements in exchange rates and interest rates.[1]

Consider Japan's current account surplus. This is always equivalent to the difference between domestic investment and savings. Consequently, trends in the current account can be analyzed by examining investment and savings trends.

Two types of investment and savings trends exist: those that change exogenously and those that change endogenously. An example of the former would be a change in preferences for saving, since such preferences are generally taken to be exogenous. An example of the latter would be a change in savings in response to a change in interest rates, since savings in this case are responding to a change in another variable, namely, interest rates.

It is also possible for a domestic savings surplus to arise endogenously in response to movements in overseas variables. For example, when a consumption boom occurs in the United States, demand for Japanese goods increases, and a surplus in Japanese savings arises due to the improved business climate that increased exports bring about. Furthermore, when the U.S. savings shortage resulting from the consumption boom brings about high interest rates, this induces higher Japanese interest rates, leading to an even larger savings surplus. At the same time, the high U.S. interest rates cause the dollar to appreciate against the yen, and a current account surplus emerges in response to the savings surplus.

While savings behavior is itself endogenously determined to a sub-

---

[1] For further detail on the following analysis, see: K. Ueda, "The Japanese Current Account Surplus and Fiscal Policy in Japan and the U.S.," Zaisei Kinyu Kenkyujo Discussion Paper No. 2, December 1985; K. Ueda, "Current Account and Exchange Rate: a Savings/Investment Balance Approach," *Kinyu Kenkyu,* Vol. 4, No. 4 (in Japanese).

stantial extent, its effect on interest rates and exchange rates ultimately impacts on the current account. Moreover, when interest rates are very sensitive to savings and investment behavior, it is easy to see that savings behavior can have a profound effect on the current account. Consequently, a useful method for examining the causes behind a current account surplus is to estimate exogenous components of domestic and overseas investment and savings, or net savings. These have been estimated by running simple saving, investment, and tax functions. The estimated equations are then used to construct exogenous movements of net savings of the private and government sectors in Japan and the U.S. That is, net savings are calculated at full employment and at a constant interest rate. The current account surplus is then regressed on these net savings variables and those that capture cyclical movements in the economies. This equation yields a decomposition of the current account into cyclical and non-cyclical components. The latter can in turn be decomposed into the effects of exogenous net savings variables. This is shown in Figure 9.1. (The details are explained in the Appendix.) Figure 9.1 shows the effect of each of the four net savings variables on the ratio of Japan's current account to GNP.

As can be seen from the figure, the high levels of Japanese private sector savings and the U.S. fiscal deficit are associated with Japan's current account surplus. Furthermore, it is also apparent that the reduction in the Japanese fiscal deficit and the further expansion of the private savings shortage in the United States also coincide with Japan's surplus. One inference that may be drawn is that Japanese and U.S. fiscal policies, which have been moving in opposite directions, have exacerbated the Japanese–U.S. trade imbalance.

This brings us to the following policy implications. If Japan's current account surplus is to be significantly reduced, a reduction in the U.S. fiscal deficit and/or the implementation of expansionary fiscal policy in Japan is imperative. Although monetary policy can affect the current account by changing domestic and overseas business conditions and moving the exchange rate, its impact can only be temporary given the long-run neutrality of money. It is for this reason that the need to invoke or alter fiscal policy has been stressed.

The above analysis also has important implications for exchange rates. One conclusion is that, given the asymmetric stances on fiscal policy and investment/savings behavior in Japan and the United States, it would be difficult to avoid a current account surplus in Japan of less than 2% of GNP. Taking this as the "equilibrium" level trade imbalance, it is possible to calculate an "equilibrium" exchange rate exactly compatible with such a surplus.

Figure 9.2 illustrates the actual exchange rate along with this equilib-

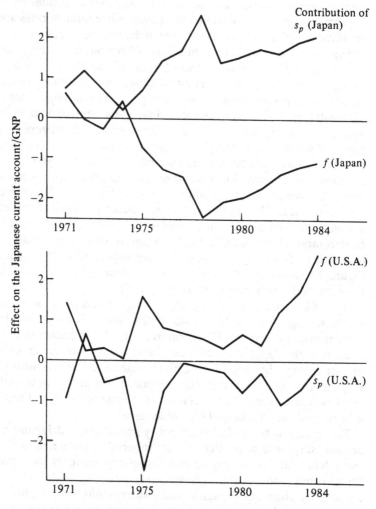

s_p: autonomous private net savings
f: full-employment budget deficit

Figure 9.1. Effects on Japanese current account of net savings in Japan and the United States.

rium rate. The equilibrium rate for the yen has been higher than the actual rate over the past few years, but the difference between the two is not great. Interestingly, in 1984 the equilibrium rate corresponded to the actual 1984 average of yen per dollar.

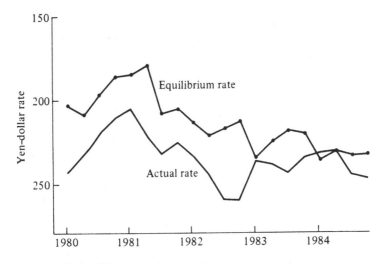

Figure 9.2. Equilibrium exchange rate.

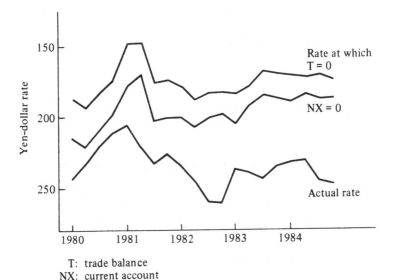

T: trade balance
NX: current account

Figure 9.3. Trade balance, current account, and the exchange rate.

For comparison, Figure 9.3 depicts an exchange rate consistent with a balance in the current account. These rates deviate significantly from the actual rate, yielding rates for 1984 of approximately 190 yen per dollar. Nevertheless, as long as there is no major change in domestic and

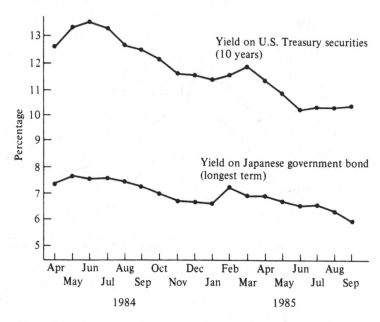

Figure 9.4. Interest rates in Japan and the United States.

overseas investment/savings balances, it is difficult to avoid a substantial Japanese current account surplus, and accordingly, it would seem more in keeping with macroeconomic logic to refer to a rate of yen per dollar as the "balanced" rate.

II.   The G5 meeting and interest rates and exchange rates

Let us look briefly here at interest rate and exchange rate movements before and after the G5 meeting in the context of a persistent Japanese current account surplus.

Interest rates and exchange rates before G5

The important features of interest rate and exchange rate movements prior to the G5 meeting are the gradual decreases in long-term interest rates in Japan and the United States since the spring of 1985 and a gradual fall of the dollar vis-à-vis the yen (see Figures 9.4 and 9.5).

A standard interpretation of this pattern runs as follows. The U.S. economy, which had shown strong growth in real GNP of 3.7% in 1983 and 6.8% in 1984, began to experience a slowdown in 1985, registering

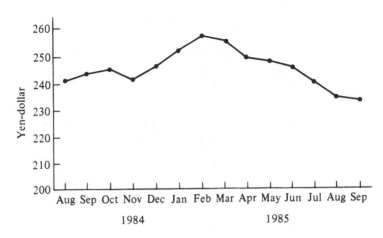

Figure 9.5. Yen–dollar rate.

0.3% growth in the first quarter and 1.9% in the second. As a result, the Federal Reserve started to ease monetary policy, bringing about lower interest rates and a slowly weakening dollar. Lower U.S. interest rates had an impact in Japan also, with long-term interest rates in particular falling.

As the arguments in the previous section suggest, however, there are other factors affecting the pattern of exchange rates and interest rates. For example, if one accepts the premise of a persistent Japanese current account surplus of about 2% of GNP, exchange rates should move toward an equilibrium rate of 230 yen per dollar.

Thus far the analysis has not touched upon the question of how long the large-scale U.S. current account and fiscal deficits can be sustained, nor what the long-term consequences thereof will be. To get a feel for the long-run effects, Table 9.1 gives a simulation of the long-term consequences of the U.S. fiscal deficit. The fiscal deficit will increase outstanding government bonds, which will in turn bring about an increase in the deficit through rising interest payments. Table 9.1 examines just how serious this effect could become under the assumption that U.S. private sector net savings and the fiscal deficit (excluding interest payments) maintain a fixed proportion of GNP. Case I assumes real growth of 2% over the next 10 years, while Case II assumes 4% growth. Interest rates have been calculated as fluctuating according to changes in the demand for funds.[2]

---

[2] For further details concerning this simulation, refer to Ueda (1985).

Table 9.1. *Simulation of the U.S. budget deficit and interest rate*[a]

Year	B/Y	BuD/Y	i
Case I			
86	0.34	0.040	10.5
87	0.37	0.044	11.1
88	0.40	0.049	11.8
89	0.44	0.056	12.8
90	0.48	0.064	14.0
91	0.53	0.074	15.6
92	0.60	0.089	17.8
93	0.68	0.111	21.1
94	0.79	0.147	24.6
95	0.95	0.196	32.1
Case II			
86	0.34	0.040	10.4
87	0.35	0.038	10.1
88	0.36	0.034	9.5
89	0.37	0.032	9.3
90	0.38	0.033	9.3
91	0.39	0.033	9.4
92	0.40	0.034	9.6
93	0.41	0.036	9.8
94	0.42	0.037	10.1
95	0.43	0.039	10.4

[a] Abbreviations: B, government bonds outstanding (holdings of private sector); Y, GNP; BuD, government deficit; i, nominal interest rate.

As is evident from Case I in the table, with a growth rate of 2%, the U.S. budget deficit as a fraction of GNP, and interest rates will begin to escalate after 4 years, reaching intolerable levels in 10 years. In contrast, a 4% growth rate (Case II) would make it possible to maintain current budget deficit ratios for some time (10 years).[3]

In other words, it should be possible over the reasonably long term to sustain an "equilibrium" fiscal deficit if the 4% growth rate assumed under Case II is realistic. In such a case, the 230 yen per dollar rate given in the previous section may be considered the long-run equilibrium rate.

[3] Of course, in both cases the relative significance of the size of the deficit will fade in terms of economic scale over the very long term. This analysis, however, rests on, as a practical issue, to what extent it actually does deteriorate over the next 10 years.

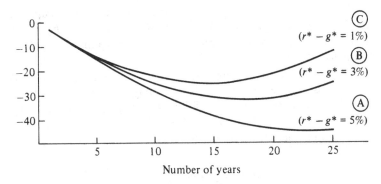

r*: interest rate on U.S. external debt
g*: U.S. real GNP growth rate

Figure 9.6. Simulating U.S. debt/GNP ratio.

If the 2% growth rate of Case II is more likely, however, then there is a strong possibility that it will not be possible to sustain the present equilibrium over the long run. In this case, an exchange rate of 230 yen per dollar cannot be a long-run equilibrium rate, and it would probably be more accurate to call it a bubble-like rate[4] that does not reflect economic fundamentals. Viewed in this way, an assessment of what is an equilibrium exchange rate differs depending on one's reading of medium- and long-term growth rates.

A similar point can be made about Krugman,[5] who warned of the long-term consequences of the U.S. current account deficit. Although the framework of his analysis differs from that above, Krugman calculated the extent of U.S. external debt that would arise as a result of the persistently strong dollar prior to G5. In particular, Krugman assumed that the dollar would depreciate (in real terms) only at the rate of 2.4%, which was the (real) interest differential between the U.S. and the rest of the world at that time. He calculated the U.S. external debt–GNP ratio for the case of 8% real interest rate and 3% real GNP growth rate. In Krugman's hypothetical case (Figure 9.6, Case A), U.S. external debt continues to increase in the next 20 years, reaching a GNP ratio of 50% at its peak. This corresponds to current Central and Latin American levels. If one assumes slightly higher growth rates[6] (Cases B and C in Figure 9.6), the seriousness of the

---

[4] See Okina (1984).
[5] See Krugman (1985).
[6] A lower real interest rate will produce the same result as a higher growth rate.

problem is considerably lowered. Both analyses, then, emphasize that medium- and long-term U.S. growth prospects are critically important for sustaining world economic conditions, including the exchange rate prior to G5.

When viewed in this light, the situation in the first half of 1985, when U.S. economic growth slowed, may be considered a period that shook confidence in the possibility of sustaining the exchange rate, fiscal deficit, and current account equilibrium of that time. It is in this context that the dollar gradually weakened.

G5 and the exchange rate

It was in the above setting that the need for a change in fiscal policy had been voiced, but there was also a growing perception of the political and economic difficulties such a move would entail. These are the circumstances surrounding the so-called G5 joint intervention in the foreign exchange markets. The movements of several economic variables, in particular the exchange rate, following the G5 meeting will be discussed next meeting.

In the analysis of exchange rate movements to follow, we shall rely on the standard asset approach.[7] According to this theory, the exchange rate is determined by (1) domestic and overseas interest rate differentials[8]; (2) expectations of the long-term exchange rate; and (3) a risk premium, which depends on the supply of various assets. An increase in the stock of foreign assets relative to domestic assets will lead to an increase in the risk premium and in turn to an appreciation of the domestic currency.[9]

It should be noted that under the assets approach, it is the demand for and supply of the stock of assets that determines the exchange rate, and the capital account is not considered to be an important variable.

[7] Concerning the asset approach, see, e.g., Fukao (1985).

[8] The standard view is that it is real interest rates that move the exchange rate because inflation rate differentials will be reflected in exchange rate expectations. However, as this process of forecast formation does not always seem to be used in the market, and given that there were no apparent great swings in the domestic and overseas inflation differentials or expectations thereof in the past several months, I will concentrate on nominal interest rates in this analysis.

[9] The Ueda paper quoted in footnote 2 works on the assumption that a risk premium does not exist and that domestic and overseas interest rates are equal. Consequently, a rise in foreign interest rates will affect home interest rates on a one-for-one basis (in real terms). It is straightforward to incorporate a risk premium into this analysis. In such a case, there is of course a strong possibility that an increase in foreign interest rates will raise home interest rates, but not to the same extent as foreign rates, thereby altering the domestic and overseas interest rate differential. This will be accompanied by a depreciation in the home currency.

The capital account is taken to be identically equal to the current account. The short-term/long-term breakdown of the capital account involves many conceptual problems and, as such, is not considered to be very useful in estimating supply and demand movements in the stock of assets.[10]

Table 9.2 shows interest rate and exchange rate movements immediately prior to and after the G5 meeting. The most prominent movements shown in Table 9.2 are the sudden jump in foreign exchange market turnover and the sudden fall in the dollar in the week that the joint intervention occurred.

Let us consider the background to the fall of the dollar. During this period U.S. interest rates were rising relative to Japanese interest rates. As a result, it is clear that a change in the interest rate differential cannot explain the dollar's movement. Judging from newspaper reports and turnover in the Tokyo market, it is evident that dollar selling interventions on a large scale took place in the Tokyo and New York markets in the week of September 23. Intervention has a direct impact on the exchange rate through the risk premium by affecting the relative supply of yen and dollar assets, but the magnitude of this direct effect has been judged to be very small by existing studies of the effects of intervention.[11]

A more important reason for the success of this intervention would seem to be that it succeeded in altering expectations of the equilibrium exchange rate. Expectations of the equilibrium rate changed for the following reasons:

1. Deteriorating forecasts for U.S. medium- and long-term economic growth had made it increasingly difficult to accept the pre-G5 rate as the equilibrium exchange rate. Uncertainty of this nature was becoming more widespread among market participants.

[10] It should also be noted that since foreign assets are traded in the assets market, both inflows and outflows arise in the capital account, there being no net changes whatsoever.

[11] According to Federal Reserve Bank of New York reports, dollar selling and yen/mark buying by the U.S. monetary authorities totaled approximately $460 million in the last week of September and the first week of October and approximately $2.17 billion in the two weeks after October 7. In addition, the dollar selling intervention by the U.S. monetary authorities from August to October used a total of approximately $3.2 billion, while funds used in interventions by other monetary authorities came to approximately $7 billion (see evening edition of the *Nikkei Shimbun*, December 5). Elsewhere, it is claimed in Ishiyama (1985) that the dollar moves by about 1 yen for every $1 billion ex ante movement of funds. Supposing that one-half of the total $10 billion used in the joint intervention was used to buy yen and sell dollars, only a 5-yen weakening of the dollar would result, making it difficult to explain the total drop in the dollar from September to October without allowing for effects due to expectations.

Table 9.2. *Interest rate and exchange rate movements prior to and after the G5 meeting*

Week	Turnover in the Tokyo market[a]	Yen–dollar rate	Long-term interest rate (Japan)[b]	Long-term interest rate (U.S.A.)[c]	Long-term interest rate differential	Short-term interest rate (Japan)[d]	Short-term interest rate (U. S.A.)[c]	Short-term interest rate differential
9/2–9/6	6001	241.5	6.13	10.61	4.28	6.38	7.75	1.37
9/9–9/13	6178	243.4	6.09	10.51	4.42	6.38	7.95	1.57
9/17–9/20	5753	241.0	5.93	10.45	4.52	6.38	7.90	1.52
9/24–9/27	8736	220.8	5.75	10.32	4.57	6.44	7.65	1.21
9/30–10/4	7353	211.9	5.57	10.42	4.85	6.44	7.70	1.26
10/7–10/11	6531	216.1	5.56	10.44	4.88	6.44	7.85	1.41

[a] Turnover of spot and swap transactions (million dollars, average per day).
[b] Yield on the 68th government bond (at weekends).
[c] Yield on treasury securities (10 years) (at weekends).
[d] Discount rate (2 months) (at weekends).
[e] CD rate (3 months) (at weekends).

2. The joint intervention made it clear that the policy authorities themselves felt that prospects for the U.S. economy were not so bright and the strong dollar was unsustainable, which added further fuel to the uncertainty mentioned in 1. And the fact that the U.S., typically unenthusiastic about intervention, was promoting such action exacerbated this effect.

As exchange rate expectations are unobservable, however, it is difficult to gauge the magnitude of this effect. While expectations of the equilibrium rate moved toward a weaker dollar from the end of September to mid-October, the actual size of the intervention itself was not large. And intervention or not, the rapid increase in weekly turnover signifies that there were still people buying large amounts of dollars who would seem to have anticipated another increase in the value of the dollar. In fact, with a widening of domestic and overseas interest rate differentials, the dollar did recover slightly in the week of October 7.

Lastly, the Japanese long-term interest rate was decreasing over this period, more rapidly than the U.S. rate. This process might have been governed by a self-fulfilling expectations process, where bond demand arising from these expectations acted to push actual prices up. Whether this is interpreted as a bubble-like phenomenon[12] or considered a very rational move controlled by an anticipated drop in the official discount rate and short-term interest rates is a very interesting point, but one that is beyond the scope of this discussion.

Monetary austerity and its effect on interest and exchange rates

Although the intervention policy conducted from the end of September to the beginning of October brought about a considerable weakening of the dollar, the dollar made a slight recovery after mid-October. It was in this context that a policy aimed at increasing short-term interest rates was implemented by the Bank of Japan. Short-term interest rates rose sharply from the week of October 21 through the following several weeks, which in turn led to a sharp drop in long-term bond prices and a significant contraction in both short-term and long-term interest rate differentials between Japan and the United States (see Table 9.3). The dollar weakened once again, with the rate settling in the vicinity of 200–205 yen from mid-November on.

[12] Assuming that people act rationally with a long time horizon, bubbles do not occur with assets such as bonds, where the coupon is fixed and a set amount is to be redeemed after a limited period expires. However, if people are myopic, bubbles may occur even with bonds.

Table 9.3. *High interest rates policy and interests and exchange rates*

Week	Turnover in the Tokyo market	Yen–dollar rate	Long-term interest rate (Japan)	Long-term interest rate (U.S.A.)	Long-term interest rate differential	Short-term interest rate (Japan)	Short-term interest rate (U.S.A.)	Short-term interest rate differential
10/14–10/18	5228	215.5	5.47	10.25	4.78	6.44	7.90	1.46
10/21–10/25	6183	214.9	6.22	10.28	4.06	7.09	7.90	0.81
10/28–11/1	8146	209.9	6.72	10.04	3.32	7.72	7.63	−0.09
11/5–11/8	9253	207.3	6.67	9.91	3.24	7.67	7.70	0.03
11/11–11/15	6620	203.4	6.98	9.97	2.99	8.00	7.80	−0.20
11/18–11/22	7651	201.8	6.49	9.76	3.27	9.06	7.75	−0.31
11/25–11/29	7556	202.1	6.17	9.70	3.53	8.06	7.75	−0.31
12/2–12/6	7091	203.0	6.22	9.74	3.52	8.09	7.90	−0.19
12/9–12/13	6432	202.3	5.85	9.30	3.45	8.13	7.65	−0.48

Note: See Table 9.1 for description of data.

The rise in long-term interest rates is easily explained if one believes that long-term interest rates move in accordance to expectations about government interest rate policy. Alternatively, if one believes that interest rate trends are often bubble-like phenomena, an example being the prior fall in long-term interest rates, the policy of increasing short-term interest rates may be interpreted as having triggered the collapse of the bubble.

Three factors may be cited as having contributed to the decline in the dollar at this time. First, the contraction of the domestic and overseas interest rate differential is an undisputed factor in the dollar's decline. Second, judging from the turnover in the foreign exchange market, dollar selling intervention on a considerable scale seems to have been conducted in the Tokyo market in the weeks of October 28 and November 4. Third, it seems that expectations of the equilibrium exchange rate moved once again toward a weaker dollar from the end of October to mid-November. As a result of the Bank of Japan's tight monetary policy and the strong intervention stance demonstrated on an international level, the market embraced the expectation that a "politically" acceptable exchange rate lay with a considerably weaker dollar. Yukinobu Oguchi of Citibank's Tokyo branch, for example, has expressed the market's sentiment at this time[13]: "As a factor influencing the level of the exchange rate, what dealers are following closely now is the so-called intention of the authorities. It's clear that this is what has pushed the rate along."

After mid-November, the yen–dollar rate settled at around 200–205 yen. Foreign exchange market turnover also contracted slightly, and the expectation that the exchange rate would remain around the 200-yen mark apparently took hold.

Movements in other variables during this period include another fall in Japanese long-term interest rates. Yields on Issue 68 government bonds peaked at 7% in mid-November, falling to almost mid-October levels of 5.5% by mid-December. Because the Bank of Japan's policy of inducing higher interest rates had run its course by mid-November, factors responsible for the October fall in interest rates began to function again. An additional factor inducing the drop in Issue 68 bond interest was the large drop in U.S. long-term interest rates, which occurred in November.

In summary, the G5 joint intervention policy, the fall of U.S. interest rates, and the Japanese tight monetary policy brought about the

---

[13] See Oguchi (1985). The third reason cited in the preceding section's analysis of changes in perception of the balanced rate in September–October, i.e., the full-scale intervention in the U.S. markets, would also seem to be closely related.

large drop in the dollar from October to November, both directly and through their effects on exchange rate expectations.

III.   Future prospects

An important issue when making projections of future trends in the world economy is how long the present weak dollar can be sustained and to what extent this will act to solve current account imbalances. It should be noted that exchange rate expectations, considered to be a major factor affecting exchange rate fluctuations, are thought to depend upon the authorities' political stance toward maintaining a weak dollar exchange rate. Should favorable economic results not be forthcoming the concept of a "political rate" itself may well collapse.

There are several important dimensions for judging future exchange rate and current account trends. I consider each of these in turn.

The role of fiscal policy

As is clear from the analysis of Section I, the most effective method of solving the issue of current account imbalance is to change U.S. and Japanese fiscal policy and in particular to reduce the U.S. fiscal deficit. Such changes in fiscal policy also have the effect of supporting the present weak dollar.

The effect of monetary policy

What if no change in fiscal policy were implemented, and only monetary measures were undertaken? Let us suppose that monetary policy is neutral in the medium and long term and as such has no impact on real variables and, furthermore, that adjustment from short term to "medium" long term is swift. In such a case, even if monetary policy succeeded in fixing the nominal exchange rate at a strong yen–weak dollar level, this would have no long-term impact on the real exchange rate. It follows, therefore, that the recent joint intervention would be of very little help in solving the issue of current account imbalance.

Now, let us suppose that even if monetary policy were neutral in the long term, adjustment to that point would take time, so that monetary policy would have real effects over a short-term period of, say, 1–2 years. Recent monetary policy trends have been interpreted as easy in the United States and tight in Japan. Two possible scenarios could result from these policies.

Scenario 1: According to standard international finance theory (the Mundell–Fleming model),[14] such policy should bring about a strong yen–weak dollar. The U.S. economy should recover due to the weaker dollar and increase its exports. If capital movements are active, there should be no great impact on domestic and overseas interest rate differentials, and the economic climate in Japan should deteriorate due to the drop in exports arising from the strong yen. Changes in the exchange rate, rather than changes in domestic and overseas economic conditions, will have a large impact on the current account, and the size of the current account imbalance should shrink.

This is the most optimistic scenario politically feasible at present. With the weak dollar being maintained, the best course is just to wait for the J-curve effect to run its course. Should the market judge this case to be a realistic one, exchange rate expectations should also settle on a weak dollar level. Care must be exercised in Japan, however, not to be tempted into implementing an overly easy monetary policy for fear of a recession because such action could induce a resurgence in the dollar by widening (temporarily) the U.S.–Japanese interest rate differential. Instead, judicious use of fiscal policy should be considered in order to avoid a decrease in demand.

Scenario 2: Coordinated monetary policy acts to improve U.S. economic conditions and dampen Japanese, but now assume that this results, as in the case of a closed economy, from interest rate fluctuations rather than through changes in the exchange rate. This corresponds to a situation where domestic and overseas interest rates do not move together, or where the exchange rate has very little impact on export and imports.

According to this scenario, the impact of exchange rate fluctuations can be offset by the current account's susceptibility to domestic and overseas income fluctuations. The current account imbalance may remain virtually unaffected or, in some cases, even increase. In such a case, the exchange rate might stabilize at a weak dollar level, but it is also possible that the dollar will stage a comeback, or plummet suddenly, due to concern about the unresolved current account problem.

Other factors

It is also possible for domestic and overseas economic conditions to be greatly swayed by factors other than fiscal and monetary policy. It is conceivable, in particular, that the U.S. economy could return to high

[14] See, e.g., Dornbusch (1980).

Table 9.4. Estimates of saving and investment equations

United States

	Constant	$y^*/\bar{y}^*$	p_f/p^*	C^*	$K^*/\bar{y}^*$	$\bar{R}^2$	s.e	Mean of dependent variable
$I_f^*/p_f^*\bar{y}^*$	-0.291×10^{-3} (−0.133)	0.422 (7.47)	−0.253 (−2.03)	−0.118 (−2.74)	-0.443×10^{-2} (−0.039)	0.754	0.711×10^{-2}	0.108
		$i^*(1 - t^* - n^*)$	p^*y^*/p_H					
$I_H^*p_H^*$	8.80 (1.25)	−20.6 (−0.271)	0.0358 (5.02)			0.363	5.56	43.9
		$y^* - G^*/p^*$	$(y^* - G^*/p^*)_{-1}$ BuD*/p*					
S^*/p^*	−9.87 (−2.63)	0.284 (7.88)	−0.0663 (−1.76)	0.294 (4.66)		0.991	5.69	178.5

Japan

	Constant	$y/\bar{y}$	$p_f/\bar{p}$	C	$K/\bar{y}$	$\bar{R}^2$	s.e	Mean of dependent variable
$I_f/p_f\bar{p}$	-0.628×10^{-2} (−0.029)	0.660 (3.67)	−0.261 (−6.48)	−0.120 (−2.67)	−0.133 (−3.22)	0.637	0.171	0.226
		$i - n$	py/p_H					
I_Hp_H	−150.7 (−0.101)	−164.7 (−0.542)	0.0598 (6.12)			0.282	575.9	6850.7
		$y - G/p$	$(y - G/p)_{-1}$	BuD/p	$W/(B + W)$			
S/p	27588.3 (1.35)	0.581 (7.35)	−0.249 (−2.95)	0.259 (1.21)	−0.434 (−1.48)	0.954	1265.6	31427.5

Note: t-statistics are in parentheses.

Symbols: p^*, GNP deflator (U.S.), 1972 = 100; p, GNP deflator (Japan), 1975 = 100; y^*, real GNP (U.S.), 1972 billions of dollars; y, real GNP (Japan), 1975 billions of yen; y^*, full-employment real GNP (U.S.), billions of dollars; $\bar{y}$, full employment real GNP (Japan), billions of yen; I^*_f, fixed investment of private sector (U.S.), billions of dollars; I_f, fixed investment of private sector (Japan), billions of yen; I^*_H, housing investment of private sector (U.S.), billions of dollars; I_H, housing investment of private sector (Japan), billions of yen; G^*, expenditures of total government (U.S.), billions of dollars; G, expenditures of total government (Japan), billions of yen; BuD*, government deficit (U.S.), billions of dollars; BuD, government deficit (Japan), billions of yen; K, capital stock (Japan), billions of yen; p^*_f, private fixed investment deflator (U.S.), 1972 = 100; K^*, capital stock (U.S.), billions of dollars; p_f, private fixed investment deflator (Japan), 1975 = 100; p^*_H, private housing investment deflator (U.S.), 1971 = 100; p_H, private housing investment deflator (Japan), 1980 = 100; i^*, interest rate on Aaa Corporate Bond (U.S.); i, interest rate on Telephone and Telegraphic bond (Japan); n^*, growth rate of GNP deflator (U.S.); n growth rate of GNP deflator (Japan); r^* = average personal income tax rate (U.S.); W, regular wages; B, bonuses. Here C = $[(r + \delta)(1 - k - uz)] (1 - u)]$, where r = real interest rate calculated by i – growth rate of private fixed investment deflator, δ = depreciation rate, k = rate of investment tax credit, u = corporate tax rate, z = present value of depreciation, and, C^* is defined similarly.

growth rates, or fall into recession, depending on autonomous consumer and investment trends.

If U.S. economic growth is substantial, this factor might dominate the movement of the current account, resulting in a situation similar to scenario 2; that is, a widening of the current account imbalance. In such a case, it is also likely that a strong dollar would reemerge. Conversely, should the U.S. economic climate deteriorate, the current account imbalance should contract. Moreover, it should be noted that despite a decrease in the current account imbalance, there is the possibility of trade friction worsening due to deterioration in U.S. economic conditions alone.

Joint intervention policy was a success in terms of realigning the strong dollar, but there still exist many uncertain issues such as whether the present dollar level can be sustained and whether the current account will contract. As a result, there remains an acute need to study such issues further to improve future policy initiatives.

Appendix

a. Net private savings variables used in Section I are constructed by estimating simple savings and investment equations. The results of estimation are shown in Table 9.4. The investment equations are of the standard type, and the savings equations include budget deficit variables in order to estimate the degree to which people are forward-looking [see Ueda (1985) for details].

The estimates are then used to calculate the autonomous parts of private net savings, which are labeled s_p in Figure 9.1. In this appendix an asterisk (*) denotes data for the U.S.A. To do this I substitute full-employment GNP (explained below) wherever actual GNP appears in the estimated equations. The real interest rate is assumed equal to a constant of 3.1% – the average of U.S. and Japanese real rates over the last 10 years.

b. Net savings of the government sector of Japan and the United States ($-f$ and f^*) are calculated as follows. De Leeuw and Holloway (1983) present an estimate of the U.S. federal government deficit at full employment. I estimate the full-employment deficit of the state and local government by running the actual deficit on a time trend and a GNP gap variable. (The full-employment GNP series is taken from de Leeuw and Holloway.) This result is added to the de Leeuw and Holloway estimate to obtain the full-employment deficit of the general government. The Japanese full-employment GNP and deficit of the general government are constructed in the same way as for the United States (Ueda 1985).

c. Based on these estimates of private and government autonomous net savings in Japan and the United States, s_p, s^*_p, $-f$, and $-f^*$, the following current account equation is estimated, which is used to carry out the simulation reported in Figure 9.1:

$$NX = 0.0911 + 0.529(s_p - f) - 0.136(s^*_p - f^*)$$
$$(1.07) \quad (5.09) \qquad\qquad (-5.28)$$

$$+ 0.234\frac{y^*}{\bar{y}^*} - 0.321,\frac{y}{\bar{y}}, \quad \bar{R}^2 = .851,$$
$$(2.94) \quad (-2.72)$$

$$\text{s.e.} = 0.631 \times 10^{-2}, \rho = -0.501$$
$$\phantom{\text{s.e.} = 0.631 \times 10^{-2}, }(-1.77)$$

where NX is the Japanese current account (relative to full employment GNP); s_p and s^*_p are defined in (a) above; $- f$ and $- f^*$ are defined in (b) above; $y/\bar{y}$ and $y^*/\bar{y}^*$ are the ratios of GNP to full employment GNP in the United States and Japan, respectively. Furthermore, $\bar{R}^2$ is the corrected coefficient of determination; s.e. is the standard error of the equation and ρ is the estimate of the first-order serial correlation coefficient.

References

Dornbusch, R. (1980). *Open Economy Macroeconomics,* Basic Books, New York.

de Leeuw, F., and T. Holloway (1983). "Cyclical Adjustment of the Federal Budget and Federal Debt," *Survey of Current Business,* December.

Fukao, M. (1983). "The Theory of Exchange Rate Determination in a Multi-Currency World," *Monetary and Economic Studies,* Bank of Japan, Vol. 1, No. 2.

Krugman, P. (1985). "Is the Strong Dollar Sustainable?" NBER Working Paper No. 1644, June 1985.

Oguchi, Y. (1985). "The Yen Appreciation: Is It Up to the Speculators?" *The Shucan Economist* (in Japanese), December 17, Maimichi Shinbunsha, Tokyo.

Okina, K. (1984). "Rational Expectations, Bubbles and Foreign Exchange Market," *Monetary and Economic Studies,* Bank of Japan, Vol. 2, No. 1.

Ishiyama, Y. (1985). *Recent International Capital Movements* (in Japanese), a report of the study group on softnomics Ministry of Finance, Tokyo.

Ueda, K. (1985). "The Japanese Current Account Surplus and Fiscal Policy in the U.S. and Japan," Discussion Paper No. 2, Institute of Fiscal and Monetary Policy, Ministry of Finance.

Discussion

ROBERT CUMBY

Ueda addresses two important questions of extreme current interest. First, what are the factors underlying the large current-account surplus in Japan, and the large current-account deficit in the United States? Second, why did the dollar decline after the first quarter of 1985, and why was the drop in the dollar so sharp around the time of the G5 meeting in New York?

The general conclusions of the chapter are that as a result of the savings propensities in the United States and Japan, along with underlying rates of capital accumulation and the fiscal policies adopted by the two governments, a Japanese current-account surplus of at least 2 percent of GNP is likely to persist for several years to come. In addition, although the decline in the dollar after the first quarter of 1985 is plausibly attributable to a slowing of the U.S. economy and to a narrowing of interest rate differentials, these factors cannot explain why such a large drop occurred following the G5 meeting. In order to understand that change in exchange rates, the chapter looks to changes in expectations concerning the future values of exchange rates. The conclusions drawn are very reasonable ones which provide useful insights into macroeconomic developments in these two countries. I would now like to analyze the main points of the chapter.

The first section of the chapter is devoted to discussing current-account developments in the context of national savings and investment rates. The discussion revolves around the GNP accounting identity, which states that the current-account surplus must equal the difference between national income and expenditure. Equivalently, the current-account surplus (CAS) is the difference between national savings (S) and investment (I):

$$CAS = S - I$$

This identity tells us that a realized current-account surplus must be associated with an excess of savings over investment. It is useful to break national savings into private sector savings (S^p) and the government budget surplus ($T - G$):

$$CAS = (S^p - I) + (T - G)$$

Not only can one use these relationships to look at the public sector and private sector savings and investment behavior that corresponds to current-account imbalance, but one can also use these in a macromodel as a description of the relationship between planned savings and investment of the public and private sectors when the market for national output is in equilibrium. The chapter takes advantage of both uses.

It is essential to examine current-account behavior in the framework of savings and investment decisions if we are to understand the behavior of the current account. There may be a temptation to focus on particular industries or commercial policies, as is common in much of the discussion of these issues that one encounters. However, the U.S. current-account deficit and the Japanese current-account surplus has very little to do with imports of baseball bats or exports of computer chips. If we want to examine long-run patterns in current-account behavior, it is sensible to suppose that an economy is fully employed, and therefore at each level of expenditure, a commercial policy that restricts imports will cause a terms-of-trade improvement. Only to the extent that this terms-of-trade change affects the difference between income and expenditure will the current account be affected by the restrictive commercial policy.

Ueda discusses the results of some simulations based on an estimated macromodel, which point to high Japanese savings propensities and a large structural fiscal deficit in the United States as accounting for the bulk of the Japanese current-account surplus. In addition, much of the increase in the Japanese current-account surplus in recent years corresponds to a reduction in U.S. private sector savings relative to investment and to a reduction in the Japanese structural budget deficits. Based on these results, the chapter concludes that, as a result of the savings propensities of the two countries, their underlying rates of capital accumulation, and their respective fiscal policies, a Japanese current-account surplus of 2 percent of GNP is likely to persist for several years. A change in the fiscal policies pursued by the two countries is necessary if there is to be any policy-induced change in the Japanese current-account surplus beyond this.

I find these conclusions extremely plausible, but my appetite has been whetted. I would like to see more. Although the results of the simulations presented in Figures 9.1–9.3 are quite reasonable, it would still be nice to know more about the model and estimation procedures employed in order to make sure I am not drawing conclusions because they reinforce my own prejudices and my own prior casual empiricism. In addition, some previous discussion has focused on the role of an investment boom in the United States as an explanation for the U.S. current account deficit. As a result, it would be useful to separate private savings from investment in the discussion. Doing so would be useful since the viability

150   Discussion by R. Cumby

of the U.S. deficit should be affected by the degree to which the deficit reflects the financing of productive investment.

The chapter next turns to a discussion of the dollar–yen exchange rate and concludes that, given conditions in 1984 and early 1985, a rate of 230 yen per dollar was consistent with the sustainable Japanese current-account surplus of 2 percent of GNP. This rate corresponds to the 1984 average dollar–yen rate. Presumably, Ueda implicitly means a real exchange rate equal to the average 1984 value when he discusses 230 as a sustainable rate. Again, whereas this conclusion is plausible, the black box is even harder to see through here than it was previously, and it is difficult to evaluate this conclusion.

If the dollar value of the yen in 1984 was sustainable, why did a big decline in the rate occur after the first quarter of 1985? Ueda points to a slowdown in the U.S. economy as the important factor in this decline for three reasons. The first two are standard. A slowdown in the U.S. economy can be expected to bring down interest rates somewhat and thereby weaken the dollar and, in addition, the chapter argues, lead to an easing of Fed policy and further weaken the dollar. The third factor is somewhat more involved. The chapter presents some simulations that examine the long-term consequences of the U.S. budget deficit. These simulations assume that private savings and the budget deficit (excluding interest payments) are a given fraction of GNP and show that a slowdown in U.S. growth to 2 percent per year would lead to a national debt–GNP ratio of 1 along with a total budget deficit of 20 percent of GNP in 10 years. The chapter finds this to be unsustainable. A growth rate of 4 percent, on the other hand, produces simulation results Ueda finds sustainable. The conclusion is then that the slowdown of the U.S. economy undermined confidence in the viability of the exising dollar–yen rate and created expectations of a weakening dollar over the long run.

Although it is reasonable that the slowdown in the U.S. economy lead to an expected depreciation of the dollar in terms of the yen, and the simulation results suggest deficit levels that require sizable adjustment, we do not want to take them too literally. Why, for example, should the savings rate remain constant while the debt–GNP ratio rises by a factor of 3 and the budget deficit rises from 4 to 20 percent of GNP? One does not need to accept extreme versions of debt neutrality to question the constancy of the private savings rate in the face of such changes. The intertemporal budget constraint cannot be completely ignored.

Although the general direction of the movement of the dollar–yen rate during 1985 can be explained by the factors discussed above, as

Ueda notes, it is difficult to use them to explain the sharp drop that immediately followed the G5 meeting in the fall. There was no abrupt change in U.S. growth or the Fed's apparent response to it, which occurred coincidentally around the time of the meeting. The timing of this drop seems difficult to explain without attributing a causal role to the meetings. This presents us with a problem. The best evidence we have suggests that the effect of sterilized intervention is small and short lived. For example, Karen Lewis has estimated that sterilized intervention of the magnitude that followed the G5 meeting should bring the dollar down by much less than 1 percent.[1] If we accept existing evidence, what was it about the G5 meeting that caused the dollar's fall? The chapter points to a change in expectations about the equilibrium value of the dollar–yen rate and suggests three reasons for that change in expectations. The first reason is the lower growth alluded to above, which has difficulty explaining the timing of the fall. The second is that the intervention signaled authorities agreement that a strong dollar was not sustainable. The third is that there was a shock value associated with U.S. participation in the intervention. It is difficult to see how this third reason can be the explanation of the behavior of exchange rates, however. It seems odd that the shock of observing the U.S. engaging in a policy measure having little or no effect on exchange rates should itself cause a substantial change in exchange rates.

Since exchange rates are not exogenous variables and neither are expectations of future exchange rates, we should look at what might be behind a change in expectations about the future equilibrium value of the dollar. The second explanation can be interpreted as viewing the G5 meeting and the actions that followed it as signaling future changes in policy. Indeed, the discussion in the chapter of the behavior of interest rates and exchange rates after the G5 meeting is consistent with this sort of an interpretation. When the dollar recovered after mid-October, the Bank of Japan acted to raise short-term interest rates in a successful attempt to stem the dollar's rise. This aspect of the effect of the G5 meeting is very interesting and warrants future study. It seems that this kind of announcement effect might be the best way to reconcile the sharp movement in exchange rates that followed the G5 meeting with the evidence that sterilized intervention has little or no effect on exchange rates.

If the G5 meeting served to change expectations about future policies that will reinforce a "politically acceptable rate," unless such policy

---

[1] Karen K. Lewis, "Risk Aversion and the Effects of Sterilized Intervention," Working paper, New York University, Graduate School of Business Administration, 1985.

measures are actually implemented, this change in expectations is likely to be reversed. Intervention alone is not sufficient to maintain that rate. The chapter points to the central role that fiscal policy must play in ratifying the change in exchange rate expectations and the weaker dollar. It argues that the apparent easing of monetary policy in the United States and the tighter monetary policy in Japan will succeed in ratifying a lower nominal dollar–yen rate but can be expected to bring about a lower real dollar–yen rate only temporarily. In addition, monetary policy will have only a short-lived effect on the current account. A tighter fiscal policy in the United States, on the other hand, will ratify a lower dollar and will reduce the current-account imbalance.

Discussion

RICHARD C. MARSTON

I would like to focus on the concept of the "equilibrium yen–dollar rate," which lies at the center of Ueda's analysis, and then suggest another concept of equilibrium that may be more relevant in the period ahead.

Ueda rightly emphasizes the importance of deficient saving, by both the government and private sectors in the United States, in explaining the recent strength of the U.S. dollar. He defines an equilibrium exchange rate as one consistent with current as well as currently projected levels of government budget deficits (and net dissaving by the private sector). I would argue, however, that a second concept of exchange rate equilibrium is ultimately more important. That is the equilibrium exchange rate consistent with whatever budget deficits, and their associated current account imbalances, are *sustainable* in the long run. I will later give some estimates of where that long-run rate should be.

First, however, I would like to point out that Ueda's equilibrium rate may have changed quite sharply in the last 6 months. The reason is that projections of U.S. government deficits have declined sharply since last August. In August 1985, the non-partisan Congressional Budget Office (CBO) predicted that the U.S. budget deficit would be $285 billion in 1990. In February 1986, the CBO revised the projection for 1990 down to $120 billion. This is a very sharp reduction, primarily due to reduced military spending in the most recent budget resolution, reduced domestic spending, and lower interest rates. Even if the CBO estimate turns out to be excessively optimistic, prospects for reduced deficits under the Gramm–Rudman law are much better than last summer. For those of us who believe, as Ueda does, that the dollar's rise was due primarily to U.S. deficits (helped along by decreased deficits by other countries like Japan), the improvement in prospects for the U.S. budget should go hand in hand with a fall in the "equilibrium" value of the dollar (using Ueda's definition).

Ueda reports the sharp fall in the yen price of the dollar from 240 to 211 during the last two weeks of September 1985. I would like to be able to attribute this fall to revisions in the U.S. budget deficit, but the timing is way off. And the timing is also bad for attributing much of it to the fall in the price of oil. The fall in the yen–dollar rate coincides instead with a dramatic shift in intervention policy, the G5 agreement for coordinated intervention reached during the weekend of September 21–22. How did a change in intervention policy have such a dramatic effect on exchange rates? To answer that question, first note that the intervention was most likely *sterilized;* that is, if the intervention took its usual form, it did not lead to changes in national money supplies (at least in Japan and the United States). There are two alternative channels by which such sterilized intervention can affect exchange rates:

1. intervention can alter the relative supplies of U.S. and Japanese securities, thereby changing the risk premia on these securities, and
2. intervention can give rise to an "announcement effect," signaling future changes in *monetary* policy (or changes in other macroeconomic policies).

In the latter case, the intervention might signal the intention of the U.S. authorities to ease monetary conditions (either unilaterally or in concert with other G5 nations as they did in early 1986).

The Jurgesen Committee of 3 years ago, after studying the statistical evidence from a score of studies, concluded that there is little evidence that buying and selling securities, without changing money supplies, can have much effect on exchange rates. If we believe the evidence on which that conclusion is based (it is not as overwhelming as some have suggested), then we are left with announcement effects alone.

The evidence which Ueda presents concerning the effects of the G5 intervention is very intriguing. During the first 2 weeks following the start of the intervention, the yen price of the dollar fell by 30 yen despite the fact that the long-term interest differential rose by 30 basis points and the short-term differential fell by only 26 basis points (Table

9.2). That seems to suggest that announcement effects were quite important during this period.[1] We cannot be more precise than that without more accurate information on intervention activities.

With further falls in the yen–dollar rate since September, we are now faced with a question opposite to that we all faced in 1985. Instead of asking "is the strong dollar sustainable," we ask "is the weak dollar sustainable?" It is here that the concept of an equilibrium exchange rate becomes crucial. Along with many other economists,[2] I believe that current budget deficits in the United States are simply not sustainable in the long run. Whether through the Gramm–Rudman law or through other means, the U.S. budget will be brought under control. Only then will it be possible for the United States to restore and maintain current account balance. The concept of exchange rate "equilibrium," which I prefer, is one based on a *sustainable* current account position. In the case of the United States, a sustainable position either means a balanced current account or one with a reasonably small deficit. What it also surely requires, moreover, is a trade account much closer to equilibrium than it is today. That in turn requires that the dollar be restored to something close to its former level of competitiveness. In fact, the dollar must fall even further than that, since the United States now must service its debt, or at least cannot benefit from the substantial interest payments provided to it in the past because it was then a net creditor.

How far must the dollar fall in terms of the yen–dollar rate? I would argue that at the very least the United States must return to the level of competitiveness with Japan that it enjoyed in the early 1970s.[3] That requires a much lower yen–dollar rate than is commonly supposed. Recent estimates of the equilibrium yen–dollar rate quoted in the *New*

---

[1] According to Morgan Guaranty Trust, *World Financial Markets,* January 1986: "The success of the intervention last fall, in contrast with that undertaken last January, stemmed from the hints in the G-5 agreement of greater consistency to come in the economic policies of the major countries" (p. 1). A few days after the G-5 announcement, Harris Bank summed up sentiments in the market as follows: "As the credibility of these nations with respect to these policy objectives fades or grows in coming weeks, the dollar should recover or continue to soften, respectively–intervention alone will probably not be sufficient to dominate the markets" (*Foreign Exchange Weekly Review,* September 27, 1985, p. 4).

[2] As an example, see "Symposium on the Exchange Rate," in *The Brookings Papers on Economic Activity,* 1985:1, 199–262.

[3] In chapter 3 Krugman points out that the increases in oil prices that occurred twice during the 1970s should affect Japan more than the United States, thus reducing the relative competitiveness of Japan. I make no attempt to adjust for oil prices here (which in any case have fallen in real terms recently). But in a recent study ("Real Exchange Rates and Productivity Growth in the United States and Japan," NBER Working Paper, June 1986), I provide estimates of how much changes in the prices of oil and other raw materials have combined with chamber in productivity to alter real exchange rates defined in terms of different price series.

Table 9.5. *PPP comparisons: U.S. and Japanese prices, Actual exchange rates and PPP values based on 1973 relative prices*[a]

		Based on general price indexes		Based on manufacturing prices only		
					Value	Unit
				WPI	added	labor
Year	Yen per dollar	CPI	WPI	manufactures	manufactures	costs
1973	272	272	272	272	272	272
1974	292	305	301	292	296	307
1975	297	312	284	267	262	318
1976	297	322	285	268	252	300
1977	269	327	273	256	237	291
1978	210	315	247	234	227	266
1979	219	294	236	221	211	239
1980	227	279	243	220	192	210
1981	221	266	226	203	180	201
1982	249	257	225	200	173	183
1983	238	253	218	195	171	181
1984	238	248	212	191	167	175

[a] PPP values calculated using relative version of PPP based on 1973.
Source: IMF, International Financial Statistics and unpublished IMF data.

York Times have been based on consumer price indexes (CPIs) in the
United States and Japan. Because of the much greater rate of productivity growth in the export sector of Japan, however, the CPI in Japan
considerably overstates the prices of export goods in Japan. To obtain
an estimate of the equilibrium exchange rate, we must use relative
export prices or, since export prices are not available for the United
States over a long enough period, we use the relative prices of manufactured goods (which figure so prominently in trade).

In Table 9.5, I present some calculations of purchasing power parity
(PPP) exchange rates based on different price series. All of the calculations use the relative version of PPP with 1973 chosen as the base year.
(Thus the calculations assume that the United States must return to the
level of competitiveness found after the Smithsonian realignments of
1971 but prior to the first oil shock.[4]) Although the calculations suffer

[4] In the paper referred to in footnote 3, I obtain similar results using equations explaining
trends in real exchange rates over the 1973–83 period (measured as the ratio of U.S. to
Japanese prices). I find, e.g., that the real exchange rate based on the value-added
deflator for traded goods should have fallen by over 35% relative to the real exchange rate
based on the CPI just to keep U.S. traded goods competitive with those of Japan.

from all of the familiar problems associated with PPP calculations, they are nonetheless quite revealing.

If we rely on CPIs, we find that the yen must *depreciate* to almost 250 per dollar in 1984 (the last year for which data are available for all of these price series). Using wholesale price indexes (WPIs), which are more heavily weighted toward manufactures, we find a much lower value of 212 yen per dollar. The estimated values for this rate are still lower when the prices of manufactured goods alone are employed. The PPP value for 1984 based on the wholesale price index for manufactures is 191 yen per dollar, that based on the value added deflator for manufactured goods is 167 yen per dollar, and that based on unit labor costs in manufacturing is 175 yen per dollar. There is no need to decide which of the series for manufacturing is the most reliable (although I would prefer to rely on those based on the value-added deflator or unit labor costs since wholesale price indexes usually reflect a limited subset of goods); all point toward a yen–dollar rate in 1984 significantly below 200. If we were to allow for further productivity growth in the succeeding 2 years and adjust for changes in the CPI (a series available with only a short lag), we would obtain an estimate of the equilibrium rate in 1986 very close to that provided by Krugman (Chapter 3).

The message to be conveyed by these PPP comparisons is that the dollar's recent fall is by no means excessive. Estimates based on PPP are not reliable enough to indicate whether 140 or 170 yen is an equilibrium value in 1986. But these estimates do suggest that we are much closer to equilibrium, defined in the sense of international competitiveness, than we were as late as September 1985.

PART III

Trade policy

CHAPTER 10

Costs and benefits to the United States of the 1985 steel import quota program

DAVID G. TARR

Introduction

U.S. trade policy on steel

During the past 15 years the United States steel industry has enjoyed a significant amount of special protection from imports.[1] From 1969 to 1974 Japan and the European Economic Community negotiated "voluntary restraints agreements" (VRAs) that limited their exports to the United States.[2] In 1978 the administration initiated the "trigger price mechanism" (TPM) as part of its program for the steel industry.[3] The TPM was, in principle, to have established a minimum price below which imports could not enter without being subjected to an expedited antidumping investigation.[4] In 1982 a major effort was undertaken by the majority of the integrated U.S. steel producers to obtain tariff protection under the antidumping and countervailing duty laws.[5] Despite the fact that the Department of Commerce (DOC) made either a negative determination of subsidies or a "de minimus" or insignificant determination of subsidies for a significant portion of the European Economic Community[6] (possibly eliminating the ability of countervail-

---

[1] This is in addition to tariff protection, which in 1983 was about 5.6 percent.

[2] For an analysis of the effects of the VRA see Jondrow (1978). He finds that the VRA was not binding after 1972; also see Crandall (1981, pp. 103–7).

[3] See the report of the Solomon (1977) task force.

[4] Crandall (1981, Chapter 5) finds that the TPM induced an increase in import prices by approximately 9 percent. See the analysis of Tarr in the FTC steel report (Duke et al. 1977) for an evaluation of the distributional and efficiency consequences of the TPM compared with tariffs or quotas; and see Barnett and Schorsch (1983, pp. 239–42) for an evaluation of the TPM's role in the public policy debate on steel.

[5] The TPM was dropped when these cases were filed. See Exhibit 4 of the United Steelworkers-Bethlehem Petition to the ITC (1984) for a comprehensive list of the antidumping and countervailing duty cases that have been filed.

[6] The DOC made a negative determination of the existence of subsidies for six of the eight Federal Republic of Germany (FRG) producers and an affirmative but de minimus finding of a 0.235 percent subsidy rate for Peine-Salzgitter. The DOC also made negative determinations for the Netherlands firm and for 14 small British firms. In

ing duties to restrain imports due to additional supply from unrestrained suppliers), the European Community (EC) agreed to quotas on steel exports of specific products under the U.S.–EEC arrangement.

In early 1984, the United Steelworkers of America and Bethlehem Steel Corporation petitioned the U.S. International Trade Commission (USITC or ITC) for relief from imports under Section 201 of the Trade Act of 1974. In that "petition" they asked for quotas on imports of carbon and alloy steel products such that imports would be at most 15 percent of domestic apparent consumption.[7] Also in 1984, there was legislation before Congress (the Fair Trade in Steel Act of 1984) that would utilize quotas to limit imports of steel to 15 percent of domestic apparent consumption for 5 years.[8]

On June 12, 1984, the ITC (by a 3–2 decision) voted that "industries" representing 74 percent of domestic shipments were injured.[9] On July 11, 1984, the ITC recommended to the president that quotas be imposed on almost all of these products (over 97 percent by tonnage).[10]

The president, in response to the affirmative decision by the ITC on the petition, rejected quotas through the 201 process; but he directed U.S. Trade Representative William Brock to negotiate with foreign governments to voluntarily restrain their exports.

After the president's program was announced, Congress passed, in the Trade and Tariff Act of 1984, a nonbinding "sense of the Congress" that imports should be reduced to between 17 and 20.2 percent of U.S. domestic apparent consumption and authorized the president to negotiate agreements to achieve that goal. The bill also provides that continuation of the import relief in any year is contingent on the major steel companies committing "substantially all of their net cash flow from steel operations to reinvestment and modernization of their steel industry."[11] These provisions appear to be the Congressional sub-

---

addition, it found small subsidies for the last FRG producer (1.131 percent), for the two Luxembourg producers (0.539 and 1.523 percent), and for two Belgian firms (2.165 and 0.348 percent). See the statement of Malcolm Baldridge, Secretary of Commerce, "Steel Countervailing Duties," August 25, 1982.

[7] See the petition at page ix.

[8] See Congressional Budget Office (1984) for an analysis of the effects of this legislation.

[9] See official transcript of the proceeding before the USITC, June 12, 1984, in carbon and certain alloy steel products and see Tarr (1984) for an estimation of the costs and benefits of a 15 percent quota on these products.

[10] See the statement by Commissioner David B. Rohr, "Remedy; Carbon Steel," July 11, 1984.

[11] Since most firms are already exceeding this requirement, the latter restraint is not considered onerous. See New York Times, "Steel Rule's Effect May Be Limited," October 15, 1984, pp. D1, D6. The 20.0 percent figure is the president's goal for imports when semi-finished products are included.

stitute for the Fair Trade in Steel Act of 1984, but the Trade and Tariff Act of 1984 indicates that if the president's program fails to achieve its goals, Congress will consider appropriate action.

Prior to the announcement of the new restrictions, there were already in place some formal and possibly informal quantitative restraints on steel imports.[12] In October 1982, the United States and the EC agreed to limit EC exports of certain carbon steel products to the United States to specified percentages of U.S. consumption, and the U.S. companies withdrew the antidumping and countervailing duty petitions they had filed against the companies in the EC.[13] South Africa and Mexico have also agreed to limit their exports of steel into the United States.[14] In addition, the United Steelworkers-Bethlehem Petition alleges that the "level of exports presently flowing from Japan to the United States [is] based on informal undertakings by the Japanese to the U.S. government." Bethlehem provided details of these undertakings when it stated: In 1983, "The United States Trade Representative negotiated a voluntary restraint promise on steel exports with Japan. As a result, the American steelmakers withdrew their 301 case against Japan."[15] Japan was said to provide a quarterly "weather forecast" to the U.S. government in which it provided its estimate of the next quarter's steel shipments to the United States.[16] Thus, the European Community, Mexico, South Africa, and possibly Japan were already limiting their exports to the United States.

In December 1984, the administration announced that agreements had been reached with Japan, South Korea, Spain, Brazil, South Africa, Mexico, and Australia. By August 1985, agreements with Czechoslovakia, Finland, East Germany, Hungary, Poland, Romania, and Venezuela were also reported.[17] By late 1985, the European Commu-

---

[12] The estimates in this chapter are for the additional effects of 18.5 percent quota, given that these quantitative restraints are already in effect. Although deadweight losses to the world economy are affected by the existing quantitative restraints, estimates of additional deadweight losses and consumer losses in the United States, which are the focus of this chapter, are unaffected by the existing quantitative restraints. See Tarr and Morkre (1984, Appendix 6) for an explanation.

[13] 47, *Federal Register*, 49058, October 29, 1982.

[14] See *New York Times*, September 19, 1984; *Wall Street Journal*, September 1984; and William Brock, "Press Briefing," The White House, September 18, 1984, p. 6.

[15] See Bethlehem Steel Corporation, "A Chronology of the Steel-Import Problem; 1959–1983," booklet 3902, 1984.

[16] See "Steel Curb Consensus Forming," *New York Times*, August 27, 1984, pp. D1, D4. Japan, however, has made no formal announcement that it is restraining its steel exports to the United States, as it has, e.g., with automobiles. In fact, the data suggest that Japan may have ceased restraining its exports in 1984, possibly in anticipation of a formal restraint through the 201 process.

[17] See *American Metal Market*, August 29, 1985.

nity agreed to extend its restraints on steel exports to the United States,[18] and a quota for Canada was being considered.

The exact level of imports permitted under the new agreements is not known. However, the administration has not changed its goal of restraining imports to 18.5 percent of domestic apparent consumption (excluding semi-finished).[19] Thus, this level of restriction is taken as indicative of the level of restraint likely to be achieved, and the costs and benefits of this level of restriction are estimated in this chapter.

Summary of results

The annual costs of such a quota to U.S. consumers is estimated to be $1,131 million. The annual inefficiency costs to the economy, under the usual method of quota allocation where the foreign countries receive the quota rights, is estimated to be $803 million. Part of what U.S. consumers lose is transferred to domestic and foreign producers. United States producers gain $441 million per year, and foreigners extract $573 million per year in quota rents. These estimates are summarized in Table 10.1.[20]

In order to obtain some perspective on the quantitative importance of the benefits of the quota in relation to the costs, cost–benefit ratios are provided as well as estimates for the costs of the quota per job created. For each job protected in the steel industry by the 18.5 percent quota, the annual cost to consumers is $113,662; the annual inefficiency cost to the economy for each job created by the quota is $80,682. These estimates are presented in Table 10.2. The benefits of the quota are measured by the present value of the saved earnings losses of workers who would otherwise have been displaced. For the purposes of this comparison, the present value of the costs to consumers and losses to the economy are taken over 5 years.[21] It is found that the quota imposes $5 billion and $3.5 billion in costs to consumers and inefficiency costs to the economy over 5 years, respectively, while $143 million in earnings losses are saved. Thus, for every dollar of earn-

---

[18] *Official Journal of the European Communities*, Vol. 28, L 355, December 31, 1985.
[19] 49, *Federal Register*, 36814, September 20, 1984; Brock, footnote 14, p. 10; *Wall Street Journal*, December 20, 1984; and *Washington Post*, December 20, 1984.
[20] It may be appropriate to adjust these estimates for the terms-of-trade effect. The employment of a methodology that is favorable to the protectionist argument yields a maximum estimate of the welfare gain from the terms-of-trade effect of steel quota imposition. That value is $72.694 million (in 1983 dollars). This would reduce the cost to the economy to $706.887 million. See Tarr and Morkre (1984, Chapter 2 and its appendix) for an explanation of the calculations.
[21] Benefits are measured as the value of deferring the earnings losses. See Section II ("Benefits of the quota" and "Cost–benefit ratios") for details.

Table 10.1. *Estimates of costs and gains from 18.5 percent quota on carbon and alloy steel products (excluding semi-finished) (millions of dollars)*

	Annual costs (base year *a* dollars)	Annual costs (1983 dollars)	Present value of costs over 4 Years (1983 dollars)
Consumers' losses	1,131	1,098	3,981
Losses to the U.S. economy	803	780	2,827
Gains to U.S. producers	441	428	1,552
Quota rents to foreigners	573	557	2,018

*a*The base year is September 1983 through August 1984.
Source: Bureau of Economics, Federal Trade Commission.

ings losses saved by otherwise displaced workers, consumers lose $34.60, and the U.S. economy has excess or inefficiency losses of $24.57. These estimates are summarized in Table 10.3.[22]

Methodology

Differentiated product

The first issue one must decide is whether to treat imported steel products as homogeneous with or differentiated from domestic steel products. The most reasonable assumption appears to be to treat imported and domestic steel products as differentiated. Jondrow et al. (1976) have observed that foreign steel appears to have to sell at a discount to be marketed in the United States. In explaining this situation, they argue that foreign and domestic steel products are differentiated for a number of reasons. For example, one must order foreign

[22] All of these estimates tend to underestimate the costs of the 18.5 percent limitation on imports. One reason for this is that no adjustment was made for the possibility of monopoly restriction of output if a quota was in place. Although we have not investigated the likelihood that monopoly output restrictions would occur in the steel industry if a quota were imposed, we note that with a quota, the domestic industry could increase its profits if it could restrict its output below the competitive level. (See Corden, 1971.) If it does so, there are additional costs to consumers and to the economy. More dramatically, however, there would be fewer jobs created. This would substantially increase cost per job created and the cost–benefit ratios. In fact, Corden (1971, pp. 203–6) has shown that if the quota is equal to the original imports, then domestic output and employment will necessarily fall. This is because there is only the monopoly restriction effect and no import substitution effect.

Table 10.2. *Annual costs to consumers and inefficiency costs to U.S. economy for each job saved by quota*[a]

Losses to consumers per job saved	$113,622
Losses to the economy per job saved	$ 80,682

[a]Costs are in base year (September 1983 through August 1984) dollars.
Source: Bureau of Economics, Federal Trade Commission.

Table 10.3. *Costs, benefits, and cost–benefit ratios for each dollar of earnings losses saved by the 18.5 percent quota*

Costs: present value of costs over 5 years[a]	Benefits: earnings losses saved[a]	Cost–benefit ratios
$4,960.422 (to consumers)	$143.334	$34.60
$3,522.344 (to the economy)	$143.334	$24.57

[a]Figures shown are in millions of base year dollars, where the base year is September 1983 through August 1984.
Source: Bureau of Economics, Federal Trade Commission.

steel further in advance and await delivery. Thus, if one relies on foreign steel, a larger inventory must be held with higher associated warehousing and interest costs. Moreover, they argue that domestic suppliers implicitly offer greater security of supply. Additionally, the econometric estimates of Robert Crandall (1981) argue for the acceptance of a differentiated product model.[23]

Model specification

The model is depicted graphically by the supply and demand framework in Figure 10.1. Panel A is the market for the domestic product, and panel B is the market for the imported product.

Since the products are related, the demand curves depend on the price of the competing good as well as having the usual own price of dependence. That is, the price of the competing import good is a parameter in the demand curve for the domestic good and conversely.

[23] See Crandall (1981, pp. 129–32).

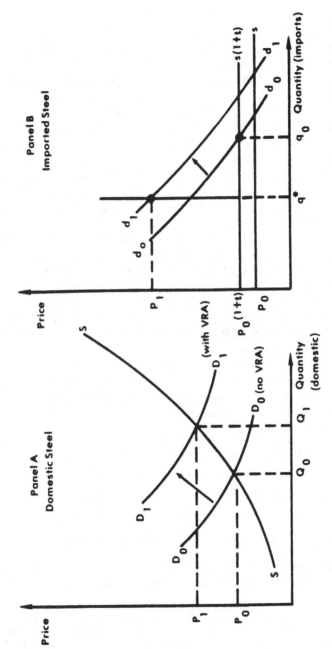

Figure 10.1. Effects of imposing a quota on a differentiated import, product with a rising domestic supply curve.

We have explained the basics of this model in our monograph on import restrictions.[24]

The dynamic adjustment to a new equilibrium after the imposition of a quota may be *intuitively explained* as follows. (Throughout this chapter we adopt the convention of using uppercase letters for prices and quantities of the domestic good and lowercase letters for the imported good.) Prior to the quota, equilibrium is at (P_0, Q_0) for the domestic good and (p_0, q_0) for the imported product, determined by the intersection of D_0 and S for the domestic good and d_0 and $s(1 + t)$ for the imported good (where t is the existing tariff rate). With the imposition of an import quota of $q = q^*$, the price of imports will rise to where quantity demanded equals quantity supplied. This is determined by the intersection of the supply relation at $q = q^*$ and the demand function for imports, d_0. The higher price for imports, however, induces an increase in demand for domestic steel, that is, a shifting out and to the right of the domestic demand curve D_1. This causes a higher price of domestic steel to result. This higher domestic price induces an increase in the demand for imported steel, resulting in a new higher price for imports. The new higher import price is analogous to the higher import price induced by the imposition of the quota, so a new round of shifts in demand is progressively smaller, and the process is convergent.[25]

To model these interactive effects explicitly requires specification of demand equations for both goods, a supply equation for the domestic good, and the price at which the imported good is supplied. The demand equations must incorporate the cross elasticity effect of the other good's price. Thus, the following specification is assumed:[26]

$$\ln Q = a + e_1 \ln P + e_2 \ln p \qquad \text{demand for domestic steel} \qquad (1)$$

$$\ln q = b + e_3 \ln P + e_4 \ln p \qquad \text{demand for imported steel} \qquad (2)$$

$$\ln Q = c + e_5 \ln P \qquad \text{supply of domestic steel} \qquad (3)$$

$$s(q) = p_0(1 + t) \qquad \text{supply price for imported steel} \qquad (4)$$

$$f(p) = q^*, \qquad p \geq p_0(1 + t) \qquad \text{supply relation under a quota.} \qquad (4^*)$$

Equations (1) and (2) are the demand curves for the domestic and imported goods, respectively. Equation (3) is the supply curve for the

[24] See Morkre and Tarr (1980, Chapter 2).

[25] The discussion of this paragraph is only for pedagogical purposes. No assumptions are made regarding the dynamic adjustment path to a new equilibrium. The analysis below is "comparative statics," and the model is specified by equations (1)–(4).

[26] We select a specification that is linear in the logs because the econometric estimates upon which we rely employed this specification.

domestic product. The coefficients e_1 and e_4 are the own elasticities of demand, e_2 and e_3 are cross elasticities of demand, and e_5 is elasticity of supply.[27] Equation (4) states that the price at which the imported good is supplied is $p_0(1 + t)$, where p_0 is the delivered price of imports excluding tariffs and t is the existing tariff rate. Equation (4*) applies with a quota in effect, rather than equation (4). It states that if imports are limited to a quantity q^*, then exactly q^* will be supplied at any price, provided price exceeds or equals the import supply price of $p_0(1 + t)$.

Clearly, there are variables affecting the equilibrium prices and quantities other than those explicitly modeled in equations (1)–(4). In the context of a comparative statics exercise, it is appropriate to hold these other variables constant. Thus, the other variables that affect the equilibrium are subsumed in the specified constants of the equations.

Elasticity assumptions

The best estimates available for own and cross price elasticities of demand are in Robert Crandall's book.[28] Utilizing Crandall's elasticity estimates means that equations (1)–(4) become

$$\ln Q = a - 1.5 \ln P + 0.6 \ln p, \tag{1'}$$

$$\ln q = b + 4 \ln P - 4.5 \ln p, \tag{2'}$$

$$\ln Q = c + 3.5 \ln P, \tag{3'}$$

$$s(q) = p_0(1 + t), \tag{4}$$

$$f(p) = q^*, \qquad p \geq p_0(1 + t). \tag{4*}$$

Selection of base year prices and quantities

We selected as a base year the most recent 12-month period for which we had data. Thus, the base year is the 12 months ending in August 1984. The prices and quantities were chosen as follows.

The petition asked for relief only on carbon and alloy steel mill products (excluding stainless and tool steel products). The USTR implied that it would be the products with which the petition was concerned that would be the object of the negotiations,[29] so it is appropri-

---

[27] In a model in which the domestic industry has sufficient time to vary all inputs, one would assume that the industry could expand output at close to constant costs, i.e., e would be very large. A shorter time period is assumed here.

[28] See Crandall (1981, p. 131).

[29] William Brock, "Press Briefing," September 18, 1984, p. 7.

ate to limit the quantity data to carbon and alloy steel mill products. In addition, it would be appropriate to exclude semi-finished products, since the 18.5 percent goal for imports excludes semi-finished steel products.[30] Monthly data on carbon, alloy, and stainless domestic steel mill products shipments, exports, and imports (by product) were obtained from the American Iron and Steel Institute (AISI) for the months of September 1983 through August 1984.[31] Subtracting exports from domestic shipments yields domestic shipments for domestic consumption, which is the desired quantity demanded as Q in equations $(1')-(4')$. Domestic carbon and alloy shipments for domestic consumption, excluding semi-finished products, were 72.164 million short tons during the year September 1983 to August 1984. Thus, Q = 72.164 million short tons in equations $(1')-(4')$. Imports of carbon and alloy shipments excluding semi-finished products over the same period were 23.034 million short tons. Thus, q = 23.034 million short tons in equations $(1')-(4')$.

The price data were based on data available in various 1984 issues of the *Monthly Report on Steel Statistics* by the USITC. The domestic price is a composite price of many steel products.[32] The value of $539 per short ton was taken as representative of the base year, that is, P = $539 for the base year.

For the price of imports we start with the unit value of the 15 categories of products subject to the U.S.–EC arrangement. This customs value of $335 per ton should be more representative of carbon and alloy steel products than all steel mill products (which includes the relatively expensive stainless steel products).[33] The customs value does not include transportation, insurance, and some brokerage fees, which must be added to arrive at the delivered price, p, in equation (4). A survey of the estimates of these additional charges has been done in our FTC staff steel report.[34] The best estimate for these charges, taken from that survey, is 15.5 percent of the customs value. A recent report by the ITC on transportation costs, however, reveals that freight rates

---

[30] 49, *Federal Register*, 36814, September 20, 1984.

[31] Although these data are not published in the *Annual Statistical Report* of the AISI, they are available in mimeo form.

[32] The ITC data on composite domestic steel prices are reproduced from *Iron Age* magazine. An *Iron Age* official stated, in a telephone interview, that the composite price excludes stainless steel. Thus, the product mix should be representative of the products we are estimating.

[33] See USITC (1984, p. 7). Since data for the complete base year were unavailable, we used the customs value of these products for the first 6 months of 1984.

[34] See Duke et al. (1977, Appendix 3B).

for iron and steel products have declined by about 1.5 percent since the publication of our FTC staff steel report.[35] Thus, we adjust the customs value of $335 upward by 14.0 percent to arrive at $382.

Tariff rates on carbon and alloy steel products were estimated by ITC staff at 5.6 percent in 1983. Due to Tokyo round cuts, however, they are expected to decline by roughly 0.3 percent per year over the next 5 years.[36] Thus, we take 5 percent as a representative tariff rate that is expected to prevail over the next several years. Thus, the delivered price of imports including tariff is $p = \$399$.[37]

The estimated new equilibrium

The domestic price and quantity (in thousands of short tons) for the base year are ($P = \$539$ and $Q = 72,164$); the price, including tariffs, and quantity (in thousands of short tons) of imports are $p = \$399$ and $q = 23,034$. Assuming that our model described by equations (1′)–(4) accurately depicts the process of price and quantity determination, the price and quantity solutions for 1983 are a particular solution to equations (1′)–(4′). One may substitute these particular price and quantity values into equations (1′)–(3′), leaving these equations in three unknowns: a, b, and c. Solving them yields $a = 23.9362$, $b = 18.7428$, and $c = -3.9190$.

With the imposition of a quota, equation (4) would no longer apply; rather, equation (4*), which states that imports are limited to a fixed quantity q^*, applies. To assess the effects of an 18.5 percent quota, we solve for that value of q that yields imports at 18.5 percent of apparent consumption.[38] This yields $q^* = 16.381$ million short tons. Substituting $q = 16.381$ million, and the above solutions for a, b, and c into equations (1′)–(3′) and solving simultaneously yields the estimated new equilibrium after the imposition of the quota: $P = \$545$, $Q = 74,800$, $p = \$434$, and $q = 16,381$, where the quantities are in thousands of short tons. These solutions are depicted in Figure 10.2.

---

[35] See USITC (1983, p. 6). The USITC study does not include transportation costs from the plant to the port or from the port in the United States to the end user. For that reason, the total value of these charges exceeds that which the ITC was estimating.

[36] These estimates were obtained from ITC staff.

[37] Since tariff rates are calculated on customs values only, we take (0.05)($335) = $16.75. This value added to the delivered price of $382 equals $399 when rounded to the nearest dollar.

[38] This is accomplished by solving for q from $q/(Q + q) = 0.185$.

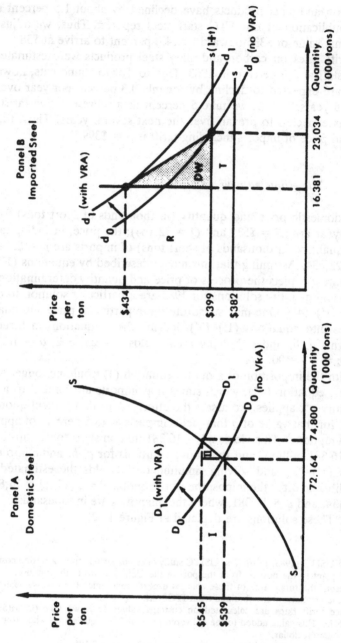

Figure 10.2. Estimated effects of an 18.5% quota on carbon and alloy steel mill products (excluding semi-finished).

The gains and losses from the quota and costs to consumers and the economy

Costs to consumers and the economy

The analysis of costs to consumers and to the economy begins with an estimate of the reduction in consumers' surplus as the measure of the value of consumers' losses from the imposition of the tariff.[39]

How to estimate the change in consumers' surplus is not immediately obvious since two markets, not just one, are involved, and the demand curves in both markets have changed. An *American Economic Review* article by Burns (1973), however, applies precisely to this situation,[40] and the Burns analysis is employed below. As a result of the quota, the lost consumers' surplus is equal to the rectangle I and triangle II in panel A plus the rectangle R and Triangle DW in panel B of Figure 10.2. The four areas together sum to $1,130.7 million.

Define deadweight losses as

$$DWL = \Delta CS + \Delta PS + \Delta T,$$ (5)

where ΔCS = change in consumers' surplus,
ΔPS = change in producers' surplus, and
ΔT = change in tariff.

That is, the deadweight loss is the amount lost by consumers that is not captured or redistributed to other sectors of the domestic economy.[41] It is lost to the economy and is in that sense a "deadweight" loss imposed by the tariff.

The areas I and II, bounded by broken lines in panel A, are equal to the gain in producers' surplus from the quota.[42] Quantitatively it is

---

[39] Alfred Marshall (1920, p. 124) defined consumers' surplus as follows: "[The consumer] derives from a purchase a surplus of satisfaction. The excess of the price which he would be willing to pay rather than go without the thing, over that which he actually does pay, is the economic measure of this surplus satisfaction. It may be called consumer surplus."

[40] Willig (1976) has shown that this measure is a good measure of welfare changes.

[41] Deadweight losses to the domestic economy may be decomposed into three parts: production distortions that are losses attributable to resources being used to produce the good in question that could be used more valuably elsewhere; consumption distortions that are losses attributable to consumers purchasing other goods that they value less highly than the good in question at the lower pre-quota price; and quota rents that are captured by foreigners. See Morkre and Tarr (1980, Chapter 2) for details.

[42] Producers' surplus is defined entirely analogously to consumers' surplus. The difference between the price at which a producer would be willing to supply the product rather than not supply it and the price he actually receives is a measure of producers' surplus.

calculated as $6 × 72,164,000 + $6(2,636,000) ($\frac{1}{2}$) and equals $440.892 million.[43] Producers are willing to supply at a price read off the supply curve but are able to receive $545 instead. This is equal to the lost consumers' surplus in the domestic market, so there are no deadweight losses attributed to the domestic market resource shifts.[44]

The rectangle R in panel B is equal to the value of the quota rents captured by the foreigners. The foreigners sell the quota amount of 16,381,000 short tons. They are willing to supply this quantity at a price read off the tariff inclusive supply curve, that is, at $399. Instead, under the usual method of quota allocation, where foreign countries receive the quota rights, they are able to receive $434 per short ton. The difference of $35 per ton is the rent they receive per ton of sales, which is attributable to the quota. This value equals $573.34 million.

The triangle DW (which is dotted in panel B of Figure 10.2) is equal to $\frac{1}{2}$ × $35 × (23.034 − 16.381) million = $116.43 million. It represents deadweight loss because it is part of lost consumers' surplus but is not redistributed to other sectors of the economy either as producers' surplus or as tariffs. It is pure inefficiency loss in that it is captured by no one.

An additional area of deadweight loss is the rectangle T, which is equal to $17 × (6.653) million = $113.101 million. This area represents tariff revenue that was formerly collected by the U.S. Treasury but is now captured by no one. It does not represent an additional loss to consumers as a result of the quota, since consumers lost this amount under the tariff.[45] The results of these calculations are summarized in Table 10.1.

Benefits of the quota

If a quota is imposed, a number of jobs in steelmaking would be created. An estimate of the number of jobs created can be based on

---

[43] In this formula, we have taken the traditional approach and approximated area II by a triangle. If we actually worked with the supply curve specified in equation (3) and the values for which we have solved, area II would be

$$\int_\alpha^\beta [545 - \exp(-c/3.5)\, Q^{1/3.5}]\, dQ,$$

where $\alpha = 72,164,000$, $\beta = 74,800,000$, and $c = -3.919$. This integral equals approximately $8.7 million as opposed to $7.9 million for the triangle.

[44] This is the traditional method of estimating these quantities and is in the spirit of Harberger's (1971) analysis, since there is no difference between the price and what any producer is willing to supply at the margin. Moreover, Wisecarver (1974) has established that the above analysis is not altered by the fact that steel is a derived demand.

[45] For simplicity of analysis, we take the tariff to be an equivalent specific tariff that raises the price to $399.

the results in the previous section which indicated that the 18.5 percent quota will result in an increase in domestically produced steel shipments of 2.636 million short tons. Based on data from the American Iron and Steel Institute, an additional 3.775 employees would be required to produce an additional 1,000 short tons of steel mill products. Assuming this ratio would be maintained implies that 2.636 million additional tons of steel produced will result in 9,951 additional jobs. This estimate is derived in the following manner.

If the average product of labor and the marginal product of labor differ, as would be expected to occur if the supply curve is not flat, the marginal product is superior to the average product for an estimate of the additional jobs required to produce additional output. This is true because the marginal product is defined as the additional output obtained from an additional unit of labor.

In 1982, 61.567 million short tons of steel mill shipments required 289,437 employees; in 1981, 88.450 million short tons of steel mill shipments required 390,914 employees.[46] Thus, the reduction in output of 26.883 million short tons from 1981 to 1982 resulted in the reduction of employment of 101,477 employees. This implies that, on average, an additional employee produced 264.9 tons of steel per year. We take this number as an approximation of the marginal product of labor, that is, the change in output divided by the change in labor employment over the previous year is the proxy for the marginal product of labor. Taking the reciprocal yields 3.775 as the marginal amount of labor required for an additional 1,000 tons of steel.

Utilizing the estimates of Section II, this means that the costs to consumers for each job created is $113,622 per year; the costs to the economy for each job created is $80,682 per year. These estimates are summarized in Table 10.2.

Cost-benefit ratios

Following the methodology developed by Morkre and Tarr (1980, pp. 16–19), benefits are taken as the adjustment costs of workers who otherwise would have been displaced. These adjustment costs are measured by the earning losses of displaced workers.

Jacobsen (1978) has estimated the earnings losses of workers displaced from a number of manufacturing industries, including steel. For most industries the substantial losses occur in the first 2 years after

---

[46] American Iron and Steel Institute, 1982, *Annual Statistical Report.*

displacement; for many industries losses continue in the subsequent 4 years. Thereafter earnings losses have usually vanished.

The introductory section of this chapter revealed that protection has been afforded to the steel industry in episodes. That is, unlike textiles, which has a history of continuous protection since the imposition of the multifiber arrangement, carbon steel has had protection for a period of about 5 years, followed by free trade for a number of years, followed by protection for a number of years, and so on. This is partly explained by the fact that the protection is usually justified on the basis of allowing the steel industry a period of time to "modernize" and adjust, after which it is hoped the industry will be able to compete effectively. Indeed, the president asked the USITC to make an annual report on the industry's modernization and adjustment efforts[47]; and the Trade and Tariff Act of 1984 requires industry reinvestment of cash flow (with possible termination of the program if the requirement is not met) and terminates authorization for the administration's program after 5 years. This suggests that the new program of protection will last for a number of years and terminate. In what follows, we assume the restraints will be lifted after 5 years.[48]

In steel, Jacobsen estimates that displaced workers lose 46.6 percent of their earnings in the first 2 years after displacement and 12.6 percent in the subsequent 4 years. The average total compensation of a steel employee in 1983 was $38,574.[49] Suppose, as a result of imposing a quota, a steelworker is never displaced. Then, taking a discount rate of 7 percent[50] yields a present value of $499 million in cumulative saved earnings losses (benefits) from the quota. After termination of the quota, however, the marginal output of the domestic industry, which was induced by and produced jobs only because of the quota, would be eliminated. Thus, those workers who are employed because of the quota would be expected to be displaced after the quota is terminated. This means the benefits of the quota are the deferral of the displacement costs for 5 years. That is, as a result of a quota, the costs of

---

[47] 49, *Federal Register*, 36814, September 20, 1984.

[48] This assumption is also supported by the fact that the Fair Trade in Steel Act of 1984 proposed to remove quotas after 5 years and in a Section 201 proceeding (which started the present policy debate on steel), quotas may only be requested for a maximum of 5 years. The protection may be extended for an additional 3 years upon further petition and affirmative rulings by the ITC and the president.

[49] $38,574 = 52 × 33.4 × $22.21 (52 weeks times the average number of hours worked per week in 1983 times total hourly compensation in 1983). The 1983 days were obtained from the American Iron and Steel Institute, *Annual Statistical Report*, 1983.

[50] A relatively high real discount rate such as this one will lower the cost–benefit ratios. This is because the costs to consumers do not change over time and eventually vanish. Thus, the cost–benefit ratios may be thought of as conservative.

adjustment will not be incurred in the first 6 years starting immediately but rather in the 6 years following the 5 years of protection.

By taking the appropriate present values, one can calculate that the present value of the cumulative earnings losses of 9,951 steelworkers who would be displaced after 5 years of protection is $356 million in 1983 dollars. If they were displaced immediately, that is, no protection were granted, the losses would be $499 million. The difference of $143 million is the benefit of the protection, that is, it is the value of deferring the earnings losses for 5 years.[51]

The present value of the losses to consumers from imposing the proposed quota over 5 years is $4,960.422 million, and the present value of the losses to the U.S. economy over 5 years is $3,522.334 million. Comparing this with $143.334 million in benefits yields that for each dollar of earnings losses saved by the quota, consumers lose $34.60 and the economy loses $24.57. These estimates are summarized in Table 10.3.

Conclusion

This chapter has estimated the costs to consumers and to the economy of imposing a quota on imported carbon and alloy steel mill products at the 18.5 percent level. It was found that the costs to U.S. consumers exceed $1 billion annually, and the inefficiency costs to the U.S. economy exceed 0.8 of the $1 billion annually. Terms-of-trade costs may

---

[51] If steel is an "infant" industry that needs a period of protection after which it will compete with foreign competition effectively, then the $499 million estimate is the appropriate one. Steel, however, has been produced in large amounts in the United States for many decades and is thus not a likely candidate as an infant industry. If an adjustment assistance program is offered to workers, in lieu of a quota, the earnings losses may underestimate the full social costs if the labor benefits available have the effect of lowering the wage rate the industry needs to pay to attract workers. This arises when workers anticipate that their compensation includes their expected benefits under an adjustment assistance program. In this case, domestic supply increases, and the effect is similar to a unit subsidy given to industry. There would be deadweight production inefficiencies caused by the increase in steelworkers under the trade adjustment assistance program; however, these effects are expected to be relatively small and are ignored in our analysis. Finally, we will have overestimated the actual costs saved if a quota results in recalling workers who have been unemployed for some period of time. If they have been out of work for 1 year, or possibly in a new job and return to the steel industry, then they would already have incurred adjustment costs over that 1 year. Their, or their co-workers', subsequent displacement in 5 years will involve incurring the full adjustment costs at that time. The benefit is not of deferring the adjustment for 5 years as was assumed above; rather it is the difference between the remaining adjustment costs of adjusting today and the full adjustment costs 5 years from now. To the extent that this is significant, the true benefits of granting protection are lower than we have estimated.

reduce these numbers by up to $73 million. Despite these rather significant amounts, a number of assumptions were made in the estimation process that imply that the estimates are conservative, that is, the true costs to the economy and other relevant measures are higher than those indicated.

References

American Iron and Steel Institute, *Annual Statistical Report*, Washington, DC, various years.

Baldrige, Malcolm (1982), "Steel Countervailing Duties," Statement of the Secretary of the Department of Commerce, U.S. Department of Commerce, August 25.

Barnett, Donald, and Louis Schorsch (1983), *Steel: Upheaval in a Basic Industry*, Ballinger, Cambridge, MA.

Burns, Michael E. (1973), "A Note on the Concept and Measure of Consumers' Surplus," *American Economic Review*, 63(3), 335–44.

Congressional Budget Office (1984), *The Effects of Import Quotas on the Steel Industry*, U.S. Congress.

Corden, W. M. (1971), *The Theory of Protection*, Oxford University Press, New York.

Crandall, Robert (1981), *The U.S. Steel Industry in Recurrent Crisis*, Brookings Institution, Washington, DC.

Duke, R., R. Johnson, H. Mueller, P. D. Qualls, C. Rousch, and D. Tarr (1977), *The United States Steel Industry and Its International Rivals. . . , Bureau of Economics Staff Report to the Federal Trade Commission, USGPO, Washington, DC.*

Harberger, Arnold (1971), "Three Basic Postulates for Applied Welfare Economics: An Interpretive Essay," *Journal of Economic Literature*, 9(3), 785–97.

Jacobsen, Louis S. (1978), "Earnings Losses of Workers Displaced from Manufacturing Industries," in *The Impact of International Trade and Investment on Employment*, William DeWald (ed.), Proceedings of a Conference on Department of Labor Research Results, USGPO, Washington, DC.

Jondrow, James (1978), "Effects of Trade Restrictions on Imports of Steel," in *The Impact of International Trade Investment on Employment*, William DeWald (ed.), Proceedings of a Conference on Department of Labor Research Results, USGPO, Washington, DC.

Jondrow, James, et al. (1976), "Forms of Competition in the Steel Industry," Public Research Institute of the Center for Naval Analysis, in mimeo.

Marshall, Alfred (1920), *Principles of Economics*, 8th ed., London, Porcupine Press.

Morkre, Morris E., and David G. Tarr (1980), *The Effects of Restrictions on United States Imports: Five Case Studies and Theory*, Bureau of Economics Staff Report to the Federal Trade Commission, USGPO, Washington, DC.

Rohr, David B. (1984), "Remedy: Carbon Steel," Commissioner's Statement, USITC, July 11.

Solomon, Anthony (Chairman of the Task Force) (1977), "Report to the President (on) A Comprehensive Program for the Steel Industry," in *The Administration's Comprehensive Program for the Steel Industry*, Hearings before the subcommittee on Trade of the Committee on Ways and Means, House of Representatives, January 25 and 26, 1978, USGPO, Washington, DC.

Tarr, David (1984), "Estimation of the Costs to the U.S. Economy and to Consumers of the Imposition of a Fifteen Percent Quota, Equivalent Tariff and Adjustment Assistance for Carbon and Alloy Steel Mill Products," Supplemental Filing by the Federal Trade Commission to the USITC on Investigation No. TA-201-51, June.

Tarr, David, and Morris Morkre (1984), *Aggregate Costs to the United States of Tariffs and Quotas on Imports*, Bureau of Economics Staff Report to the Federal Trade Commission, USGPO, Washington, DC.

United Steelworkers of America and Bethlehem Steel Corporation (1984), "Petition Under Section 201 of the Trade Act of 1974 and Subpart B of Part 206 of the rules of the USTIC," submitted to the USITC in mimeo.

U.S. International Trade Commission (USITC) (1982), "Certain Steel Products from Belgium, Brazil, France, Italy, Luxembourg, the Netherlands, Romania, the United Kingdom and West Germany," USITC Publication 1221, February.

      (1983), "Transportation Costs of U.S. Imports," USITC Publication 1375, April.

      (1984), "Monthly Report on Selected Steel Industry Data," USTIC Publication 1567, August.

Willig, Robert D. (1976), "Consumers Surplus Without Apology," *American Economic Review*, 66(4), 589–97.

Wisecarver, Daniel (1974), "The Social Costs of Input-Market Distortions," *American Economic Review*, 64(3), 359–72.

Discussion

LAWRENCE J. WHITE

The theory of international trade and comparative advantage teaches us that under most circumstances artificially imposed impediments to international trade raise prices to consumers and impose real costs on the domestic economy, which decreases social welfare. David Tarr has provided a specific estimate of these costs for the recent quotas imposed on the import of carbon and alloy steel into the United States.

Tarr finds that these costs are large. Consumers are paying significantly higher prices for domestic and imported steel as a consequence of these quotas. In part, these higher prices represent transfers from consumers to the owners of steel companies and to steelworkers. But the higher prices mostly imply net losses (net costs) to the U.S. economy. These losses result from the transfer of rents to overseas producers and from the inefficient allocation of domestic resources that follow from the higher prices.

Tarr's estimates are probably conservative; the losses from protectionism are probably even larger. For example, his calculations do not include the effects of a separate set of import restrictions on specialty steels, including stainless steels. Further, he has not included as a cost the wastes of lobbying and of other expenditures by protected parties aimed at preserving (or strengthening) their protected positions.[1]

What are the political motives that underlie such protectionist actions? Usually, they are aimed at protecting specific job slots and protecting the incomes of the holders of these job slots. Appropriately, Tarr calculates the costs to consumers and the costs to the economy per job slot preserved and per dollar of income protected.

Before I discuss the estimates, it is worth emphasizing two basic economic truths concerning the effects of protectionism. First, tariffs and/or quotas on imports cannot improve the net balance of trade. The fundamental identities of macroeconomic ensure that the saving and investment rates of the U.S. economy will determine the net balance of trade. As long as our economy continues to have low saving rates and high investment rates, we will continue to attract capital from abroad and (concurrently) will continue to run large deficits on our current account (which are the real counterpart to those capital inflows). Under our current regime of flexible exchange rates, an impediment that discourages imports but that does not alter the basic saving and investment flows will simply cause the dollar to appreciate vis-à-vis foreign currencies, discouraging exports and bringing the net trade balance back to where it was before the impediment was imposed.

Second, and a corollary to the first proposition, import protectionism is unlikely to be a net creator of jobs for the U.S. economy. Protection can protect specific job slots in the protected industry, but it does so at the expense of job losses in actual or potential export industries. The net effect for total employment is likely to be negligible.

But, of course, the protectionism itself is not harmless. It imposes

[1] See, e.g., Krueger (1974) and Posner (1975).

real costs on the economy–through inefficiency and through transfers to overseas producers. Tarr estimates that these real costs are about $80,000 per job slot preserved in the steel industry. These costs per job slot are higher than the estimates of the costs of protection in some other industries but lower than the costs estimated for yet others.[2] This last result is only mildly comforting, however.

Further, Tarr finds that the real cost per dollar of income transferred to steelworkers who would otherwise have to find another job is quite high: around $25 per dollar transferred. The real costs of ordinary income transfer programs–such as food stamps, Aid to Families with Dependent Children, or Social Security–are dwarfed by comparison. Even if we acknowledge that steelworkers who remain employed and stockholders of steel companies will benefit from the income transfers, we still find that the economy loses around two dollars for every dollar transferred; and ordinary income transfer programs still look good by comparison.

One interesting question that Tarr does not pursue is the net income distribution consequences of this protection–that is, a comparison of the incomes of those who ultimately have to pay higher prices for products embodying the higher priced steel and the incomes of the workers (and stockholders) who are being protected. I suspect that the net effects are regressive: that is, on a net basis poorer people are being taxed (through higher prices) so as to maintain the incomes of richer people. I base this suspicion largely on the fact that wages and benefits in the U.S. steel industry, even after the recent "givebacks," are still appreciably higher than the average level of wages and benefits in the U.S. economy.[3] But it would be comforting to be able to confirm this suspicion through a set of computations that would involve a melding of an input–output table (to determine the end-product uses of steel), a set of consumer expenditure surveys (to determine the consumption patterns of individuals at different incomes), and an income distribution table. A quick survey of the relevant literature and of knowledgeable colleagues did not reveal any such study for any instance of import protection.[4] I hope that this gap in our knowledge of the equity consequences of protectionism will be remedied in the next few years.

[2] For estimates for other industries, including autos, textiles, citizens band radios, color televisions, and sugar, see Morkre and Tarr (1980), Gomez-Ibanez et al. (1983), Tarr and Morkre (1984), and US ITC (1985).

[3] See Crandall (1981, pp. 34–8) and Barnett and Schorsch (1983, p. 68).

[4] Fielke (1971) shows that the incidence of import duties in general is mildly regressive when only their impact on consumption is examined. He does not make the further comparison of "who pays and who receives."

Finally, I would like to focus on a puzzle in the political economy of import protection that has recently begun to trouble me. The U.S. government's protection for steel has largely been in the form of quotas. (The same has been true for a number of other protectionist efforts, including protection for textiles and autos.) The quotas, of course, limit the supply of imports and cause their prices to rise. But given the methods that we use to administer the quotas, we let the foreign exporters capture the rents from this artificial scarcity.

Thus, by using quotas of this type, our government is imposing much larger losses on our economy than if we used equivalent tariffs (which would capture the rents in the form of tariff revenues for the U.S. Treasury) or even (if the quantity certainty of quotas is deemed desirable) if we auctioned the quota rights to domestic importers. In the language of international trade geometry, we have converted small "deadweight loss triangles" into much larger "giveaway loss rectangles." In Tarr's calculations, over 70 percent of the net loss to the U.S. economy is in the form of the loss of quota rents to foreign exporters.

Why do we do this to ourselves? Why, when we engage in protection, do we insist on "shooting ourselves in the foot" to an even greater extent than necessary through the use of quotas? Consider the following paradox: If a senator or member of congress were to vote for a program of tariff protection combined with the automatic transfer of the tariff proceeds to the foreign exporters, he or she would likely be voted out of office at the first opportunity; critical newspaper editorials might even suggest the need for an immediate psychiatric examination. But legislators regularly advocate and vote for quota protection programs that achieve exactly the same effects. And they are regularly re-elected, without any calls for psychiatric examinations. Why?

I can suggest some possible answers: Perhaps the legislators believe that consumers will be able to identify price increases with tariffs more easily than with quotas. Perhaps the GATT's emphasis on tariffs has made it easier for governments to impose quotas. Perhaps the transfer of the scarcity rents to the foreigners is necessary as a bribe to dampen their opposition and forestall retaliation. I do not find any of these explanations wholly convincing. I hope that political economy theorists and empiricists will turn their attention to this puzzle.

In closing, it is important to emphasize that adaptation to change – rather than outright resistance – is one of the keys to a vibrant and growing economy in a changing world. The U.S. economy and polity must learn to adapt to change, not resist it. As David Tarr has demonstrated, the costs of resistance through protection are high indeed.

References

Barnett, Donald F., and Louis Schorsch (1983), *Steel: Upheaval in a Basic Industry*, Ballinger, Cambridge, MA.

Crandall, Robert W. (1981), *The U.S. Steel Industry in Recurrent Crisis: Policy Options in a Competitive World*, Brookings Institution, Washington, DC.

Fielke, Norman S. (Fall 1971), "The Incidence of the U.S. Tariff Structure on Consumption," *Public Policy*, 19, 639–52.

Gomez-Ibanez, Jose A., Robert A. Leone, and Stephan A. O'Connell (1983), "Restraining Auto Imports: Does Anyone Win?" *Journal of Policy Analysis and Management*, 2 196–218.

Krueger, Anne O. (June 1974), "The Political Economy of the Rent-Seeking Society," *American Economic Review*, 64, 291–303.

Morkre, Morris E., and David G. Tarr (June 1980), "The Effects of Restrictions on United States Imports: Five Case Studies and Theory," Staff Report, Bureau of Economics, U.S. Federal Trade Commission.

Posner, Richard A. (August 1975), "The Social Costs of Monopoly," *Journal of Political Economy*, 83, 807–28.

Tarr, David G., and Morris E. Morkre (December 1984), "Aggregate Costs to the United States of Tariffs and Quotas on Imports," Staff Report, Bureau of Economics, U.S. Federal Trade Commission.

U.S. International Trade Commission (USITC) (February 1985), "A Review of Recent Developments in the U.S. Automobile Industry, Including an Assessment of the Japanese Voluntary Restraint Agreements," Publication No. 1648.

Discussion

MITSUAKI SATO

As I understand it, the United States requested other governments to voluntarily restrain steel exports to the United States rather than impose quotas because, I assume, President Reagan wanted to stick to his avowed free-market stance. Voluntary restraint agreements have effects similar to import quotas, and the costs and benefits of such trade restrictions are obvious. As Tarr has detailed, these measures impose a tremendous cost on the American consumer and affect the entire economy negatively.

Why, then, did Japan agree to the U.S. government's request? The reason is simple: Japan judged that unless the foundation of the U.S. steel industry solidified, sound development of international trade in steel could not be achieved and development of the world economy would be hampered. Along with the United States and the European

Community, Japan is a top producer of steel in the free world and wishes to avoid any situation that might damage the sound development of steel trade and the prosperity of the world economy.

For this reason, Japan actively participated in the program, as requested by the United States, of restraining steel exports and has faithfully observed the proposed terms. As a result, Japan's exports of steel to the United States totaled 6.4 million tons in 1984 and 5.2 million tons in 1985, and in 1986 the total is estimated to be around 4.5 million tons.

There are a few other developments that should be noted. The 30 percent rise of the yen against the dollar that took place between the fall of 1985 and early 1986 has and continues to have a positive effect on the American steel industry. Also, the price reductions resulting from excessive competition among domestic steel manufacturers are, I understand, now being corrected. If all this is helping the U.S. steel industry regain its health, that is good news to Japan and all other countries that have worked to make the voluntary restraint agreements effective.

However, some questions remain. Is the U.S. steel industry using the funds generated by protectionist measures – voluntary restraint agreements *are* protectionist – for capital investment to modernize its plants and equipment? Is it phasing out obsolete and excess facilities? Is it correcting the wage levels that are too high in comparison to those of other industries? If it is not, the sacrifices necessitated by voluntary restraint agreements and the time limit of 5 years will make little sense. Serious attempts by American steel companies to rationalize and modernize themselves are called for, especially in view of the aggressive competition from newly industrialized countries.

In a broader context, the question raised by Tarr might be analyzed not only from the standpoint of the relief to the steelworkers versus the losses to the consumer and the whole economy by using demand and supply curves, but also from a macroeconomic viewpoint. In macroeconomic terms it is particularly important to consider how voluntary restraints affect such things as inflation, the international competitiveness of domestic industries that use steel products, and entrepreneurship within the steel industry, in addition to terms of trade. Needless to say, steel is not the only industry where such considerations must be made when a protectionist measure is taken.

Next, I would like to comment on a couple of points in Tarr's otherwise excellent chapter with which I disagree. First, Tarr said that as a result of the voluntary restraint agreements, U.S. imports of steel declined by 6.653 million tons while domestic demand increased by 2.636

million tons. My question is: How do we account for the difference? Could it be explained as the substitution effect of the resulting steep price rises? Even if it could, the difference strikes me as too large.

Second, Tarr says that in the absence of VRAs on steel 9,961 workers would have become immediately unemployed and a total of $499 million would be lost accordingly, whereas with the VRAs in force the total loss in the 5-year period would be $356 million. Thus, Tarr says, the introduction of the VRAs would save $143 million over a period of 5 years. I find this argument odd. On the one hand, the absence of VRAs would not have meant an immediate loss of 9,961 workers – the loss would have occurred gradually – and on the other hand, introduction of VRAs would mean preservation of an excess labor force and high wage rates. I would argue that without VRAs rationalization and modernization would be carried out faster, thereby lessening the losses.

In addition, the domestic price rise in Figure 10.2 is shown to be as small as $6 per ton, from $539 to $545. In fact, though, the domestic price rose by as much as $60. If that was the case, figures indicating the effect on the consumer and the economy might have to be revised upward.

Finally, Tarr seems not to have taken into account the losses sustained by the U.S. economy as a result of the supply shortages caused by voluntary restraint agreements of certain products – products that are either not produced in the United States or are so undesirable on the quality side as to be unusable. Such losses were estimated to amount to $1 billion, according to a report General Electric Company submitted to the U.S. Trade Representative in April 1984.

These are, however, minor points. I found Tarr's analysis very persuasive. Generally, the United States has been making the same argument on the voluntary export restraints on automobiles that Japan has been observing at the request of the U.S. government. Overall, protectionism of any kind has a negative effect on the consumer *and* the economy of the country that adopts it. We also know that protectionism has a detrimental effect on the world economy as a whole.

CHAPTER 11

Limits of trade policy toward high technology industries: the case of semiconductors

THOMAS A. PUGEL

The semiconductor industry is among the fastest growing and most technologically dynamic of all manufacturing industries. Semiconductors are increasingly pervasive in their product applications. They are creating new levels of performance in consumer, industrial, and military products; thus, they appear to be the basis for a new "industrial revolution."

Since the industry's beginning, U.S. firms have been dominant in terms of sales and technological innovation, but the competitiveness of Japanese firms has been rising. For a number of years U.S. firms have complained about the unfair competitive practices of Japanese firms and the unfair policies of the Japanese government. In 1985 these complaints became formal trade actions – three dumping suits and a petition charging unfair trade practices. In addition, U.S. firms continue to accuse Japanese firms of illegally copying U.S. technology – two new major infringement suits were filed in 1985 and early 1986.

This chapter describes and analyzes U.S.–Japanese semiconductor trade frictions and these formal actions against Japanese firms and the Japanese government. It focuses on an examination of the U.S. national economic interest in semiconductors, which may be different from the interests of the firms in the U.S. semiconductor industry. It discusses the implications of this analysis for U.S. government policy toward the industry. The analysis includes an examination of the applicability of the new theory of strategic trade policy to the industry, as well as a discussion of more traditional considerations in the formulation of government policy.

A major conclusion of the analysis is that there is a national interest in the U.S. production of semiconductors, but this interest is not the same as that of the firms in the industry, and it is not the same as that posited in the theory of strategic trade policy. Rather, the national

This chapter was written while the author was a Visiting Professor at the School of International Politics, Economics and Business of Aoyama Gakuin University.

interest is based on the technology externalities created by the industry and on the importance of semiconductor technologies to the competitiveness of U.S. producers of systems products that use semiconductors. In essence, the latter basis involves a modification and extension of the theory of strategic trade policy.

The analysis has clear implications for desirable changes in U.S. government policy. The policy should aim to support and encourage activities to create and bring to market new semiconductor technologies. Such a policy of positive assistance enhances the international competitiveness of the U.S. semiconductor industry in a manner consistent with the national interests in technology externalities and user industries. Import protection and anti-dumping actions are not desirable because they are not consistent with these national interests. Improved access to the Japanese market is desirable for U.S. firms, but there is little evidence of any Japanese government or business practices that the U.S. government can legitimately complain about. Rather, U.S. firms must be willing to invest to improve their position in a highly competitive market.

The semiconductor industry

The value of world production of semiconductors has grown by about 16 percent per year over the last 25 years. Secular real growth has been higher than 16 percent, because prices of semiconductor devices tend to fall, sometimes dramatically. However, the industry is also very cyclical. The value of world production fell by 13 percent from 1984 to 1985, as the industry experienced its worst recession in its history.

As shown in Table 11.1, the worldwide value of semiconductor production is estimated at $28.7 billion in 1985. About 18 percent of this was accounted for by captive producers, those that produce semiconductors completely or almost completely for in-house use, and the rest by merchant firms. Discrete devices such as transistors and diodes account for a declining share of world production. Integrated circuits (ICs), which contain a number of elements (each functioning as a transistor or diode) on a single "chip," account for a rising share of world production of semiconductors, 79 percent in 1985.

National production

Table 11.1 also shows production by the home base of the producing firm for 1980 and 1985.[1] The U.S.-based firms, both merchant and

---

[1] Presentation of data on the semiconductor industry is difficult. Serious problems of definition arise, including the distinctions between merchant and captive producers, as

captive producers, accounted for 58 percent of world semiconductor production in 1985, a decrease from 66 percent in 1980. The U.S. share of world IC production also fell from 74 percent to 62 percent. The share of Japan-based firms has risen from 22 to 33 percent for all semiconductor production and from 19 to 30 percent for ICs.[2] The shares of Western European firms and firms in the rest of the world were essentially unchanged, although several South Korean firms are aggressively investing to achieve entry into the production of advanced ICs. The share of captives in total U.S. production of ICs varies somewhat from year to year and was 33 percent in 1985. As shown in Table 11.1, the United States and Japan are also the two major consumers of semiconductors, accounting for about three-quarters of world consumption in 1985.

Japanese firms have captured substantial shares in the world markets for a number of IC products, especially dynamic random access memories (DRAMs). They captured about 40 percent of the world merchant market for 16K DRAMs in the late 1970s, about 60 percent of the market for 64K DRAMs in the early 1980s, and about 90 percent for 256K DRAMs in the mid-1980s.

Technology and business behavior

Business behavior in the semiconductor industry is strongly influenced by its technology. Two aspects of this relationship are of major importance to the subsequent discussion of trade frictions in the industry. These two are the implications of learning economies for pricing and the implications of rising IC complexity for investment requirements, learning, and interactions with systems producers.

Learning economies and pricing: The production process for semiconductors, especially for ICs, is considered one of the most complex and

---

well as the issues of determining the national identity of production by multinational firms and of currency translation. U.S. government sources are not particularly useful, so that estimates by private organizations must be cited. The source of data shown in Table 11.1, the Integrated Circuit Engineering Corporation, categorizes three firms as U.S. based although they are owned by European parents (Signetics by Philips, Fairchild by Schlumberger, and Interdesign by Ferranti) and one firm as European based although its corporate headquarters are in the United States (ITT). This is standard practice, but it may be noted that reclassification of these firms according to the base of their parent headquarters would alter the shares cited in this paragraph. For instance, reclassification would lower the U.S. share and raise the European share of world IC production in 1985 by 4 percentage points.

[2] Further discussion of the rise of Japanese firms can be found in Pugel, Kimura, and Hawkins (1984).

Table 11.1. *Semiconductor production and consumption in millions of dollars*

Region and product	Production[a] 1980	1985	Consumption[b] (1985)
United States[c]	11,135	16,135	14,285
IC	9,055	13,975	12,075
Merchant	6,360	9,300	7,400
Captive	2,695	4,675	4,675
Discrete[d]	2,080	2,160	2,210
Japan	3,680[e]	9,350	8,000
IC	2,290[e]	6,800	5,800
Discrete	1,390	2,550	2,200
Western Europe	1,620	2,550	4,950
IC	710	1,375	3,675
Discrete	910	1,175	1,275
Rest of world[f]	320	650	1,450
IC	130	400	1,000
Discrete	190	250	450
Total	16,755[e]	28,685	28,685
IC	12,185[e]	22,550	22,550
Discrete	4,570[g]	6,135	6,135

[a]According to the home base of the producing firm, as categorized by the Integrated Circuit Engineering Corporation. Several U.S. firms owned by European firms are considered U.S. based.
[b]Production by U.S.-based captives is allocated to U.S. consumption, including $460 million of captive discrete production-consumption.
[c]Includes Canada.
[d]Includes both merchant and captive production and consumption.
[e]Japan IC production for 1980 uses revised data presented in Integrated Circuit Engineering Corporation (1986), Figure 1-9, and all totals are adjusted accordingly.
[f]Excluding the Soviet Union and Eastern Europe.
[g]Revised data presented in Integrated Circuit Engineering Corporation (1986), Figure 1-9, show a total of $4,460 million. No attempt is made to incorporate this small revision because no regional detail is presented for the revision.
Sources: Adapted from Integrated Circuit Engineering Corporation (1981) and Integrated Circuit Engineering Corporation (1986), Figures 1-3, 1-9, and 1-11.

exacting high-volume processes in all industry. Regardless of how carefully the process is performed, some of the chips prove to be defective. The ratio of usable chips to the total possible is called the yield. The yield achieved depends on many factors, but substantial learning economies (or experience effects) appear to exist. A general rule used in the industry is that cumulative unit cost falls by about 30 percent as cumulative output doubles.

Pricing in the industry is affected on the one hand by the transient monopoly power that an innovative firm creates for itself and on the other hand by the economics of learning economies. In an industry subject to learning economies, there is an incentive to price below current average cost because incremental or marginal cost is often below average cost and because additional sales made now will contribute to the achievement of additional learning economies.[3] Although current profit will be lower, and possibly negative, future cost will be lower and profit higher. This pricing strategy is called forward pricing or penetration pricing.

Complexity: The complexity of IC design – the scale of integration – has risen dramatically since the invention of ICs in about 1960. The number of active elements on the most advanced chips has approximately doubled every year. The most advanced ICs widely produced for commercial sale in 1986 are called very large scale ICs (VLSI), and ultra-large scale ICs, those with the equivalent of one million or more active elements, are beginning to appear for commercial sale.

Rising complexity has several implications for business behavior. One implication is the increasing cost and difficulty of designing and producing the most advanced ICs.

Research and development (R&D) expenses can exceed $100 million for the design of an advanced microprocessor and its accompanying software. In response to the rising costs of innovation, semiconductor firms are becoming more aggressive in achieving the returns to innovation. Licensing and cross-licensing are increasingly used, and many such agreements exist between U.S. and Japanese firms. The cost and risk of innovation also increasingly are being shared through technology agreements and joint ventures between semiconductor producers, often those from different countries.

The capital investment necessary to establish a production facility for advanced ICs is also rising and by 1986 appears to be $100 million or more.[4] In addition to the rising financial investment, production of increasingly complex ICs is increasingly challenging. Learning must occur with respect to the refinement of generic production processes to achieve adequate yields with smaller feature sizes, as well as with respect to the production of specific devices. It is believed that learning

---

[3] See Spence (1981).

[4] Discussion of rising capital requirements can be found in Organization for Economic Cooperation and Development (1985) and Semiconductor Industry Association (1983).

about a more advanced production process is best achieved using mass production of standard chips, especially such memory chips as DRAMs, static random access memories (SRAMs), and erasable-programmable read-only memories (EPROMs).

A second implication of rising complexity involves the relationship between the semiconductor producer and the systems firm that is the consumer of semiconductors. Rising complexity allows a systems product to consist of a small number of ICs, so that the IC designs essentially determine the characteristics and performance of the systems product. Better coordination between IC design and systems design is needed, and it can be achieved in several ways. One is through backward integration by systems producers in order to control and guard the IC designs that differentiate their products. Another is the improvement of technical interactions between merchant semiconductor suppliers and their customers. Close relationships between the merchant and the customer are often strengthened by formal technology development contracts or minority equity investments.

Recent trade and related actions

For over a decade up to 1985, increasing liberalization characterized U.S. and Japanese policies toward international trade (and foreign direct investment) in the semiconductor industry. While the U.S. and Japanese governments periodically held talks on semiconductor issues, no formal trade actions had ever been initiated against Japanese firms or the Japanese government. As shown in Table 11.2, several events early in 1985 suggested that the year would see further liberalization of trade in semiconductors. In February the market-oriented, sector-selective (MOSS) talks between the U.S. and Japanese governments began for the electronics industries, including semiconductors. MOSS talks, which were also pursued for three other sectors in 1985, were designed to resolve many sectoral trade issues, including some mundane or technical, at one time and in one forum, through orderly but firm negotiations. In addition, on April 1 the United States and Japan simultaneously eliminated their tariffs of 4.2 percent on semiconductor imports.

However, in late 1984 the semiconductor industry entered the worst recession in its history. U.S. concern about Japanese competition in the United States and other countries had been rising as Japanese firms increased their shares of these markets, and such concern became severe as prices of commodity products plunged in the face of declining demand. Clear indications of rising frictions surfaced in May,

Table 11.2. *Trade and related actions (1985–86)*[a]

Month and year	Action
February 1985	Market-oriented, sector-selective (MOSS) talks for the electronics industries begin between the U.S. government and the Japanese government.
	Intel files suit against NEC, charging copyright infringement of microprocessor microcode.
April 1985	The United States and Japan simultaneously eliminate tariffs on imports of semiconductors.
May 1985	The Japanese government enacts the Act Concerning the Circuit Layout of Semiconductor Integrated Circuits.
June 1985	The U.S. government extends the right to obtain protection for IC designs under the 1984 Semiconductor Chip Protection Act to Japanese semiconductor firms.
	The Semiconductor Industry Association (SIA) files a petition asking the U.S. government to investigate unfair trade practices under Section 301 of the 1974 Trade Act, alleging Japanese practices to deny U.S. firms access to the Japanese market and Japanese practices conducive to dumping in the U.S. market.
	Micron Technology files suit against seven Japanese firms, alleging dumping of 64K DRAMs in the U.S. market.
August 1985	The U.S. International Trade Commission (USITC) issues a preliminary finding that imports of 64K DRAMs from Japan are injuring U.S. producers.
	The Office of the United States Trade Representative accepts the SIA petition and begins a Section 301 investigation of unfair trade practices by Japan.
	Simultaneously, all semiconductor issues involved in the Section 301 investigation are removed from the MOSS talks. The U.S. government and the Japanese government begin separate talks on the issues raised in the Section 301 investigation.
September 1985	Intel, National Semiconductor, and Advanced Micro Devices file suit against eight Japanese firms, alleging dumping of EPROMs in the U.S. market.
	Micron Technology files a $300 million antitrust suit against seven Japanese companies, alleging an attempt to monopolize the market for DRAMs.
November 1985	The USITC issues a preliminary finding that imports of EPROMs from Japan are injuring U.S. producers.

Table 11.2. *(cont.)*

Month and year	Action
December 1985	The U.S. Department of Commerce (DOC) issues a preliminary finding that Japanese firms are dumping 64K DRAMs in the U.S. market and sets preliminary dumping margins.
	The U.S. government files suit against Japanese producers of 256K DRAMs, alleging dumping in the U.S. market.
January 1986	The Act Concerning the Circuit Layout of Semiconductor Integrated Circuits is implemented, with registration of circuit designs administered by the Industrial Property Cooperation Center, a private organization.
	Texas Instruments (TI) files suit against eight Japanese firms and one Korean firm, alleging infringement of ten patents used in the design and manufacturing of DRAMs.
	The USITC issues a preliminary finding that imports of 256K DRAMs from Japan are injuring U.S. producers.
February 1986	TI files a complaint with the USITC charging eight Japanese firms and one Korean firm with unfair trade practices because of the infringement of patents for DRAMs.
March 1986	The DOC issues a preliminary finding that Japanese firms are dumping EPROMs in the U.S. market and sets preliminary dumping margins.
	The DOC issues a preliminary finding that Japanese firms are dumping 256K DRAMs in the U.S. market and sets preliminary dumping margins.
	NEC files suit against TI alleging infringement of patents used in the production of DRAMs.
April 1986	The DOC issues a final ruling affirming that Japanese firms are dumping 64K DRAMs and sets final dumping margins.
	Toshiba files suit against TI alleging infringement of patents used in the production of DRAMs.
May 1986	The USITC issues a final ruling affirming that imports of 64K DRAMs are injuring U.S. producers. The collection of anti-dumping duties begins.
	The U.S. government and the Japanese government reach agreement on the broad outline of a settlement of the Section 301 investigation.
July 1986	The U.S. government and the Japanese government reach a detailed agreement on semiconductor trade, under which the U.S. government suspends the Section 301 investigation, the EPROM dumping investigation, and the 256K DRAM dumping investigation.

*This table reflects developments through the end of July 1986.

when the U.S. government suggested to the Japanese government that it advise its firms to restrain the levels of their semiconductor capital investment. Some U.S. semiconductor firms also began to suggest that the United States should institute temporary quotas on the import of certain ICs.

In June the trade association of U.S. semiconductor producers presented a petition to the U.S. government alleging unfair trade practices, and a U.S. firm filed a dumping suit. The trade frictions turned into formal trade actions against Japanese firms and the Japanese government. This section of the chapter describes the major trade and related actions that occurred in 1985 and the first half of 1986, focusing on the three areas of dumping suits, protection of proprietary intangible assets, and unfair trade practices. Each discussion includes an analysis of some of the economic issues raised with respect to the application of each type of action to the industry.

Dumping suits

Three dumping suits were filed in 1985 against Japanese firms exporting ICs. As shown in Table 11.2, these suits involved 64K DRAMs, EPROMs, and 256K DRAMs. Dumping is defined in U.S. law as selling imports at a price in the U.S. market below fair market value. Fair market value is defined as the price charged in the home country or third country export markets, or constructed value, the latter equal to the fully allocated average cost of production plus a profit margin.

Each suit follows a standard procedure prescribed by law. After a petition is filed alleging dumping and injury to domestic industry due to this dumping, the U.S. International Trade Commission (USITC) investigates the claim of injury, and the U.S. Department of Commerce (DOC) simultaneously examines the existence and extent of dumping. Each issues both a preliminary finding and a final determination. The preliminary findings are intended largely to eliminate frivolous suits.

The anti-dumping law specifies that the comparison between the U.S. price of the import and the foreign price is the preferred method to determine the existence of dumping. However, if the U.S. price is below the foreign cost of production (which is essentially constructed value excluding the profit margin), comparison with constructed value is required.

The DOC prefers to obtain cost data directly from the foreign firm. Constructed value equals materials, labor, and other fabrication costs plus general selling, administrative, and related costs (which must equal at least 10 percent of the first set of costs) plus a profit margin (which must equal at least 8 percent of the first two sets of costs) plus packing and related distribution costs. If the DOC cannot obtain such data from the foreign company, it uses the best available data.

If the preliminary finding of the USITC affirms injury and the DOC issues a preliminary finding that dumping exists, a bond equal in value to the preliminary dumping margin – the percentage by which fair market value exceeds the U.S. price – must be posted for all imports brought into the United States between the dates of the preliminary finding and the final determination of the margin.

If the DOC is using constructed value based on data submitted by the foreign firm, DOC accountants and related experts examine the data submitted and discuss the data with the firm before the final determination is issued. Their goal is to verify the data and to make reasonable adjustments to bring the data in line with the U.S. definitions of constructed value. Adjustments are necessary especially in the allocation of overheads needed to calculate fully allocated average cost.

If both final determinations rule that injury and dumping exist, duties equal to the dumping margins found in the DOC's final determination are collected on all subsequent imports from the foreign firm. In addition, anti-dumping duties are collected on the imports that occurred after the preliminary findings were issued, up to the amount of the bonds posted, with a refund of any excess of the amount of bonds posted over the amount due under the final ruling of dumping margins.

The DOC must review the dumping ruling at least once per year. The foreign firm may request a review, based on recent data, at any time after the final determinations. The review could reduce or eliminate the duties if it finds that the margins of dumping have been reduced or eliminated.

The three dumping suits: On June 26, 1985, Micron Technology filed a petition against seven Japanese companies charging dumping of 64K DRAMs at a margin of 94 percent.[5] This was the first dumping suit ever filed against imports of Japanese ICs, although possible dumping by Japanese firms had been discussed in 1978 and 1981–2.

In a related action, in September Micron filed a $300 million private antitrust suit charging that these Japanese firms were attempting to monopolize the market for DRAMs through a "predatory invasion and seizure of the United States market," after which the Japanese firms would raise prices.

[5] "Micron Files Petition Against Japanese Firms," *Wall Street Journal*, June 28, 1985.

On September 30, 1985, Intel, National Semiconductor, and Advanced Micro Devices (AMD), three of the ten largest producers of EPROMs in the world, filed suit against eight Japanese firms charging dumping of these ICs in the U.S. market at margins over 50 percent.[6] Two major U.S. producers of EPROMs, Texas Instruments (TI) and Motorola, did not join in the petition. Both produce EPROMs in Japan and presumably export some back to the United States.

A major piece of evidence related to this suit was a memo sent from the Hitachi U.S. office instructing its U.S. salesmen and distributors to underbid its U.S. competitors (and Fujitsu) by 10 percent and continue to do so until an order was won. The memo guaranteed a profit margin to the sellers. Although Hitachi admitted that the memo was sent, it stated that the memo was not authorized and did not reflect company policy. It subsequently circulated an official memo disavowing the first memo.

On December 6, 1985, the U.S. government filed suit against Japanese producers of 256K DRAMs, charging dumping in the U.S. market. This suit was only the second time ever that the government filed a dumping suit itself, without waiting for U.S. producers to file a petition. At the time of the filing there were only two U.S. firms, TI and Micron, producing 256K DRAMs for merchant sale, and TI based much of its production in Japan. The government also suggested that the suit applied to the next generations of DRAMs, the 1M and 4M.

In all three suits, the petitioner alleged dumping based on sales at prices less than constructed value, and the Japanese firms denied any sales at less than fair market value. In all three the USITC issued a preliminary finding of injury and the DOC issued a preliminary finding that dumping existed. The preliminary dumping margins varied across the Japanese firms included in each case, with a low of 9 percent and a high of 94 percent for 64K DRAMs, a low of 22 percent and a high of 188 percent for EPROMs, and a low of 20 percent and a high of 109 percent for 256K DRAMs.[7] In the 256K DRAM case, the DOC also accepted that the dumping margins applied to the imports of 1M DRAMs because a small amount of market sales of these new ICs existed, but the DOC dropped 4M DRAMs from the finding because no commercial sales existed.

[6] "Three U.S. Firms File Trade Complaint Against Japan Semiconductor Makers," *Wall Street Journal*, October 1, 1985.
[7] "Agency Finds Japanese Are Dumping Certain Semiconductors on U.S. Markets," *Wall Street Journal*, December 4, 1985; "Japanese 'Dumping' Some Microchips in U.S., Commerce Department Rules," *Wall Street Journal*, March 12, 1986; "Japan Is 'Dumping' Second Major Type of Microchip in the U.S., Agency Rules," *Wall Street Journal*, March 14, 1985.

In the 64K DRAM case, the DOC issued a positive final determination of dumping in April 1986, and the USITC issued a positive final determination of injury in May 1986. Thus, in May the U.S. government began to collect anti-dumping duties varying from 12 to 35 percent on imports of 64K DRAMs from the various Japanese firms.[8] In July the other two suits were suspended before any final determinations were issued, as part of the negotiated final settlement of the unfair trade practices case.

On the application of the anti-dumping law to the semiconductor industry: The application of the anti-dumping law to the semiconductor industry brings up well-known questions concerning this law. In addition, because of specific conditions in the industry, the application also raises issues that are less often considered.

As is well known, the application of the anti-dumping law does not take into account customer interests in the United States. Rather, the definition of injury refers solely to the domestic producing industry. Consumers presumably benefit from low-priced imports, regardless of whether the price is above, below, or equal to prices or average production costs in other countries. Two of the dumping cases involve DRAMs, a product with application in a large number of systems products and especially intensive use in computer products. If these suits succeed in raising the U.S. prices of DRAMs to levels that at least equal average foreign production costs but are above the prices of these ICs in foreign markets, the international cost competitiveness of systems products, perhaps especially computer products, produced in the United States and incorporating these ICs will decline. The logic of effective protection cannot be ignored.

A major economic issue with respect to the application of the anti-dumping law is the standard of fair market value based on fully allocated average cost plus a set profit margin. This standard brings up issues of the measurement of such a cost and of the model of price determination that it implies.

Measuring the fully allocated average cost is a challenging task for an employee fully familiar with a company's accounting system and methods of production, marketing, and other functions. It is substantially more difficult for an outsider. The DOC experts must make allocations of overheads and modifications to the data supplied by the foreign firms. There are no apparent biases in this procedure, but

---

[8] "Hurdle Is Cleared in Move to Penalize Japanese Chip Makers for 'Dumping,' " *Wall Street Journal,* April 25, 1986.

differences of opinion nonetheless can easily arise. The allocation of overheads is important for ICs because direct manufacturing costs account on average for only about half of a product's total cost[9] and because a number of products are often produced in the same factory using substantial amounts of common equipment.

In addition, a rather special problem in determining fully allocated cost arises in the semiconductor industry. The average cost of production depends crucially on the yield achieved in the fabrication process. This yield varies not only because of unexpected events but also because of learning economies. Although there is some indication that for products such as DRAMs the yields may rise rather quickly to reasonably high levels and then perhaps continue to rise more slowly thereafter, it is still likely that yield and therefore average cost will vary over time.

In measuring average cost for IC products, the DOC typically examines a recent 6-month period for which company data are available. The DOC is willing to listen to company suggestions of unusual conditions or events. Trends may also be examined using several years of data, if they are available. Nonetheless, current yields and average costs can be substantially different from those shown in the historical record. The variation across firms in dumping margins found in the final ruling in the 64K DRAM case is rather large, and it may reflect shortcomings in the method of measuring cost rather than true differences in cost levels.

Furthermore, the model of price determination implied by the dumping law seems inappropriate to the semiconductor industry. When a U.S. producer bases its pricing on the economics of the learning curve, it is called penetration pricing. It is not clear that U.S. law should call it dumping when its Japanese competitors do so. Indeed, forward pricing may be crucial to latecomers into the production of a specific IC because they start with higher cost given their lack of production experience. Pricing below average cost will probably be necessary to gain sufficient sales to eventually achieve lower unit costs.

The price determination model implied by the dumping law seems best suited to oligopoly pricing based on long-run average cost and subject to slow responsiveness to changes in demand, perhaps in order to minimize the likelihood of a breakdown in the tacit consensus to limit price competition. In contrast, pricing in the semiconductor industry is flexible and responsive to changes in cost and demand conditions. The longer run declines in cost resulting from learning econo-

---

[9] Cost estimates are presented in Integrated Circuit Engineering Corporation (1986), Figure 2-4.

mies, and the incentive to price in anticipation of the economies, has created a downward trend in prices for many ICs. The short life for each IC also makes the achievement of any consensus to limit price competition unlikely, as do the moderate levels of seller concentration in the industry, the continued entry of new firms, and the mobility across semiconductor product areas by established firms. In short, the technological and structural conditions in the industry favor substantial price competition. Pricing is also responsive to short-run changes in demand conditions. As demand rises faster than expected, capacity utilization rises and eventually approaches its short-run limit. As short-run marginal costs rise above what they otherwise would have been, prices decline less quickly or start to rise. On the other hand, if demand declines unexpectedly, prices are cut, perhaps to levels of marginal cost that are below average cost. The application of the dumping law to such an industry may reduce its contribution to national efficiency and welfare by forcing a reduction in its price flexibility. It seems unlikely that the U.S. economy would be better served by a semiconductor industry exhibiting sluggish price changes and insensitivity to changes in market conditions.

Perhaps the broadest issue in the application of the anti-dumping law is the conflict between the comparatively slow progress of due process under the law and the rather rapid and sometimes unexpected changes in conditions in the industry. Final rulings in mid-1986 were or would have been based largely on data from the first half of 1985. By mid-1986 the 64K DRAM market was in the declining phase of its life cycle, a phase usually characterized by shrinking but profitable sales for those firms that continue to produce, as other firms exit from the product to focus resources on newer products. The 256K DRAM market was expanding, as it moved into its growth phase, and as general demand recovered from the industry recession levels of 1985. Among other changes, prices were naturally firming as orders increased and capacity utilization rose. Learning economies lowered costs by raising yields. Soon after the final determinations, the Japanese firms probably could request a review that would reverse the finding of dumping, or at least lower the margins. Of course, the Japanese firms had it in their own interest to consciously raise their prices so that this review would be decided in their favor, but market forces were also pushing in the same direction. In an industry as fast changing as semiconductors, the anti-dumping law, with its emphasis on set procedures and investigation, cannot be applied quickly enough. It is probably at least partly for this reason that the U.S. government suggested that the findings in the 256K DRAM suit should be applicable to future DRAM generations. However, neither the economic or legal aspects of this proposition appear to be defensible, even if the prevention of dumping is accepted as necessary.

Protection of proprietary intangible assets

Firm-specific intangible assets are a major determinant of competitive performance in the semiconductor industry. These assets are generated by R&D activities and by the process of adjustments that result in learning economies. The assets are typically divided into product technology and process technology. Product technology refers to product design and the know-how that is required to modify or enhance such design. Process technology refers to know-how necessary to successfully manufacture semiconductors of a particular design and the know-how that is required to modify or enhance such processes.

A key issue for a semiconductor firm is the appropriability of the returns to the technology that it creates – its ability to earn returns on its investments in R&D and other technology activities. Appropriability of process technology is considered to be reasonably good, as learning economies are largely product and factory specific. Nonetheless, more basic process technology may be less appropriable because much is embodied in production machines that are marketed and because employees can change firms and carry the know-how of the process technology with them. Product technology is considered to be less appropriable because reverse engineering can be used to replicate the design at a modest cost.

U.S. firms have taken varying approaches to the protection of proprietary intangible assets. Some have filed for patents on new technology that was patentable, while others have relied more on the advantages of being the first to apply the technology and on the fact that the useful life of the technology (before it is replaced by a further advance) is relatively short, often only a few years. Much technology, such as product design, was not patentable, and the law provided only uncertain protection to such assets. Occasionally, a firm would sue its former employees for carrying technology to their new firms, but mobility of highly skilled people remains a characteristic of the industry.

The increasing investment necessary to create new designs or build new production facilities has led to an increasing concern in the industry about protecting intangible assets. In addition, U.S. firms perceive that foreign competitors, especially Japanese firms, have been able to obtain U.S. technology at a low cost and thus have an advantage in the subsequent competition in the product market. Furthermore, the Japanese firms are not part of the implicit bargain that seems to favor a liberal environment because the process technology at which they excel can be largely protected and because their employees are not mobile.

Two recent trends in the area of protection of proprietary intangible assets continued in 1985 and 1986. The first is a more aggressive use of existing laws, such as the patent and copyright laws, to enhance appropriability by penalizing infringement. The second is the enactment of new laws to create new forms of protection for technology that previously was not well protected.

Infringement suits: As part of a pattern that has emerged in recent years, two major suits were filed in 1985 and 1986 by U.S. firms alleging infringement by Japanese firms.

On February 26, 1985, Intel filed suit against NEC, charging that NEC's V20 and V30 microprocessors illegally reproduce the microcode of Intel's 8086 and 8088 microprocessors, thereby infringing on copyright protection for this microcode. NEC maintains that their microcode is of original design, although very similar to that of Intel. In addition, NEC disputes the claim that the microcode is covered by copyright protection. The microcode is the set of computer instructions that are etched onto the silicon of the chip. Intel claims that the microcode is the equivalent of a computer program and thus eligible for copyright protection, while NEC maintains that the microcode is part of the hardware and thus a physical product ineligible for copyright protection.

In January 1986 TI filed a set of suits against one Korean and eight Japanese firms, alleging infringements of ten patents used in the design and production of DRAMs. TI had cross-licensing agreements with the Japanese firms covering these patents, but the agreements expired in December 1984. In the discussions to renew these agreements, TI demanded substantially better terms, and the Japanese firms resisted. TI apparently believed that it provided this technology too cheaply, perhaps because the Japanese firms have gained such a large share of the DRAM markets in comparison with TI's share. The discussions about the renewal of the cross-licenses broke off in September 1985.

In February 1986 TI filed a Section 337 case against these firms with the USITC, charging unfair trade practices – the firms' use of TI technology without a license gives them an unfair cost advantage over TI because they have a lower cost of technology. If the USITC rules in favor of TI, the most likely remedy would be the exclusion from the U.S. market of the devices using the infringed technology. In March the USITC began its investigation, which could take up to one year.

In March NEC filed a suit in Tokyo against TI, alleging infringement of NEC patents related to DRAMS of 256K or larger. NEC sought a court order to stop manufacturing and sale of these products by TI in Japan. In April Toshiba filed a similar suit against TI covering manufacturing and sale in the United States.

As with dumping suits, a major disadvantage of infringement suits is their slow progress toward resolution. In fact, most suits of this nature are settled out of court. The suits are used to force the allegedly infringing firm to bargain toward a solution more quickly. The TI suit and the countersuits by NEC and Toshiba also appear to be aimed at influencing the terms of the new cross-licensing arrangements to be negotiated.

New laws to protect circuit design: Until recently, the circuit design of ICs had at best vague protection as proprietary property under the law. As hardware, the design could not receive copyright protection, but most designs were not sufficiently novel to be eligible for patent protection.

As the cost of creating new circuit designs has risen, semiconductor firms have become increasingly concerned about their ability to earn returns to pay back the investment in design. U.S. semiconductor firms approached the U.S. government requesting that the problem be examined and a solution found. Expert studies concluded that neither copyright protection nor patent protection is appropriate. Copyright protection lasts for much longer than is necessary or desirable, while obtaining patent protection, with its investigation into originality, takes too long to achieve and would use up too much of the scarce resources of the patent office.

In October 1984 the Semiconductor Chip Protection Act was enacted in the United States, and it was implemented in November. The act creates a new category of copyright protection for the masks containing the circuit design that are used in manufacturing the chip. The protection lasts for 10 years. The design must be registered, but there is no investigation into originality. The act provides that as a foreign country enacts similar legal protection available to U.S. firms, firms from that country can become eligible for protection under the U.S. law.

The U.S. government requested the Japanese government to enact a similar law. In May 1985 Japan enacted the Act Concerning the Circuit Layout of Semiconductor Integrated Circuits, which provides protection very similar to the U.S. law. In June the U.S. government provisionally granted Japanese semiconductor firms the right to obtain protection for their IC designs under the U.S. law, with permanent right contingent upon acceptable implementation of the Japanese law. This implementation occurred in January 1986. Several other countries, including the Netherlands, Canada, Australia, and the United Kingdom, are enacting similar laws.

Assessment: As is well known, the economics of the efficiency and welfare implications of patent and similar protection to intangible assets involve complicated trade-offs between static and dynamic effects. Perhaps all that should be expected is a reasonable legal solution. By this criterion the new laws are probably a major success. Dynamic efficiency is promoted through clear protection, although the usual issue of "how different is different?" will inevitably arise. The harm to static efficiency is reduced somewhat by the relatively short length of the protection. If the laws promote the orderly negotiation of licensing agreements for second sourcing, as they are intended to do, some amount of static inefficiency may also be avoided. For instance, the laws may promote the transfer of design technology to firms that have the lowest cost production technology.

In relation to U.S.–Japanese competition in semiconductors and the frictions that arise with respect to this competition, the laws address an issue of unfairness often raised by U.S. firms. Japanese firms excel in many areas of process technology, whereas U.S. firms excel in many areas of product design. Japanese technological strengths benefit from patent protection as well as the protection of secrecy and the firm-specific nature of incremental process innovation related to learning economies. U.S. firms had less certain protection for their technological strengths, but this protection has been strengthened by the new laws. U.S. firms can invest in product design with a higher probability of earning adequate returns on their investments, returns that can accrue as a larger share of the market for the specific IC product, revenues from licenses for second sourcing, or other benefits from licensing (or similar arrangements such as joint ventures), including access to competitors' technology.

Unfair trade practices

On June 14, 1985, the Semiconductor Industry Association (SIA) filed a petition with the Office of the United States Trade Representative (USTR) requesting relief from unfair trade practices and policies of the Japanese government under Section 301 of the 1974 Trade Act. The SIA petition raised two major charges. First, U.S. semiconductor firms face barriers to access to the Japanese market because of the previous use of severe restrictions against imports and foreign direct investment (FDI), with the effects of the restrictions still being felt,[10] and because the Japanese government previously created and now tolerates a market structure conducive to collusion and reciprocal dealing arrangements that effectively exclude outsiders. Second, Japanese firms engage in capacity expansion races that lead to periodic overcapacity and the dumping of semiconductors in the U.S. market.

Section 301 gives the U.S. government broad powers to investigate allegations of unfair trade practices by foreign governments and to seek remedies. Section 301 was amended in 1984 to include restrictions on market access as a basis for complaint and action. After a preliminary examination to determine that a case existed, the USTR in August accepted the petition and began its investigation. The main issues in the case can be summarized by contrasting the positions of the SIA and the Electronic Industries Association of Japan (EIAJ).[11]

Market access: Most of the discussion of issues in the case focused on market access. The SIA offered as a major piece of evidence the fact that the U.S. share of the Japanese semiconductor market has changed little since the early 1970s, remaining at a level close to 10 percent. This share is much lower than the U.S. share of any other national or regional market. The SIA contrasted this with the growing Japanese share of the U.S. merchant market, which by 1984 was 17 percent.

The SIA argued that the low, relatively unchanging U.S. share of the Japanese market is strong evidence of barriers to market access. Although strict restrictions on imports of semiconductors, especially ICs, and on FDI into Japan by foreign semiconductor firms had been liberalized by 1976, the SIA charged that a variety of countermeasures were used by the Japanese government to offset the effects of the liberalizations. These countermeasures included the encouragement of specialization in devices produced by each Japanese firm, pressure to buy Japanese products, the encouragement of cooperative R&D, production, and sales, and the provision of subsidies to programs with clear commercial objectives. The government also restricted entry of Japanese firms into semiconductor production and concentrated its subsidies among certain firms in order to create a concentrated Japanese semiconductor industry in which the large producers are also the major consumers of semiconductors in Japan. Device specialization

[10] For estimates of the effects, see Finan and Amundsen (1985).
[11] Positions as stated in the various filings – Semiconductor Industry Association (1985a–c) and Electronic Industries Association of Japan (1985a,b).

then leads these large producer-consumers to trade extensively among themselves, with the power to exercise a "buy Japanese" bias and otherwise to control access to the market by outsiders.

The SIA charged that the Japanese government tolerates this market structure and these trading practices rather than investigating possible violations of the anti-monopoly act or similar laws. At the least, the Japanese government thus condones the barriers to access, and the recent elevation plans for the semiconductor industry drawn up by the Ministry of International Trade and Industry (MITI) suggest continued guidance and promotion of coordination and cooperation. In addition, the Japanese government has failed to adhere to an agreement it reached in 1983 with the U.S. government to encourage semiconductor users to enlarge the opportunities for U.S.-based suppliers and to develop long-term purchasing relationships with them in order to increase U.S. participation in the Japanese market.[12] The U.S. market share did not rise.

The EIAJ responded to these charges by the SIA. The EIAJ maintained that the announcement of the countermeasures was necessary to gain political support for the liberalizations. However, MITI never enforced concerted action by the semiconductor industry – there was no division of production and no effective prohibition on entry. The only effective measures were the government support of and subsidies to cooperative R&D projects. These measures represent a domestic subsidy of a type permitted by the General Agreement on Tariffs and Trade (GATT) and related international norms of acceptable policies pursued by national governments. Indeed, the U.S. government provides much larger funding to various U.S. semiconductor R&D projects. Although these U.S. projects are directly concerned with creating technology for defense applications, they generate clear commercial spinoffs.

The EIAJ argued further that there is nothing illegal under Japanese law about the structure or conduct of the Japanese industry. U.S. firms presented no specific evidence of illegality, and there is no evidence of collusive behavior in product sales or purchasing and no evidence of reciprocal trading agreements. The cooperative R&D undertaken is not anti-competitive. The extent of device specialization by Japanese firms is not that high, and in any case the device specialization that does exist is the result of competition and the need to achieve low-cost

---

[12] Recommendation II.3 (1) of "Recommendations of the U.S.–Japan Work Group on High Technology Industries: Semiconductors," November 2, 1983, endorsed by the Japanese Government with intent to implement. See Semiconductor Industry Association (1985a).

production. Intense competition is also evident in pricing by Japanese firms.

The EIAJ presented a number of reasons for the failure of U.S.-based firms to capture a larger share of the Japanese market (and also disputed the estimates of market shares offered by the SIA). Although some U.S.-based firms, such as TI and Motorola, are successful in Japan, Japanese buyers generally perceive U.S. devices to be of lower quality and reliability than Japanese devices and U.S. firms to be less reliable in delivery, less helpful with technical services, and less willing to redesign products and renegotiate agreements. The lack of manufacturing facilities in Japan, a decade after liberalization, can explain much of the difference between U.S. firm shares in Japan and those in Europe.

In short, the EIAJ maintained that the Japanese market is open. The trading practices that the SIA complained about represent the private purchasing decisions of each Japanese semiconductor user. Legal private practices are not actionable under Section 301. In accordance with the 1983 agreement, the Japanese government did encourage Japanese firms to purchase semiconductors from U.S.-based firms, but Japanese decision makers remained unconvinced of the attractiveness of most U.S. products.

Injury and relief: The SIA concluded its case with its statement of injury to the interests of the United States and its requests for relief. The SIA claimed that the denial of access to the Japanese market has diminished the revenues of U.S. firms and thus reduced internal funds available for R&D and other investments. Furthermore, a lower level of sales limits the ability to achieve learning economies and scale economies. In pursuing capacity expansion races, the Japanese firms use their domestic sales base to reduce their risk. Overcapacity and periodic dumping result. The Japanese share of the U.S. market rises. U.S. firms are driven out of the production of certain products, especially DRAMs and EPROMs, that are generally used to master new levels of process technology. The decline of U.S. merchant producers of semiconductors will force U.S. systems producers to rely on Japanese semiconductor producers who also compete with them in the systems markets. The Japanese firms will use this position to capture the markets for the systems products, to the detriment of the U.S. national economic interest and U.S. national defense and security.

In response, the EIAJ noted that, in addition to its previous denials of the SIA evidence and logic, the "injury" to the U.S. industry was largely the result of the decline of U.S. demand for semiconductors, especially the sudden decline in demand by computer makers. Furthermore, Japanese firms face the same risks that U.S. firms do in making investment decisions. Japanese firms differ in that they use longer time horizons to justify investments, but investment decisions by Japanese firms are responsive to short-run shifts in market demand. Japanese investment spending levels were revised downward substantially during 1985.

The SIA requested that the U.S. government under Section 301 seek five elements of relief from the Japanese government. First, the Japanese government should effectively encourage its semiconductor users to purchase from U.S. firms, as it already agreed to do in 1983. The SIA suggested that the effectiveness be judged solely by results – long-term commitments to purchase U.S. semiconductors and a dramatic rise in the U.S. share of the Japanese market. Second, the SIA requested the implementation of a system for gathering data on Japanese costs of production and monitoring the prices of Japanese exports to swiftly act against any Japanese dumping of semiconductors in the U.S. market. Third, the SIA called for improvements in the collection of data on worldwide semiconductor trade and sales. Fourth, the SIA called for long-term reforms to assure that the semiconductor market in Japan responds freely to market forces. Finally, the SIA sought an investigation by the Japan Fair Trade Commission into possible violations of the anti-monopoly act by Japanese semiconductor firms. If the Japanese government did not cooperate with these requests for relief, the SIA suggested that the U.S. government take various unilateral actions to secure relief.

The EIAJ did not seem to oppose the third and fifth points, and there was little discussion by either side of the meaning of the fourth point. The EIAJ sharply disputed the suitability of the first two requests. The EIAJ suggested that the first request is equivalent to demanding a guaranteed share of the Japanese market rather than equal market opportunities. It would also violate the most-favored-nation principle of the GATT. The second request would be largely unworkable in an industry subject to such rapid changes in technology and costs. In any case, it is equivalent to minimum price controls, with the obvious economic disadvantages of such controls. Finally, the EIAJ noted that the logical relief for the SIA to seek was a radical restructuring of the Japanese industry because this structure was the heart of the SIA complaint. Such a restructuring would include severing of vertical integration, prohibitions or limits on interfirm trading, and an end to Japanese government encouragement to and support of cooperative R&D projects. Such relief could not be justified, especially given the continued existence and perhaps growing importance of these practices in the United States.

Government-to-government negotiations: As required by law, the USTR pursued negotiations with the Japanese government regarding the issues raised by the investigation. These issues were removed from the MOSS talks on the electronics industries in August, although certain other issues regarding the semiconductor industry continued in the MOSS forum.

In the talks related to the Section 301 case the Japanese government proposed to implement a floor price mechanism as a simple and workable way to prevent low-priced exports to the United States. The U.S. government rejected this proposal because it would not actually monitor or prevent dumping by high-cost firms and because it might assure excessive profits to low-cost firms.

The U.S. government instead supported the adoption of a cost-price-monitoring system applied company by company and requested that the prices of all sales by Japanese semiconductor producers be monitored in relation to cost levels. This request for monitoring of all Japanese prices seemed to be related to several objectives – to prevent U.S. users from buying low-priced Japanese devices outside of the United States in order to circumvent the protection against dumping by the Japanese firms themselves, to prevent foreign users from gaining a competitive advantage against U.S. user firms, and to enhance the price competitiveness of U.S. devices in the Japanese and other foreign markets.

In relation to market access, the U.S. government proposed that the Japanese government commit itself to assuring that U.S. semiconductor firms achieve a substantial and growing share of the Japanese market. The U.S. government stated that vague assurances of improved access for U.S. firms would not be adequate. The Japanese government at first suggested that it would only commit itself to efforts resulting in a gradual increase in the U.S. market share.

In May 1986 the U.S. and Japanese governments reached a broad agreement to resolve the complaints raised in the Section 301 case. Continuing negotiations produced a detailed agreement in July 1986. Under the agreement the Japanese government is committed to take actions to encourage Japanese semiconductor consumers to purchase more foreign semiconductors, thereby expanding the U.S. share of the Japanese market by the early 1990s. Although no share is specified, an unwritten target of about 20 percent appears to exist. The agreement also establishes a cost-price-monitoring system for Japanese semiconductor exports; and, as noted previously, the U.S. government suspended investigation of the two dumping cases that had not been completed.

Comments on market shares and market access: Many of the points of contention in the Section 301 cases are typical of those that arise in trade disputes and antitrust cases. For instance, injury can be attributed to declines in market demand or to unfair foreign competition, and certain behavior can be viewed as competitive or anti-competitive.

Before the analysis of the broad issues of national interest, efficiency, and welfare presented in the next section of the chapter, three specific issues raised in the case deserve comment. These are the measurement of market shares, the reasons for the low U.S. share of the Japanese market, and the 1983 agreement by the Japanese government to encourage purchase of U.S. semiconductors.

The measurement of market shares was a contentious issue in the case. The SIA presented estimates for all semiconductors and excluded captive production-consumption from its estimates of the Japanese share of the U.S. market. The EIAJ argued that discrete devices and ICs represent two different markets and that the focus should be on ICs. The EIAJ also argued that captive production-consumption should be included in calculating the size of the market because it does represent consumption that could be sourced from outside merchant firms.

It is not clear that ICs and discrete devices should be combined into a single market, but it seems reasonable that discrete devices should not be totally ignored. At the same time, the SIA claim that captive production should be ignored is not supportable. The SIA claimed that U.S. captive production is almost completely of nonstandard devices, but IBM and AT&T appear to produce large quantities of standard devices such as memory chips. Furthermore, the fact that captive production is of nonstandard devices does not remove it from the available market. Many merchant firms produce nonstandard devices, and they presumably could supply the demands of the captive consumers. The SIA included merchant production and sale of nonstandard devices in its market estimates – there is no logical reason not to include captive production-consumption as well.

Table 11.3 presents estimates of the shares of U.S.-based firms and Japanese-based firms in each other's market. The U.S. shares of Japanese consumption are shown for all semiconductors and for ICs only. The U.S. shares in ICs are higher than those for all semiconductors, but both have changed little over the last decade and are lower than U.S. shares in other foreign markets. U.S. captive production-con-

Table 11.3. *U.S. and Japanese shares of each other's consumption (1976–83)*[a]

Year	U.S. share of Japanese consumption		Japanese share of U.S. IC consumption
	All semiconductors	ICs	
1976	11	16	1
1978	10	16	2
1980	12	16	5
1983	11	15	7

[a]U.S. consumption includes captive consumption.
Sources: Adapted from Semiconductor Industry Association (1983), Figure V, and Integrated Circuit Engineering Corporation (1984), p. 10.

sumption is included in calculating the Japanese shares of the U.S. market. These shares are shown for ICs only, but the shares for all semiconductors would be similar. The Japanese share of U.S. IC consumption has been rising since the late 1970s. It remains lower than the U.S. share of Japanese IC consumption, but if current trends continue, it could equal or exceed this U.S. share by the late 1980s.

There seems to be substantial agreement among observers about the competitive strengths and weaknesses of U.S. firms in the Japanese market. The sales of U.S. firms are largely limited to those devices for which they have a clear advantage in product technology and to other devices at times when Japanese producers find themselves short of supply capacity. The Japanese operations of U.S. firms report profitable sales but do not capture a large share of the total market. The lack of competitiveness of other products–those in direct competition with comparable Japanese designs–is largely related to perceptions by the purchasing decision makers in Japanese user firms that U.S. devices are of lower quality and reliability. These decision makers may also view U.S. firms as being less reliable in delivery (especially those firms without a production base in Japan) and as providing less helpful customer service (especially those firms without a technical service center in Japan). Although U.S. firms dispute the reality of the differences, the perceptions persist. Furthermore, one or more Japanese semiconductor firms are usually willing to invest in any product area that promises a reasonable market size, so that U.S. firms' advantages in product technology are continually under attack.

Within this setting the Japanese government accepted an agreement in 1983 to encourage Japanese semiconductor users to enlarge the sales opportunities for U.S. producers. Although no formal trade actions were in process, the U.S. government did make presentations to the Japanese government regarding the lack of openness of the Japanese market. The Japanese government presumably did not accept these arguments but probably believed that some agreement would be useful to reduce U.S. pressures.

The Japanese government encouraged more importing of U.S. semiconductors in early 1984 with some success, and this effort was aided by the tight supply conditions in Japan for many devices at that time. Subsequently, the forcefulness of its encouragement apparently declined. Thus, the single strongest legal argument in the SIA petition seems to be the shortcomings in the efforts of the Japanese government with respect to this agreement.

The failure of the U.S. market share to expand also appears to be related to the structure of decision making in the large Japanese electronics companies. The efforts of the Japanese government and the knowledge of U.S. pressure apparently have convinced many top managers of these companies of the wisdom of expanding purchases of U.S. semiconductors, at least as a short- or medium-term tactic to deflect U.S. criticism. But purchasing decisions are made by systems engineers and similar people many levels below. These decision makers are resistant to expanding their purchases of U.S. semiconductors, given their rather negative perceptions of U.S. product and service quality and their direct responsibility for assuring the effective functioning of their systems products.

The U.S. national economic interest

Although the legal issue of injury in an anti-dumping suit is injury to domestic producers, injury in a Section 301 case regarding unfair trade practices is broader. Indeed, in its petition, the SIA discussed injury to the U.S. national interest. More generally, the design of government policies toward an industry requires analysis of the national economic interest.

This section presents an examination of the relationship of the semiconductor industry to the U.S. national economic and related interests in order to determine the basis for government policies affecting the industry. Traditional economic considerations are discussed first, and the possible application of the new theory of strategic trade policy next. The section then presents an extension of the strategic approach to the indirect effects on user industries.

Traditional economic considerations

Based on traditional economic (and related) considerations, at least four arguments in favor of government protection for or assistance to the U.S. semiconductor industry can be identified and evaluated. These involve the terms of trade, employment, national defense and security, and the generation of external economies. Each might justify some form of government intervention, although the best form is often not intervention in international trade patterns. Each consideration is evaluated individually – interrelationships are of some importance, but they are not discussed explicitly.

Effects on the terms of trade: It is well-known that improvement in the terms of trade – the relationship between the prices a country receives for its exports and the prices it pays for its imports – is a valid economic argument for a country to intervene in its international trade pattern, subject to a number of caveats. Two concerns have been raised regarding the semiconductor industry and the U.S. terms of trade. First, foreign government assistance to foreign semiconductor firms promotes an import-competing industry in the foreign country, and this drives down the price (and volume) of U.S. semiconductor exports. Second, if foreign firms succeed in driving U.S. firms from the industry, these foreign firms may then have monopoly power and raise their prices in the United States.

The first argument suggests the need for U.S. retaliation. Yet, the optimal retaliation is not obvious. Assistance to the U.S. industry would serve to further depress U.S. export prices and the U.S. terms of trade. The optimal response by the United States seems to be efforts to prevent the foreign government from promoting their industry in the first place. Furthermore, substantial intra-industry trade occurs in semiconductors, so that prices of U.S. imports of certain devices are also likely to fall as a result of the foreign government assistance to its semiconductor firms. The net impact on the U.S. terms of trade may be relatively small.

The second argument, concerning the development of foreign monopoly power, suffers from its speculative nature when applied to the semiconductor industry. Japanese firms, although cooperating in limited areas such as specific research projects, otherwise appear to compete vigorously for sales. It seems very unlikely that they could reach some kind of agreement to restrain their competition even if they came to dominate the world industry as a group. Furthermore, several policy responses would be available if this did occur, including the application of U.S. antitrust laws or tariffs to reduce the extent of foreign monopoly profit (and perhaps encourage U.S. firms to reenter the industry).[13] Indeed, it is not clear that sufficiently high barriers to entry exist to permit the Japanese firms to jointly monopolize the industry.

Employment: A political argument often heard in favor of protection for or assistance to a domestic industry is the need to preserve domestic jobs. It is not necessary to develop the economics of this argument, which are far from supporting it. Rather, the need to preserve employment in the U.S. semiconductor industry simply has not been raised to any noticeable extent.

In 1983 U.S. merchant firms employed 128,000 people within the United States, a relatively small number of workers. About 46 percent of these workers are executive, professional, and clerical.[14] Most of these employees are skilled and suffer little from the frictions of finding a new position that afflict less skilled production workers. Given that a number of the production workers are also skilled and relatively mobile, much less than half of the U.S. workforce is in danger of suffering from pronounced difficulties if forced to change employers. Furthermore, U.S. merchant firms employed 142,000 workers outside of the United States in 1983. About 92 percent of this foreign employment is engaged in production and assembly.[15] In short, the international division of labor has proceeded within U.S. companies – protecting domestic employment is not much of an issue in the industry.

National defense and security: Electronics are increasingly and by now overwhelmingly important to weapons systems and other elements of the U.S. national defense and security. Semiconductors are of great importance because they form the basis for these electronics systems. The discussion of the relationship to national defense thus raises many of the same issues raised subsequently in the section that discusses the extension of the theory of strategic trade policy to user industries. It may also be noted that national defense does not require that an entire merchant industry be protected or supported. Several U.S. merchant

---

[13] Brander and Spencer (1981).
[14] Finan and Amundsen (1985), Table 2-14.
[15] Finan and Amundsen (1985), Table 2-14.

firms focus on supplying the defense market, and these presumably already have substantial protection from foreign competition because of procurement practices. Furthermore, U.S. captive producers have been major contributors to defense research and production.

The generation of external economies: Industries that create and apply new technology usually generate external economies because the firms investing in the new technology cannot appropriate its full social value. As discussed previously, the semiconductor industry does suffer from some lack of appropriability, although recent changes in laws and company policies to more carefully safeguard proprietary technology may be raising the appropriability achieved by the industry. In the face of such externalities, a case exists for some form of government intervention. It is usually presumed that too little investment in new technology occurs without government assistance. However, there is at least a theoretical case that too much investment can occur if firms compete aggressively to achieve innovations and the subsequent economic returns that arise even with partial appropriability. It is certainly possible that the semiconductor industry falls into this latter category, but this possibility is not explored further here.

A major issue for a national government in designing an intervention in response to technology externalities is the extent to which the national economy benefits from the externalities. It is very likely that these externalities do not stop at the national border.[16] In the semiconductor industry this is clearly true for externalities associated with device design and application. Process technology may also be subject to some international externalities because of international trade in equipment and some disembodied transmission of process ideas and know-how. To the extent that externalities are international, the incentive for the domestic government to provide assistance to the industry is reduced, and the hope that foreign governments will provide such assistance is raised. Thus, in the semiconductor industry some level of U.S. government support for investment in new technologies is probably appropriate (subject to the caveat mentioned above), and the United States should encourage the Japanese government to do the same. Indeed, a case can be made that the United States gains much benefit from the willingness of the Japanese government and firms to invest in semiconductor technology and production that create international external economies but earn barely a normal private return to such investments.

[16] Krugman (1984b).

Strategic trade policy

A new theory of trade policy focusing on dynamic competition in oligopolistic industries has recently been developed by a number of economists.[17] This theory emphasizes that the use of trade and other government policies can benefit a country by altering the outcome of international competition in imperfectly competitive industries in favor of its producing firms.

The approach usually considers an industry in which fixed costs create scale economies, with either constant or declining marginal production costs. Scale economies (or other, often unspecified entry barriers) limit the number of competing firms to a small number (often only one from each country). The limited number of firms results in the achievement of excess returns, with the oligopolistic equilibrium often determined using a Nash–Cournot solution.[18] The governments are able to commit themselves to policies that then have an impact on the decisions of firms about whether to enter into production, how much to produce, and what levels of other activities, especially R&D, to undertake.

The national economic interest is usually measured by the rather standard criterion of welfare as the sum of domestic consumer surplus plus the excess returns to domestic producers (which may accrue not only as profit but also as higher wages for labor, and so forth) plus any government tax revenues or minus any government subsidy payments. The government may use different policies, including protection against imports, subsidies to domestic production, subsidies to exports, or subsidies to R&D.

In such a setting it is possible for a national government to use its policies not only to assist its own firms but also to send a signal to foreign firms that deters them from engaging in R&D or production (or at least that lowers the foreign levels of these buisness activities). Because domestic firms then gain a larger share of the world market and a larger share of the global excess returns, the country may enjoy an increase in its welfare. In the general case it is not assured that the nation benefits because changes in consumer surplus and government revenues must also be considered. Furthermore, protection of the domestic market may allow domestic firms to dominate foreign markets

---

[17] Spencer and Brander (1983), Dixit (1984), Brander and Spencer (1984, 1985), and Dixit and Kyle (1985) are among the important articles. In many ways this theory represents an extension of the traditional concept of the infant industry. It can also be viewed as an application of the theory of the second-best policy in the presence of a distortion, in this case imperfect competition.

[18] Some conclusions are sensitive to the choice of solution concept. See Eaton and Grossman (1986).

as well, if marginal costs decline with output achieved. In this case import protection becomes export promotion.[19]

The theory has a strong resemblance to common descriptions of Japanese government policy toward its semiconductor industry. The government used its policies strategically to assist its industry to become internationally competitive, through temporary protection against foreign competition and subsidies to R&D. Japanese firms are now gaining global market share from U.S. (and European) firms. The logic of the model suggests that retaliation by the U.S. government may be in the U.S. national interest, by assisting its firms to gain back market share and excess returns.

The model is subject to a number of theoretical qualifications, but the most direct reason to doubt its applicability as a guide to U.S. policy toward the semiconductor industry is an empirical one. Although Japanese government policy may have assisted Japanese firms to gain market share, the excess returns do not appear to exist.[20] Although it is not possible to measure economic profits exactly, the history of the semiconductor industry indicates that firms have earned an accounting rate of return that is about average for all manufacturing, on average over the business cycle.[21] Labor earnings appear to be at their competitive levels, although some highly skilled employees do have high earnings. In short, excess returns appear to be transitory and modest at best. The lack of excess returns is not surprising. The moderate level of seller concentration, moderate level of entry barriers, and rapid changes in technology already mentioned make restraints on competition difficult to achieve. In addition, a number of governments are assisting their industries, enhancing the return-depressing competition. It is possible that in the future the Japanese companies may find a way to restrain competition and achieve excess returns, but this does not appear to be likely.

In the absence of excess returns, the theory does not support the use of government policy. The government can assist its industry to gain market share, but only with a loss of national welfare due to the economic distortions (inefficiencies) accompanying such a policy.

An extension and modification: dynamic competition in user industries

Although the theory of strategic trade policy may not apply directly, the case presented by the SIA suggests an extension and modification

---

[19] Krugman (1984a).
[20] Kreinin (1985) also discusses this point. For a theoretical analysis of one possible situation, see Dixit (1985).
[21] See the analysis in Webbink (1977).

that may be relevant. The extension focuses on the importance of semiconductors in determining the functioning of many electronics systems products and thus in determining the international competitiveness of these products. The suggestion is that U.S. producers of systems products will suffer declines in global market share following the decline of the U.S. semiconductor industry. Although the decline of the semiconductor industry itself may not directly harm U.S. economic welfare, the decline of the systems products industries would. Excess returns are likely to be earned in some of these industries because of a smaller number of global competitors and higher entry barriers. IBM might be an example of a company that enhances U.S. national welfare by earning excess returns from foreign markets. In addition, these industries generate externalities through new technology, and a number of them are important to national defense efforts.

The model begins with the premise that Japanese competition in semiconductors either drives U.S. semiconductor firms out of the business or forces them to abandon commodity products such as DRAMs, SRAMs, EPROMs, and other memory products. In the latter case, the U.S. firms instead focus on the production of application-specific ICs (ASICs) or similar products exploiting U.S. strengths in design but produced in short runs without much ability to gain either product-specific learning economies or rapid learning about new process technologies. Thus, the focused U.S. firms lose the scope economies of using commodity products to gain new capabilities in process technology.

If the U.S. semiconductor firms have been driven completely from the market, then U.S. systems producers depend on Japanese semiconductor firms not only for commodity semiconductors but also for the ASICs and similar products that give the U.S. systems their distinctive character and international competitiveness. The Japanese semiconductor suppliers are also integrated into the production of systems products. They have some incentive not to supply U.S. systems firms with the most advanced semiconductor technology, or at least to delay delivery, in order to improve the international competitiveness of their systems divisions.[22] Indeed, this incentive is particularly strong to the extent that excess returns can be earned most easily at the systems level. In addition, the design of ASICs and similar products usually requires substantial pre-production cooperation between the systems firm and the semiconductor producer. Japanese semiconductor firms

---

[22] South Korean consumer electronics firms claim that Japanese firms use such practices with respect to ICs for consumer goods applications. The need to overcome this problem appears to be one reason the Korean firms are investing to integrate backward into advanced IC production.

also have the incentive to pass on knowledge of new U.S. technology gained in this way to their systems divisions. Thus, the U.S. firm could suffer a reduction in the appropriability of its new technology.

If U.S. firms remain in the semiconductor business but focus on ASICs and similar products, the U.S. systems firms can avoid many of the disadvantages and risks of dealing with the Japanese firms. However, this will only delay their demises. Eventually U.S. firms cannot supply these semiconductor products at as low a production cost or as high a level of complexity as can Japanese firms because of the relative decline in U.S. capabilities in process technology.

In either case the international competitiveness of U.S. systems firms will decline. U.S. national welfare will decline because of the loss of excess returns and loss of externalities.

The model is complex, but the outcome of a decline in the competitiveness of U.S. systems firms is not implausible. Nonetheless, there are several major questions about the validity of the approach as a guide for U.S. government policy.

First, the extent to which U.S. firms will suffer cost or process disadvantages by focusing away from commodity products is not established. There is a belief that the disadvantages would be large, but a number of firms already focus on ASICs and similar products. These firms appear to compete successfully for business. Furthermore, to the extent that there are substantial scope economies to producing commodity products, these provide the incentive for U.S. firms to continue to produce these products even if a profit cannot be earned on them alone. In the presence of scope economies, what is usually called cross-subsidization is a rational competitive strategy for a profit-maximizing firm.[23] Of course, sufficiently severe Japanese competition will force U.S. firms to cease production of commodity products.

Second, U.S. systems firms have strong incentives not to completely shift their purchases of ASICs and related products to the integrated Japanese producers, for exactly the reasons stated – the dangers of relying on the Japanese firms. The major issue is then whether acceptable alternative sources of supply exist. Some U.S. semiconductor firms are likely to survive, and U.S. systems firms can support the technology and production capabilities of these U.S. producers through such contractual arrangements as minority equity investments, technology contracts, and joint ventures. These arrangements are increasingly being used as a method to correct possible infirmities in the relation-

---

[23] The existence of scope economies is another reason that the application of the anti-dumping law based on fully allocated cost is not economically appropriate.

ship between the semiconductor producer and the buyer-user. In the area of ASICs another aspect of the evolution of contractual relationships is the ability to separate actual production from the design of the IC and the generation of the photomasks used in its production. Specialization in this case may lead to low-cost, high-quality production, with IC designs more securely controlled by the semiconductor user. Other new contractual arrangements could appear if U.S. systems firms actually were to face a scenario such as that presented in the model.

U.S. systems firms also may be able to order from "safe" Japanese semiconductor firms – those without direct interest in their specific systems business but strong interest to gain semiconductor business. For producers of computers, firms such as Sony or Tokyo Sanyo might be less risky sources. In addition, other Japanese firms are potential entrants into the semiconductor industry, perhaps in joint venture with U.S. firms. Several U.S. firms produce in Japan, including TI, Motorola, and Fairchild. These firms also could represent surviving and less risky sources of semiconductor supply for U.S. systems firms.

Furthermore, a number of U.S. systems firms have become captive producers of semiconductors, largely to avoid the problems of dealing with outside suppliers that are cited in the model. The model may not apply to such captive producers as IBM, AT&T, Digital Equipment, NCR, and General Motors. Nonetheless, smaller U.S. systems firms that do not have captive production are often considered among the most innovative. Even if the model applies only to them, the U.S. national interest could be harmed.

Other considerations related to the national interest

Several other considerations are relevant to the possible application of models of strategic trade policy to the semiconductor industry. In some cases these are also related to issues that arise in the traditional analysis of trade policy.

First, the models of strategic trade policy assume that the national identity of the claimants to the excess returns are the same as the national base of the firm. The fact of multinational ownership and operation of many companies makes this identification less clear. Indeed, in the semiconductor industry several firms often considered U.S. based are in fact owned completely by foreign companies, and the growing importance of international joint ventures also complicates the identification process.

Second, the models of strategic trade policy are often presented as partial equilibrium solutions and thus may ignore important constraints imposed by the general equilibrium of the economy.[24] Any assistance to the semiconductor industry draws away some resources from their alternative uses. This may be an especially important issue for skilled people such as scientists and engineers available in limited and inelastic supply. Rather than the mutual decline posited in the extention of the strategic model discussed in the preceding section, there may rather be a trade-off between the size of the U.S. semiconductor industry and the size of related electronics industries. This raises a subtle issue of the national interest, especially if excess returns can be earned or externalities achieved in a number of these industries.

Third, the models suffer from an inability to specify types of policies and levels of their application that would be reasonably successful in optimizing (or even in raising) national welfare, based on the kinds of information and analytical capabilities available to the government.[25] This widens the scope for political pressure on such decisions and encourages the socially wasteful use of resources in rent-seeking activities.

Finally, in general, other governments have an incentive to retaliate or deploy practices simultaneously in response to use of strategic trade policy by any one government. This noncooperative solution is not jointly optimal. A cooperative government approach to the formulation of such policies is preferable. Of course, achieving such cooperation is not easy. It involves negotiation over appropriate actions and the division of benefits as well as incentives not to cheat on any agreement reached.

Conclusions

The discussion in the preceding section suggests that some national economic interest in the national production of semiconductors exists. The industry generates externalities that benefit the economy, even though these may also confer international benefits. The decline of the U.S. semiconductor industry poses a risk for U.S. systems producers. Their ability to rely on Japanese and other foreign semiconductor producers is not assured. At times the most advanced ICs may not be made available quickly, so that foreign firms can create advantages for their own systems division or local customers. In addition, interactions between U.S. systems firms and their foreign suppliers about new

---

[24] See Dixit and Grossman (1984).
[25] For additional discussion of this point, see Kreinin (1985).

design or application ideas may not be so smooth, and the risk exists that these ideas may leak out. Although it cannot be proven that the decline of the U.S. semiconductor industry will result in a decline in the competitiveness of U.S. firms producing systems products, the potential loss is large enough that the possibility must be taken seriously.

The analysis of the national interest also suggests the types of government policies toward the semiconductor industry that would enhance national economic welfare. The focus on the ultimate importance of the user industries indicates that import protection is not desirable. The benefits to the semiconductor industry would be more than offset by the harm to the systems products industries that paid higher prices and perhaps lost some access to advanced foreign semiconductor products. Indeed, although some member firms have suggested a need for some form of import protection, the SIA as a group has not requested protection.

Application of the anti-dumping law to semiconductors, especially if actions are based on foreign production cost, can easily have the same effects on user industries as outright protection. U.S. prices are raised above prices in other markets. Such an application also is inconsistent with the economics of pricing in the industry. Forward pricing is done in anticipation of cost reductions. Scope economies imply that the production of advanced ICs that allow learning about new production processes need not separately cover its costs to be profitable for the firm. Pricing in the industry is sensitive to demand variations. In addition, the application requires the difficult measurement of fully allocated cost in an industry with substantial indirect costs and substantial use of shared production equipment. Furthermore, the resolution of a dumping case moves slowly relative to the pace of change in the industry.

Two possible methods to speed up the implementation of countervailing actions against dumping have been proposed recently. First, the U.S. government suggested that the decision in the 256K DRAM suit be applied to future generations of DRAMs. It is not clear how this is possible or why it is desirable. Second, the SIA has requested the implementation of a cost-price-monitoring system for Japanese IC exports to the United States, and such a system is included in the governmental agreement resolving the Section 301 case. To the extent that it is effective, the system at times could raise U.S. prices above foreign prices and harm U.S. users of semiconductors. On the other hand, the system may prove to be rather unworkable or ineffective because of its administrative complexity or because ways are found to circumvent the price monitoring.

Access to foreign markets clearly can contribute to the health of the

U.S. semiconductor industry. Japanese government policies probably did provide assistance to the Japanese industry to develop, and protection against imports and FDI was a major part of this assistance. U.S. semiconductor firms also derived major benefits from U.S. government programs, especially the procurement of ICs in the early and mid-1960s. Such proportionately large assistance is in the past for both countries.

The SIA's assertion of current unfair trade practices by the Japanese government is supported by little evidence. While the SIA claimed that the low U.S. share of the Japanese market is evidence of unfair trade practices that are subtle and nontransparent, other explanations are at least as plausible. Japanese firms have developed upon a strong national economic base, with an abundance of skilled and educated labor and an abundance of financial capital seeking investment opportunities. The firms have been willing to invest, not only in production capacity, but also in the development of technology. Although rather low, the Japanese shares of the U.S. and other foreign markets have been rising rather quickly, an indication of the competitiveness of Japanese firms. In the absence of clear evidence of governmental barriers to market access or anti-competitive business practices, the SIA request for the achievement of a much larger share of the Japanese semiconductor market implies an attempt by the U.S. government to alter private business practices in Japan that are arguably pro-competitive, consistent with the economics of the industry, and successful in terms of the business performance of the Japanese semiconductor producers and users.

The U.S. government should insist that the Japanese government abide by its 1983 agreement to encourage purchases of U.S. semiconductors. The agreement resolving the Section 301 case affirms such encouragement, but a specific target for the U.S. share of the Japanese market also appears to be an implicit part of the agreement. The concept of using a specific market share as evidence of market access is dangerous – it creates a new form of protectionism that could easily be abused by a variety of undeserving claimants. Furthermore, administration of measures to meet the share target is likely to be difficult and any gains in market share short-lived. Once the government pressure is removed, the buying firms will return to their pursuit of self-interested decision making.

The long-term success of U.S. companies in the Japanese market depends mainly on changing the perceptions of the systems engineers and others who make purchasing decisions. This is a problem of investment in promotion if U.S. quality levels are as good as U.S. firms say they are. Additional FDI into Japan by U.S. firms is probably also desirable. Such investment can signal a commitment to the market by the U.S. firm, allow it access to production and R&D resources in Japan, provide a base for monitoring technology developments in Japan, and allow it to create competitive challenges to Japanese firms in their home base.

The types of changes in U.S. government policies toward the semiconductor industry that are most desirable are those that act in concert with the basis for national economic interest in the industry. The agreement resolving the Section 301 case falls short of this standard. Rather than a cost-price-monitoring system and a forced expansion of market share in Japan, the U.S. government instead should expand its support for the activities of U.S. semiconductor firms to create and bring to market advanced technology. These activities are the basis for externalities and the enhancement of the competitiveness of the systems industries. Such assistance previously formed the major part of the SIA program for suggested changes in government policy to benefit the industry. Policy changes should be examined in the areas of tax policy and assistance to technical, engineering, and scientific education, as well as in assistance to cooperative research for projects that are not defense related. In addition, the government should continue to be responsive to the needs of the industry in protecting intangible assets, and the industry should continue to assert its rights to prevent infringements by Japanese or other firms. For instance, if necessary, the U.S. government should consider an amendment to its copyright law or chip design law to make clear that original microcode is covered by one of these laws.

The semiconductor industry is continually evolving. The severe industry recession has focused attention on the rising competitiveness of Japanese firms. It is not possible to turn back the clock on Japanese competitiveness, and it would not be in the U.S. national interest to do so. Rather, U.S. government policy should offer positive assistance to U.S. firms to enhance their ability to compete. In this way the U.S. economy can continue to benefit from the high levels of technological progress in the semiconductor industry.

References

Brander, James A., and Barbara J. Spencer, "Tariffs and the Extraction of Foreign Monopoly Rents Under Potential Entry," *Canadian Journal of Economics,* Vol. 14, August 1981, pp. 371–89.

"Tariff Protection and Imperfect Competition," in Henryk Kierzkowski, ed., *Monopolistic Competition and International Trade*. Oxford: Oxford University Press, 1984.

"Export Subsidies and International Market Share Rivalry," *Journal of International Economics*, Vol. 18, February 1985, pp. 83–100.

Dixit, Avinash, "International Trade Policy for Oligopolistic Industries," *Economic Journal*, Vol. 94, Supplement, 1984, pp. 1–16.

"The Cutting Edge of International Technological Competition," manuscript, October 1985.

Dixit, Avinash K., and Gene M. Grossman, "Targeted Export Promotion with Several Oligopolistic Industries," manuscript, 1984.

Dixit, Avinash K., and Albert S. Kyle, "The Use of Protection and Subsidies for Entry Promotion and Deterrence," *American Economic Review*, Vol. 75, March 1985, pp. 139–52.

Eaton, Jonathan, and Gene M. Grossman, "Optimal Trade and Industrial Policy Under Oligopoly," *Quarterly Journal of Economics*, Vol. C1, May 1986, pp. 383–406.

Electronic Industries Association of Japan, "Brief of the Electronic Industries Association of Japan," Before the Office of the United States Trade Representative, August 26, 1985a.

"Reply Brief of the Electronic Industries Association of Japan," Before the Office of the United States Trade Representative, November 8, 1985b.

Finan, William F., and Chris B. Amundsen, *An Analysis of the Effects of Targeting on the Competitiveness of the U.S. Semiconductor Industry*. Study Prepared for the Office of the United States Special Trade Representative, the Department of Commerce and the Department of Labor. Washington, D.C.: Quick Finan and Associates, May 1985.

Integrated Circuit Engineering Corporation, *Status 1981*. Scottsdale, AZ: Integrated Circuit Engineering Corporation, 1981.

Status 1984. Scottsdale, AZ: Integrated Circuit Engineering Corporation, 1984.

Status 1986. Scottsdale, AZ: Integrated Circuit Engineering Corporation, 1986.

Kreinen, Mordechai E., "United States Trade and Possible Restrictions in High-Technology Products," *Journal of Policy Modeling*, Vol. 7, Spring 1985, pp. 69–105.

Krugman, Paul R., "Import Protection as Export Promotion: International Competition in the Presence of Oligopoly and Economies of Scale," in Henryk Kierzkowski, ed., *Monopolistic Competition and International Trade*. Oxford: Oxford University Press, 1984a.

"The U.S. Response to Foreign Industrial Targeting," *Brookings Papers on Economic Activity*, 1984b, pp. 77–121.

Organization for Economic Cooperation and Development, *The Semiconductor Industry: Trade Related Issues*. Paris: OECD, 1985.

Pugel, Thomas A., Yui Kimura, and Robert G. Hawkins, "Semiconductors and Computers: Emerging International Competitive Battlegrounds in the

Asia-Pacific Region," in Richard W. Moxon, Thomas W. Roehl, and J. F. Truitt, eds., *International Business Strategies in the Asia-Pacific Region.* Greenwich, CT: JAI Press, 1984.

Semiconductor Industry Association, *The Effects of Government Targeting on World Semiconductor Competition: A Case History of Japanese Industrial Strategy, and Its Costs For America.* Cupertino, CA: Semiconductor Industry Association, 1983.

"Petition of the Semiconductor Industry Association," Before the Office of the United States Trade Representative, June 14, 1985a.

"Brief of the Semiconductor Industry Association," Before the Office of the United States Trade Representative, October 22, 1985b.

"Reply Brief of the Semiconductor Industry Association," Before the Office of the United States Trade Representative, November 15, 1985c.

Spence, Michael, "The Learning Curve and Competition," *Bell Journal of Economics,* Vol. 12, Spring 1981, pp. 49–70.

Spencer, Barbara J., and James A. Brander, "International R&D Rivalry and Industrial Strategy," *Review of Economic Studies,* Vol. 50, October 1983, pp. 707–22.

Webbink, Douglas W., *The Semiconductor Industry: A Survey of Structure, Conduct, and Performance.* Washington, DC: Federal Trade Commission, 1977.

Discussion

RAMA V. RAMACHANDRAN

Thomas A. Pugel has undertaken an informative survey of the semiconductor industry that highlights the changing roles of U.S. and Japanese firms in both global and regional markets, the factual and conceptual basis of recent allegations of dumping and unfair trade practices and, finally, the legal actions taken by the U.S. government and individual firms to restrain those practices. Pugel points out that the criteria used by the Department of Commerce for determining the extent of dumping or other collusive behavior are both vague and logically inadequate. He then reviews the traditional and more recent arguments for restraint of international competition and examines the legal remedies now adopted or under consideration in the light of these theories. Again he finds that it is not in the national interest to turn back the performances of Japanese industries. As another economist who shares Pugel's belief in the paradigm of neoclassical analysis, I am in deep sympathy with most of these arguments.

Having so quickly agreed with Pugel, I began to have second thoughts. If rational people can all agree on the deficiencies of the arguments for trade restraint, why is there such trade friction? David Tarr, in Chapter 10 of this volume, argued that the U.S. economy transfers to foreign steel producers a quota rent of more than $500 million. Yet, as Lawrence White noted in his comments to the same chapter, such transfers have not generated any political protests. In contrast, the allegation that the Japanese semiconductor firms do not incorporate a proper amount of depreciation for their capital equipment in determining "fully allocated average cost" is a major source of trade friction, even though the evidence is far from conclusive. Are we to conclude that the sources of trade friction are political stupidity and opportunism or is it possible that the economists are unable to incorporate relevant factors into their neoclassical models? One has also to remember that there is a third player in this competitive game, Europe. Any general theory that seeks to explain the divergences in international competitiveness must also give us an understanding of the waxing and waning of European industry.

Reflecting on these issues, it occurred to me that some tentative answers could be obtained by using a dichotomy suggested by Alfred Marshall (1920: 266) in another context. If all the alleged sources of trade friction can be classified into those that are internal to the firm and those that are external to it, then I could venture a hypothesis that friction generated by factors internal to the firm should be resolved locally while those generated by external sources are at least sympathetic candidates for governmental action.

As far as the semiconductor industry is concerned, I have noticed four types of arguments being proposed as to why the performances of the Japanese semiconductor firms are contributing to trade friction: (a) the destabilizing influence of the product cycle and its influence on relative market performance; (b) marketing policies; (c) relative advantages in product and process innovation; and (d) the cost of capital. I will discuss each argument below.

Product cycles: Product cycles affect the semiconductor firms in two different ways. First, the successive generations of semiconductor devices are characterized by increasing miniaturization and integration. Thus, we saw the progression from 1K to 256K in the last 15 years and 1M and 4M chips are in various stages of development. Because of this accelerated pace of product innovation, each of the products has a dominant role in the market for a very short period of time. The history of this cascading technological revolution is well documented and analyzed [see e.g., Tilton (1971) and Braun and MacDonald (1982)]. But the fortunes of the semiconductor industry is as much affected by another type of product cycle that I characterize as user–product cycles.

Periodically, we find the expansion of one user industry creating a dramatic increase for semiconductors. This, in turn, puts competitive pressure on the firms to increase their capacity. When the product demand slackens, as happened with video games, CB radios, home computers, and lately personal computers, the semiconductor industry is left with excess capacity. Certain firms may find themselves in financial difficulty just when their competitors are posed for the introduction of the next generation of semiconductors. If it so happens that the firms in trouble are all in one country, then the national industry is devastated by the product cycle. Malebra (1985: 111) traces the decline of the European industry to a particular set of events: Texas Instruments' victory in the bipolar logic war and the semiconductor recession of 1970–1. The Japanese industry's ability to meet the growing demand in the recovery from the 1974–5 recession is claimed to have paved the way for their subsequent prominence. The industry had another recession in 1981–2 and is currently recovering from the worst recession in its history, which began in 1984. How high would the new plateau be and how long will it be there? If the recovery leads to a long period of prosperity, much of the trade friction would disappear, as U.S. firms would lose interest in running to Washington for relief. If the recovery is short lived, then the current disputes may be nothing more than the gathering storm before the main confrontation.

Although the cyclical nature of the industry could be a proximate cause for trade friction, it cannot be the ultimate cause. If the cycles affect industries in every nation in a similar manner, then none of them enjoys a special advantage. The cyclicity argument must be supplemented by analysis as to why they have asymmetric influences on national industries and whether such asymmetry is created by factors internal to the firm or external to it.

Marketing: An argument is made that Japanese firms have enjoyed a superiority in judging consumer preferences and so avoided the mistakes made by U.S. firms in such consumer products as CB radios and watches. But it is rather strange to ask for trade restraint on this ground. Marketing abilities are strictly internal to the firm, and government should not be in the business of penalizing the competent. So far as I know, no one has attributed the problems of New Coke to Japanese malfeasance. Maybe what this calls for is a reexamination of marketing education and research in American universities.

Innovation: Another alleged source of trade friction is differing abilities of the two national industries in product and process innovations. The U.S. industry is widely believed to excel in the former whereas the Japanese superiority in the latter is generally conceded. This argument has many facets that must be clearly separated.

First, a clear distinction should be made between major innovations and subsequent incremental improvements. Second, the degree of appropriability of the innovation should be clearly identified. Can the new entrants leapfrog ahead of the original innovator or does the advantage of early production experience act as a barrier to entry? Finally, should the differences in research abilities be attributed to national traits, government policies toward industries, national educational systems, or firm-specific attributes?

After the discovery of the transistor in Bell Labs, a number of small merchant firms arose in the U.S. semiconductor industry. The availability of venture capital in this country and the procurement policies of the military are said to have aided this (Okimoto, Sugano, and Weinstein 1984). But the established electronics firms in Europe were able to catch up with American firms in the transistor phase; thus, Philips was able to produce a workable transistor within a week of the Bell announcement (Malebra 1985: 55). In contrast, the Japanese industry had a 2-year lag. It may also be noted that, according to National Science Foundation data (1976: 86), Japan has the worst record for innovation by small firms. There was no suggestion that this market structure was contributing to trade friction.

But by the 1980s the American industry was forced to share technological leadership with the Japanese while the European industry had fallen behind. The Japanese firms were helped by four factors in their efforts to attain this status. First, the government did provide protection in the early stages. Second, they seem to have avoided the disadvantages of a late entrant by exploiting new areas in consumer electronics. In this they must have benefited from their alleged marketing superiority as discussed earlier and by their lower production costs. Third, Japanese entry into computer applications was evidently helped by the indirect subsidies received through Japanese Computer Company, Ltd. (JECC). Finally, claims have been made that the Japanese industry did make incremental innovations like the development of MOS technology (Okimoto et al. 1984: 15–16).

Unlike their European counterparts, the Japanese firms seem to have succeeded in working around whatever technological barriers the American industry was able to build through their early technological leadership. There is also no clear indication that the industry in either country benefited from substantially higher governmental assistance than its competitor.

In a recent article on national science policy, Bloch (1986: 597) distinguishes among three reasons for Federal support of R&D: (i) basic research has intellectual value independent of its economic payoff; (ii) the government needs new technology for specific missions such as defense; and (iii) basic research in science and engineering contributes to the economic well-being of the society. He recognizes that support of research that would enhance the knowledge base available to industry has lagged since 1970s. He argues that the establishment of engineering research centers and basic science and technology centers through awards from the National Science Foundation would reverse this trend. Whatever the future effects of this policy may be, the recent breakthroughs achieved by Texas Instruments (*Business Week* 1986) indicate that mourning for the demise of America's technological leadership in the semiconductor industry may be premature.

Two other factors are frequently mentioned as having contributed to Japan's emergence as an international force in this industry. The lack of employment security and the corresponding disdain for loyalty to one's firm has created difficulties in creating long-term strategies in U.S. industry. It has also been argued that the best U.S. engineers prefer research jobs while their Japanese counterparts prefer production jobs and this in turn contributes to the Japanese superiority in production. Even if these arguments are true, they arise from incentives created by the firms and should be rectified by changing them.

Finally, the ability of Japanese industry to close the technology gap with the United States while the European industry kept falling behind is attributed to its national character. The industriousness, the emphasis on group discipline as compared to individualism in the work place, the emphasis on science education, and other cultural characteristics of Japanese society are mentioned in this context. In making comparisons between nations, economists face a basic dilemma. Microeconomic theory emphasizes the universality of our qualitative responses to economic incentives while assiduously holding that the exact quantitative response is strictly individualistic. Thus, it is difficult to distinguish between the typical American or Japanese decision maker. However, two independent observations can be made on cultural bias and the understanding and use of innovation. Pratten (1976: 51) notes cases where U.K. subsidiaries of multi-national firms were less successful than their continental divisions in new ventures and product development. Assuming some commonality in the organizational and incentive structure within the multinational firm, this difference could be an indicator of cultural influence. In a totally different context, Goldberg (1984) traced the differences in national response to the then revolutionary scientific ideas of Einstein. The disturbing thought that arises is whether we economists are ignoring the importance of national traits because of our inability to model it.

Two arguments are offered as to why Japanese firms may be selling below cost abroad. The first argument is based on the strategy of sliding down the learning curve by generating a high volume of sales even at a loss. Profits are made later when costs have come down and new entrants are not in a position to compete. Pugel refers to the paper by Spence (1981) suggesting that the pricing policy described above is indeed the optimal inter-temporal one. Pugel then argues that, since such a strategy is optimal both for Japanese and U.S. firms, selling below cost during the early stages should not be considered dumping. I would like to add a caveat that theoretical results in this area are extremely sensitive to assumptions. Under an alternative set of assumptions, Lasher (1979) argues that prices should always be set so as to elicit positive profits, though the rate of profits would vary along the learning curve.

This argument is carried one step further when it is suggested that Japanese firms may be selling 64K or 256K chips below cost to establish market dominance in the next stage of the product cycle. Before treating this alleged pricing policy as an unfair trade practice, one must consider two countervailing considerations. First, if penetration pricing is accepted as admissible for a specific product (as a means for exploiting the learning curve), should inter-product penetration pricing be illegal if firms find it economically advantageous? Second, the argument that leadership in one product cycle would facilitate it in the next cycle is a proposition of doubtful validity.

The other argument is that MITI's policies are creating an overproduction of priority items and this in turn leads to an export torrent. The line of reasoning implies that MITI is forcing the Japanese firms off their supply curve, in which case they should be the ones complaining about it. In the discussion of Chapter 5, it was pointed out that some Japanese firms did feel the pressure from MITI in an earlier period.

Cost of Capital: The last argument is that Japanese firms are enjoying a lower cost of capital for various reasons. Since this question was exhaustively reviewed by Theresa Flaherty and Hiroyuki Itami (Okimoto et al. 1984), I will confine myself to two comments. First, whatever institutional arrangements such as investment banking permit the Japanese to achieve this, they are not valid grounds for trade restraints unless it can be shown that there is a direct government subsidy. Second, the same is true of the argument that Japanese semiconductor firms enjoy the benefits of being part of a larger manufacturing firm with all the attendant benefits of access to internal and external sources of capital. The independent merchant firms in the semiconductor industry came into existence at the very same time that conglomerates were being formed in other sectors of the U.S. economy. The opportunity to become part of a larger firm was not unavailable to them. Recently, there have been some highly publicized marriages between American semiconductor firms and those in potential user industries and at least one public divorce (between United Technologies and Mostek). It is whispered that the professionals in semiconductor industries have developed a culture that is incompatible with those in traditional industries. Again these are problems that are best tackled by methods other than trade restraint.

The post-war period has many examples of economic problems that looked highly destructive in the short run and got resolved without any cataclysmic change in international economic order: the dollar shortage in the immediate post-war period, tensions created by complaints of racial and sexual discrimination, life-threatening pollution of our rivers and oceans, and the recent dollar glut all can be mentioned in this context. One may, therefore, rightfully wonder whether the Japanese–U.S. trade friction is not another problem that will self-destruct.

Yet over the longer history of human civilization, one sees the centers of economic power shifting around. The last phase began with the industrial revolution in England, which spread to geographically and culturally contiguous areas of Europe and North America. The inability of the rest of the world to absorb the new industrial technology acted as a barrier, protecting the industries in these countries. The striking achievement of post-war Japan seems to have been its ability to break this barrier and compete with Western nations in areas where they were traditionally dominant. Now other countries like Korea are following the Japanese lead in absorbing highly productive technology into a low-cost economy. Traditional international trade theory would suggest that the resulting expansion in trade would permit the Western and Asian nations to enjoy a new era of prosperity. But one is left to wonder whether the growth of the Pacific region is another orderly expansion of the international industrial economy or the prelude to one of those historic swings in economic power.

230   Discussion by R. S. Raubitschek

References

Braun, E., and S. MacDonald, *Revolution in Miniature*. Cambridge: Cambridge University Press, 1982.

Bloch, E. "Basic Research and Economic Health: The Coming Challenge," *Science*, May 2, 1986, pp. 595–99.

Business Week, "Texas Instruments: Off the Roller Coaster?" April 28, 1986, pp. 68–9.

Goldberg, S., *Understanding Relativity: Origin and Impact of a Scientific Revolution*. Boston: Brikhauser, 1984.

Lasher, W. R., "Dynamic Oligopolistic Pricing Strategies with Learning," Ph.D. Dissertation, Southern Methodist University, Dallas, 1979.

Malebra, F., *The Semiconductor Business: The Economics of Rapid Growth and Decline*. Madison: The University of Wisconsin Press, 1985.

Marshall, A., *Principles of Economics*, 8th ed. New York: Macmillan, 1920.

National Science Foundation, "Indicators of International Trends in Technological Trends," National Science Foundation, April 1976.

Okimoto, D. I., T. Sugano, and F. B. Weinstein, *Competitive Edge: The Semiconductor Industry in the U.S. and Japan*. Stanford: Stanford University Press, 1984.

Pratten, C. F., *Labor Productivity Differentials within International Companies*. Cambridge: Cambridge University Press, 1976.

Spence, M., "Learning Curve and Competition," *Bell Journal of Economics*, Spring 1981, pp. 49–70.

Tilton, J. L., *International Diffusion of Technology: The Case of Semiconductors*. Washington, DC: The Brookings Institution, 1971.

Discussion

RUTH S. RAUBITSCHEK

Introduction

Trade friction between the United States and its trading partners has increased in the last decade. Trade friction is no longer confined to mature industries such as steel and automobiles and is now present in high technology industries as well. In 1985 trade friction between the United States and Japan in semiconductors intensified, involving formal actions focused on three issues: the protection of intangible assets, dumping, and market access. Pugel's case study of U.S.–Japanese trade friction in the semiconductor industry provides a springboard for

I should like to thank Barbara J. Spencer for valuable discussions on strategic trade theory and suggestions on policy.

thinking about trade friction generic to high technology industries and policy options to deal with it.

This discussion is divided into two parts. First, sources of U.S.-Japanese trade friction in the semiconductor industry are examined. The second part is concerned with the new strategic trade theory and the insights it provides on trade friction in high technology industries.

U.S.-Japanese trade friction in the semiconductor industry

There are several reasons why U.S.-Japanese trade friction in semiconductors has increased and has become both intense and visible.

The semiconductor industry (SCI) is seen as an important industry because it is a large high technology industry and many industrialized nations such as Japan and the United States are shifting their focus from mature industries to high technology industries.

The SCI is a leading industry[1] in the sense that technological developments in semiconductors have a strong impact on many other industries. For example, technological advances in semiconductors have driven the development of other high technology industries such as computers and telecommunications and they have "dematurized"[2] and changed the nature of competition in several consumer goods industries such as consumer electronics and automobiles. The SCI is frequently believed to be a strategic industry, important to national security, national economic progress, and competitiveness.

The SCI is today in a very similar position to that of steel 40 years ago. The current ambitions of many nations to establish a domestic SCI are similar to those seen for the steel industry after the Second World War. In Japan, the Ministry of International Trade and Industry (MITI) now refers to the SCI as the *rice of industry*, a term that in the 1950s and 1960s had applied to steel (Ohmae 1984). As rice is the staple diet in Japan, the importance of SCI to Japan is underscored by this term.

There are differences in perceptions between the United States and Japan about the nature of competition in this industry and the role that governments have played in promoting competitive advantages for their home firms in the SCI. These perceptions carry over to other high technology industries.

One can roughly characterize the U.S. perceptions as follows. The

---

[1] The terms *leading* and *strategic industries* are taken from Nelson (1984).
[2] The term *dematurized* is taken from Clark (1983). The dematurity of an industry occurs when a radical innovation requires new product designs and new production processes shifting the industry from a mature and stable state to a more fluid state.

Japanese government has used and continues to use its policies strategically to create comparative advantages for certain of its high technology industries, including semiconductors, which in turn create competitive advantages for their firms. Perceptions are that the United States has not engaged for the most part in such actions, at least explicitly, or to such a large extent in recent years. U.S. perceptions are that in the past the Japanese had used trade policies with tangible restrictions such as restrictions on foreign direct investments (FDIs) and on imports. In the 1970s trade agreements were reached between the United States and Japan for the removal of many of these restrictions in certain high technology industries including semiconductors. Hence, the Japanese government has replaced these tangible policies with more subtle policies, such as the encouragement to specialize and to buy Japanese, which are less visible and much more institutional but just as effectively bar access to Japanese markets by foreign firms. The Japanese government also encourages cooperative R&D and provides subsidies for R&D programs with commercial objectives, policies that effectively lower R&D costs to Japanese firms. The net result of these governmental policies has been the creation of comparative advantages to Japanese high technology industries and competitive advantages to Japanese firms.

The unique characteristics of high technology industries[3] make it possible to use a broad range of subtle nontariff measures to protect and aid them. These measures include hindrance of market access through such measures as the encouragement of discriminatory government and private procurement practices, idiosyncratic standards and product certification procedures, selective import licensing, failure to protect intangible assets of foreign firms, and the subsidization of research and development.[4]

On the other hand, as Pugel points out, the Japanese perceptions are very different. The Japanese believe that current competition in the SCI is driven by private decision making. The U.S. perceptions are that the Japanese government "rigs the game" so that private decisions favor the Japanese firms. (In spirit this relates to the soft policies described in Chapter 5.)

The convergence of perceptions about the strategic importance of

---

[3] These unique characteristics of high technology industries include high R&D costs, the presence of intangible assets and the need to protect them, high levels of uncertainty, complexity in technology with numerous trade-offs between product characteristics and performance, many possibilities for product specifications and standards, dynamic cost structures, and dynamic technological advancements.

[4] For a more general discussion of nontariff barriers to high technology industries see Cohen et. al. (1985).

the semiconductor industry and the divergence of perceptions about the nature of the current sources of competitive advantages of firms are at the heart of the trade friction.

These new sources of trade friction are more difficult problems to resolve than tangible trade restrictions such as FDI and import restrictions for two reasons.

1. They are much more subtle and consequently less easy to detect and measure directly. Often there is not a specific regulation that one can point to and prove its existence. Hence analysts have to resort to unusual proxies such as changes in market shares in order to detect their existence.

2. They are also less easily subject to trade negotiations and to changes in the context of trade talks. This is because the Japanese believe that foreign requests for changes in these national and commercial policies involves meddling in the internal affairs of Japan. Furthermore, relief from them would involve a radical restructuring of Japanese industries. Some of those claims by the Japanese may in fact be true. Nevertheless, part of the problem is that in Japan, as in some other countries, internal development goals are achieved through a strategy that closely links industrial policies and international trade policies. Trade relief may indeed require internal institutional and structural changes.

Insights from strategic trade theory

The new strategic trade theory provides a framework in which to understand how industrial and trade policies can be used by governments to promote home firms, increase national income, and deter foreign competitors in high technology industries.

The spirit of the new strategic trade theory can be roughly summarized as follows. In an imperfectly competitive international market characterized by economic profits, government intervention can alter the outcome of international competition in favor of the home country's firms. Such intervention includes trade policies such as tariffs or industrial strategy policies like subsidization of R&D or exports. As a result of these policies, the home country's firms capture a larger share of the world market and economic profits and increase net national income, while a foreign country's industry is worse off because its firms capture a smaller share of the rents.

The seminal paper by Spencer and Brander (1983) shows how government support of imperfectly competitive high technology industries in the form of R&D or export subsidies can improve domestic net welfare by increasing the domestic market share. Krugman (1984a) shows that protection of domestic markets characterized by static or dynamic economies of scale can be used by firms to translate this privileged domestic position into an advantage in the export markets through lower marginal costs and higher market shares in the unprotected markets. As Krugman (1984b) points out, markets in which import protection policies act as export promotion are more characteristic of innovative, high technology industries than of mature industries such as automobiles and steel.

Pugel raises several criticisms concerning the new strategic trade theory that he suggests invalidate it as a guide to competition in the semiconductor industry. These criticisms are discussed in the literature (Dixit 1984; Krugman 1984b) and a few invite some brief comments.

As Pugel recognizes, although this point needs to be emphasized, the new trade theory does not advocate retaliation as the best solution. Or, to put it in the language of economic theory, the noncooperative outcome (retaliation) is welfare inferior to the jointly maximizing outcome.

Basically what these models show is that government intervention can promote domestic industries at the expense of foreign industries. Industrial strategy policies have a beggar-thy-neighbor aspect. The best remedy is to try to negotiate to get rid of these interventionist policies. However, it is the case that in the noncooperative solution, retaliation is usually optimal. The threat of retaliation, made credible by the knowledge that it is the optimal noncooperative solution, together with the understanding that the cooperative solution is superior to the noncooperative solution may well provide governments with the very incentives to try to arrive at a cooperative outcome. As Spencer and Brander (1983) predict, governments will be willing to undertake industrial strategy if no other government does but should be willing to negotiate limitations on such policies in the face of retaliation.

An imperfectly competitive market with excess profits is a critical assumption of strategic trade theory. Pugel argues that excess returns in the SCI are at best transitory and modest. The theory does not require that excess profits be present for the entire product lifecycle; it is sufficient that rents be present in some portion of it. Furthermore, in high technology products such as semiconductors, the issue of profit linkages over sequences of generations of a product must be considered. For example, Teubal (1982) observed increasing profitability across generations of a particular product class; he concluded that there are "interproject synergies" and that early generations of projects in high-technology industries can contribute to the profitability of later generations. The profitability of the SCI is an empirical question and studies are needed as to whether or not there are excess returns in that industry.[5]

Another frequent criticism of this theory that Pugel raises is that these models are partial equilibrium models that do not take into account that assistance to a particular industry can create a severe shortage of a particular factor of production, such as skilled labor, in other industries. This factor distortion is essentially a short-term problem, which markets will correct in the long run.

There are two important concerns that surround the new strategic trade theory. First, as Pugel points out, the danger exists that these models will be distorted and misused by vested interest groups to obtain protection for selfish gains, which will hurt the economy. This is a valid concern and this type of misuse should be guarded against. Second, certain types of retaliation such as tariffs and quotas can easily escalate into trade wars that can be extremely detrimental to all parties involved. This raises the question of what types of policies governments should consider pursuing.

In the semiconductor industry formal actions are proceeding on three issues: the protection of intangible assets, dumping, and market access. These actions can be viewed as aiming at a cooperative rather than a noncooperative (retaliatory protectionist) solution and are a step in the right direction.

So far, the most progress has taken place in the area of protecting intangible assets. As Pugel points out, the protection of intangible assets involves complicated trade-offs, and reasonable regulations are an appropriate solution.

Two factors appear to have slowed down progress on the second and third issues. These are that it is hard to establish the existence of dumping and blocked market access, and it is equally difficult to arrive at acceptable remedies.

Dumping is difficult to measure in a high technology industry because of the dynamic nature of costs and prices. Furthermore, the current legal process for relief is too slow to be effective given the fast pace of innovation in the industry. As discussed above, barriers to market access in high technology industries can be achieved through very subtle policies, and remedies may require internal institutional and structural changes.

[5] Of the two sources [Kreinin (1985) and Webbink (1977)] that Pugel references concerning the modest profitability of the SCI, only Webbink (1977) contains specific empirical information about the SCI. However, his data cover a very restricted time period (1970-5). Studies covering more recent data are necessary.

It is quite likely with the current political climate and the distress of the SCI that if some reasonable compromises on these issues are not forthcoming, protectionist measures will be sought. Furthermore, the issues of dumping and market access are likely to surface in other high technology industries and with other trading partners. Therefore, it is vital that some reasonable standards and proxies be established for proving their existence and that reasonable remedies for their relief be negotiated.

On a more global level, as Pugel points out, a promising policy route in high technology industries is the general support of commercial research and development. That does not mean that the U.S. government should try to choose specific winners and losers. Such decisions should be left to firms that are much better informed. Rather, such policies should be very general and designed to foster greater overall innovation by U.S. firms.

Conclusions

Pugel gives a comprehensive overview of trade friction between the United States and Japan in the SCI. He further raises the issue of how the United States should deal with it. This is an urgent question, not just because trade friction in SCI has intensified but also because the United States, as well as other industrialized nations, will face similar issues in most or all high technology industries. For example, Japan may very soon find itself in a position similar to the United States vis-à-vis Korea in semiconductors.

There are two major reasons why trade friction between the industrialized trading partners is likely to surface in other high technology industries:

1. Advanced industrialized countries and newly industrialized countries have come to believe that high technology industries – especially electronic components, but also computers, telecommunications, biotechnology, and synthetic materials – are an important engine for growth. Besides the obvious example of Japan, many other countries, such as Korea and other Pacific Basin countries as well as the European Economic Community countries, have begun to focus their attention on these industries.

2. Japan's success has led other countries to try to emulate it. One of the most salient characteristics of Japan's development strategy is the linking of industrial policy to trade policy. Thus, the likelihood is increasing that others will decide to follow similar strategies, especially in high technology industries, where attention is currently focused.

The danger exists that trade friction will escalate into the kind of trade wars that were seen in the 1930s if more and more countries link industrial and trade policies across the same limited number of high technology industries. Thus, it is critical that trade friction associated with high technology industries be understood and that policies are adopted that are not destructive to ourselves and our trading partners.

References

Clark, Kim B., "Competition, Technical Diversity, and Radical Innovation in the U.S. Auto Industry," in Richard S. Rosenbloom, ed., *Research on Technological Innovation, Management and Policy*. Greenwich, CT: JAI, 1983.

Cohen, Robert B., Richard W. Ferguson, and Michael F. Oppenheimer, *Nontariff Barriers to High-Technology Trade*. Boulder, CO: Westview, 1985.

Dixit, Avinash, "International Trade Policy for Oligopolistic Industries," *Economic Journal*, Vol. 94, Supplement 1984, pp. 1–17.

Kreinin, Mordechai E., "United States Trade and Possible Restrictions in High-Technology Products," *Journal of Policy Modeling*, Vol. 7, Spring 1985, pp. 69–105.

Krugman, Paul, "Import Protection as Export Promotion: International Competition in the Presence of Oligopoly and Economics of Scale," in Henryk Kierzkowski, ed., *Monopolistic Competition and International Trade*. Oxford: Oxford University Press, 1984a.

"The U.S. Response to Foreign Industrial Targeting," in William C. Brainard and George L. Perry, eds., *Brookings Paper on Economic Activity*. Washington, DC: The Brookings Institution, 1984b.

Nelson, Richard R., *High-Technology Policies: A Five-Nation Comparison*. Washington, DC, American Enterprise Institute for Public Policy Research, 1984.

Ohmae, Kenichi, "The New Technologies: Japan's Strategic Thrust," *The McKinsey Quarterly*, Winter 1984, pp. 20–35.

Spencer, Barbara J., and James A. Brander. "International R&D Rivalry and Industrial Strategy," *Review of Economic Studies*, Vol. 50, October 1983, pp. 707–22.

Teubal, M., "The R&D Performance Through Time of Young, High Technology Firms," *Research Policy*, Vol. 11, December 1982, pp. 33–46.

Webbink, Douglas W., *The Semiconductor Industry: A Survey of Structure, Conduct, and Performance*. Washington, DC: Federal Trade Commission, 1977.

Index